Cornwall

and the Coast

Mousehole and Newlyn

An England's Past for Everyone paperback

Other titles in this series:

Bolsover: Castle, Town and Colliery

Bristol: Ethnic Minorities and the City 1000-2001

Burford: Buildings and People in a Cotswold town

Codford: Wool and War in Wiltshire

Cornwall and the Cross: Christianity 500-1560

Exmoor: The Making of an English Upland

Henley on Thames: Town, Trade and River

Ledbury: A Market Town and its Tudor Heritage

The Medway Valley: A Kent Landscape Transformed

Parham: An Elizabethan House and its Restoration

Sunderland and its Origins: Monks to Mariners

Sunderland: Building a City

Cornwall
and the Coast
Mousehole and Newlyn

JOANNA MATTINGLY

Phillimore

First published 2009

A Victoria County History publication
Published by Phillimore & Co. Ltd, Madam Green Farm Business Centre,
Oving, Chichester, West Sussex, England in association with the Institute of
Historical Research at the University of London.
www.phillimore.co.uk

ISBN 978-1-86077-489-8

British Library Cataloguing in Publication Data. A cataloguing record for this
book is available from the British Library.

Typeset in Humanist 521 and Minion

We wish particularly to thank the following EPE and VCH staff for their efforts
during the production of this volume:

John Beckett – Director of the Victoria County History
Matthew Bristow – Historic Environment Research Manager
Sarah Byrne – Production Assistant
Catherine Cavanagh – Project Manager
Jessica Davies – Publications Manager
Skye Dillon – Education and Skills Manager
Nafisa Gaffar – Finance and Contracts Officer
Mel Hackett – Communications Manager
Nick Hall – Administrator
Dmitri Nemchenko – Web Manager
Alan Thacker – Executive Editor of the Victoria County History
Elizabeth Williamson – Architectural Editor of the Victoria County History

Printed and bound in Malta

Front Cover: Duck or Duke Street, Newlyn. Early colour photograph by Albert
    Kahn, 1913. The site is now a Street-an-Nowan car park. Image courtesy of
    Musée départemental Albert-Kahn.
Back Cover: Fishy designs, Trelawney's fish shop, the Strand, Newlyn. Image
    courtesy of English Heritage (Peter Williams).

Contents

Foreword

The Lands End peninsula has always been distinguished in possessing its own powerful identity, a situation which continues to this day, its population regarding their few square miles as being independent from the rest of Cornwall and even special in the context of England as a whole.

Having been fortunate enough to have been born and bred in this promontory, West Penwith as it is known, I support these prejudices strongly; the peninsula is indeed marvellous in so many ways, wild and rugged by its geological nature, and generally not too much tamed by the pressures of modern life. It is such qualities that have caused the area to attract successive waves of artists throughout the past hundred and fifty years.

The contrast between the north and south coasts is very marked, the steep rough cliffs and exposed weather of the former complementing the benign sandy beaches of its southern shore. Between the two runs a moorland plateau; granite monuments, standing stones and circles towards its western tip bequeath upon this land an air of mystery and ancient spirituality.

It is on the short east-facing coast of West Penwith that the villages of Mousehole and Newlyn are situated, a mere stone's throw from one another. Both places are permeated at dawn by uninterrupted sunlight. However, well before sunset early shade settles in, caused by the higher land behind them. This is the source of deep precocious evening shadows that envelop everything in both harbours – a dramatic contrast on days when the bay beyond basks in sunlight.

Rapid changes of weather, sun and storm mingling one with another, often in violent juxtaposition, are typical of this land that pushes into the Atlantic. The close and constant proximity of the sea is an overwhelming factor which has always dictated the realities of these villages, whose past is explored in this book with fascinating and intense detail.

I am writing today in my studio just above Newlyn harbour, the outlook so bright and blue as to match for brilliance and beauty anywhere one can imagine on earth. Mount's Bay expands generously towards the Lizard, into the English Channel and eventually the ocean.

The quays fill the foreground geometrically, their tawny darkness a reminder of the relative rarity of this overwhelming lightness. Grey days, which are quite as beautiful being possessed by gale force winds and rough seas, tend to outnumber clear skies.

These two small and vulnerable ports are crucially protected to the south by a prominent headland but the chink in their armour lies to the south-east where there is no guard against storm, fortunately rare from that quarter. At night the moon is often reflected in the waters of the Bay, appearing to race any clouds going.

I love these places for the way they have through the centuries become sewn into the granite fringe of Mount's Bay. Newlyn is still busy every day, its unselfconscious dignity preoccupied with industry, fishing and the associated skills and crafts crucial to the true survival of the place. Of late there have been ill-judged attempts to introduce tourist attractions but the surprise and joy of this little port is that people who drive through it unknowingly can miss its importance, and its present-day vigour, a unique phenomenon along all the coasts of the West Country.

In contrast, Mousehole is bereft of fishing, its four-square granite cottages now overlook the harbour blankly. The surface within its two grand quays is now covered with soft, imported, yellow sand imposed upon the edgy stones and shingle that have witnessed so much hard work, the sorting and gutting of fish, making an uncomfortable refuge for luggers by the score, resting at home from the perils of the deep. It is now a popular venue for second homes and holiday-lets. The hill towards Newlyn which until recently represented a halo of small green fields is now covered in bungalows.

This book puts into abrupt focus the necessity for a deep knowledge of history in relation to planning for the present and the future. It states in no uncertain terms the importance and excitement of the past, implying the unique character of these two little places, whose vulnerability is being tried and tested constantly under the pressures of development. This book is indeed an important and commendable achievement.

Jeremy Le Grice

Preface and Acknowledgements

Mousehole and Newlyn began as trading places, jostling for position in Mount's Bay. This book is an attempt to tell their intersecting stories and I am grateful to all the Mousehole maids and Newlyn Buccas who have helped. In particular, Margaret Perry for sharing her immense knowledge of, and research on, Mousehole and Newlyn, and Tony Pawlyn who grew up in Street an Nowan and helped to steer me through some technicalities of fishing. Matthew Spriggs co-wrote chapter 5, Eric Berry and Nick Cahill produced an architectural report on Keigwins and Mousehole and wrote text panels. Other panels were written by Andrew Langdon, Oliver Padel and Tony Pawlyn. Peter Herring helped to produce the map of the medieval parish and the late Harold Fox answered landscape queries. Tom Arkell provided much useful advice on probate records and population figures at an early stage.

Without 'Mattingly's Minions' the scope of this book would have been very much narrower. Under the leadership of Sally Pocock, key volunteers were Jean Cadby, Pat Griffith, Charlotte Murray-Taylor, Kate Newell, Pat Penhallurick, and Barbara Warwick who with many others transcribed Paul parish wills and other documents. Among those who gave us access to their houses and private archives Pat Garnier stands out. The work on wills began as a pilot project initiated by Anthony Fletcher and the Victoria County History of Cornwall Trust. We are grateful to the Heritage Lottery Fund for agreeing to fund the main phase of this project. Transcriptions of the probate records can be viewed on our website, www.ExploreEnglandsPast.org.uk/Cornwall.

Catherine Lorigan acted as general volunteer coordinator and she and Bob Wilson did sterling work on records in The National Archive at Kew. Paul Brough, Deborah Tritton and the staff of the Cornwall Record Office created a dedicated and friendly space for volunteers to work in. The University of Exeter provided resources at their Cornwall campus at Tremough and I am particularly grateful to David Rhymer for letting me work in Room101.

Many people read and commented on drafts of this book including Professor Jonathan Barry, Professor Philip Payton and Dr Bernard Deacon of the University of Exeter, Christine Edwards, my husband Alex Hooper and my father Harold Mattingly, while   Ron Hogg, Pam Lomax and Mike Sagar-Fenton saw individual chapters.

Thanks are also due to Angela Broome of the Courtney Library, Royal Institution of Cornwall; Kim Cooper and the Cornish Studies Library, Redruth; Trudi Martyn of the Cornwall Family History Society; Annabel Read, Jan Ruhrmund, Glyn Richards and John Simmonds at the Morrab Library; Alison Bevan and Jonathan Holmes of Penlee House Gallery and Museum; and Nick Johnson, Bryn Tapper, Jane Powning and the Historic Environment Service of Cornwall Council. Many others made valuable contributions: there are so many, including VCH colleagues, that it would be invidious to try to name them all: you know who you are!

Most of all my heartfelt thanks go to the local VCH of Cornwall Trust, especially the chairman, Lady Banham and the vice-chairman, the late General Sir Richard Trant, who fought so hard to keep this project alive. Without the financial support of the people of Cornwall the revival of the VCH for Cornwall would not have been possible. Finally, but by no means least, I owe a huge debt of gratitude to the administrator of the project, Coral Pepper, who besides her exceptional organisational skills has helped with every aspect including picture research and the Mounts Bay school project, for which the learning resources are available at www.ExploreEnglandsPast.org.uk/Schools. It was also Coral who thought that a barn dance led by the Newlyn Reelers would be the right way to launch this book.

Joanna Mattingly

To a Mousehole maid and a Newlyn bucca.

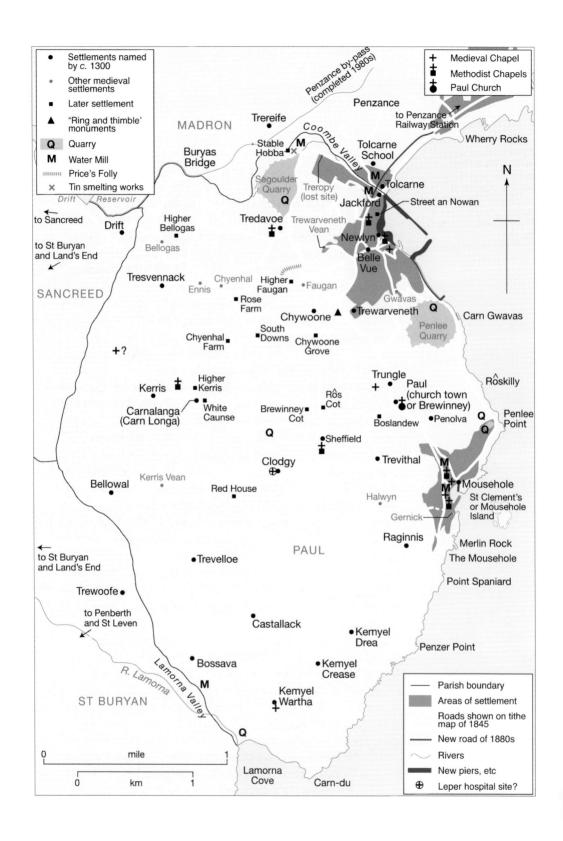

Settlements named by *c.* 1300
Other medieval settlements
Later settlement
"Ring and thimble' monuments
Q Quarry
M Water Mill
Price's Folly
× Tin smelting works

Medieval Chapel
Methodist Chapels
Paul Church

Penzance by-pass (completed 1980s)

MADRON
Penzance

Trereife
Stable Hobba M
to Penzance Railway Station
Wherry Rocks

Coombe Valley
Tolcarne School

Buryas Bridge
Segoulder Quarry Q
Treropy (lost site)
M Tolcarne
Street an Nowan

N

Drift Reservoir
Tredavoe
Trewarveneth Vean
Jackford

to Sancreed
Drift
Higher Bellogas
Newlyn
Belle Vue

Bellogas

to St Buryan and Land's End

SANCREED
Tresvennack
Chyenhal
Ennis
Higher Faugan
Faugan
Gwavas
Q
Trewarveneth
Carn Gwavas

Rose Farm
Chywoone
Penlee Quarry

Chyenhal Farm
South Downs
Chywoone Grove

+?

Trungle
Roskilly
Kerris
Higher Kerris
Rôs Cot
Paul (church town or Brewinney)

Carnalanga (Carn Longa)
White Caunse
Brewinney Cot
Boslandew
Penolva
Q Q
Penlee Point

Q
Sheffield
Trevithal

Bellowal
Kerris Vean
Red House
Clodgy
Halwyn
M M Mousehole
St Clement's or Mousehole Island

Gernick

Raginnis
Merlin Rock

PAUL
The Mousehole

to St Buryan and Land's End
Trevelloe
Point Spaniard

Trewoofe

to Penberth and St Leven
Castallack
Kemyel Drea
Penzer Point

R. Lamorna
Bossava
Kemyel Crease

M
Kemyel Wartha

ST BURYAN
Lamorna Valley
Q
Lamorna Cove
Carn-du

0 mile 1
0 km 1

Parish boundary
Areas of settlement
Roads shown on tithe map of 1845
New road of 1880s
Rivers
New piers, etc
Leper hospital site?

Introduction

Figure 1 The ancient parish of Paul shown in relation to areas of settlement, roads, religious sites and the neighbouring parishes of Madron, Sancreed and St Buryan.

The fishing villages of Mousehole and Newlyn lie on the western fringes of Mount's Bay in far west Cornwall, an area of outstanding natural beauty. From both places there are spectacular views across the bay, which is still dominated by St Michael's Mount. Backed by the high plateau of the Penwith peninsula, land communication remains problematic to this day. Sea routes were always more important and a major theme of this book is the dramatic effect of sea and terrain on the activities of local inhabitants and on the appearance and plan of their settlements. The approach adopted here is largely chronological, with chapters 5 and 9 being thematic and focusing on the Cornish language and Newlyn art colony, respectively.

There is no evidence of permanent settlement in Mousehole or Newlyn before about 1200 but they have probably been part of the parish of Paul since Anglo-Saxon times. Both towns, which seem to have been seasonal fishing settlements colonised from inland, clung tightly to coastal strips with steep cliffs rising to the high farming plateau behind. They have now spread up the steep hills, producing townscapes with dramatic variations in height. Both Mousehole and Newlyn emerge in the historic record as medieval towns, with at least four medieval chapels between them. Neither was autonomous, and the centres of local government remained inland, but Mousehole was really two towns with a shared market and fair. In chapter 1 we take a view of the inhabitants and their activities from prehistory onwards. Woven into this is the dramatic story of an unscheduled royal visit that had a major impact in shaping medieval Mousehole. We will also see how the Spanish raid of 1595 (by the remnant of the Armada fleet) had a lasting impact on Mousehole.

Chapter 2 introduces another major theme: fishing and the fish export trade. In the medieval period both Mousehole and Newlyn became significant centres of the trade and fishing is still crucial to Newlyn's economy today. The two towns were also important trading ports and key players in the medieval overseas trade of Mount's Bay, which as well as being a profitable fishing area, imported wine and salt and exported cloth and hides, with local merchants sometimes acting as middlemen. Competitive quay building began in the late 14th century at Mousehole and part of the original quay can still be seen there. Soon after, the

ure 2 The County of Cornwall the south west of England.

1

development of larger ships favoured ports that lay more securely sheltered within Mount's Bay – Marazion, Penzance and Newlyn, with the safe anchorage of Gwavas Lake playing a major role here.

The discussion of fishing is expanded into a more general maritime theme in chapter three. Although Penzance's specialisation in the luxury goods trade in the late 17th century pushed Newlyn to concentrate more and more on fish, many fisherman invested their spare cash in land and so became farmers as well. Mount's Bay was also both a key recruitment area for the Royal Navy and a haven for smugglers.

Newlyn's development, rather different from Mousehole's, is the focus of chapter 4. After the Spanish raid, a new settlement grew up at Street-an-Nowan, which effectively more than doubled the size of the town by linking it with the medieval settlement of Tolcarne and Jackford. Thereafter Newlyn developed into a four-part town with distinctive characteristics. The Newlyn river in its valley – the picturesque wooded Coombe – was the setting for several mills, and Mousehole's topography was also dominated from the medieval period by a network of rivers with fast running waters and steep drops, ideal for mills.

A chapter on Mousehole and Newlyn as last bastions of the Cornish language follows as chapter 5. The roots of this were firmly bound up with the fishing industry. Other close-knit communities like the mining areas around St Just further west also kept Cornish alive. But on the west side of Mount's Bay it was the merchant-gentry who played the greatest role in nurturing late Cornish. The two key families were the Keigwins of Mousehole and Bosons of Newlyn, both of which sadly died out with, or soon after, the language.[1]

Maritime themes continue in chapter 6 but the types of fish, areas of fishing and methods of processing have subtly changed. Round Britain fishing began in this period with the Irish fishery in the 1820s and by the 1850s a Mount's Bay fleet was annually circumnavigating Britain through the Caledonian canal, fishing in the early summer in the Irish Sea, late summer and early autumn in the North Sea and then returning home for the late autumn and winter. Old methods of pilchard curing with levers and weights were superseded by screw pressing towards the end of the 19th century and other occupations like market gardening, and quarrying were introduced.

Chapter 7 looks at the 19th-century development of the settlements into the distinctive villages we know today. Newlyn Town itself is distinguished by its narrow, sinuous, sloping streets, linked across the slope by footpaths known as gearns. Belle Vue took on the character of a gentry suburb with a few grand 18th century houses among more rural-style cottages, and late

19th-century terraces of middle-class housing eventually linked this area via the back of Street an Nowan to Tolcarne, down Chywoone Hill. Street an Nowan developed a dense network of picturesque lanes and alleys, especially in the Fradgan area, which was curtained off from the new harbour road of 1908 by industrial stores and warehouses. At Tolcarne and the Coombe, grander, late 19th- and early 20th-century houses and villas were built above the industrial and public buildings.[2]

Overlapping governmental structures – parish, manor, and urban institutions – all had a foothold in the area during this period but some rationalization took place when Newlyn was granted parochial status in 1848. However, it was still administratively part of Paul parish. Methodism was strong in both Mousehole and Newlyn, dominating education as well as religion. An Anglican fight back began with the building of a new church at Newlyn in the mid-1860s and Anglicans consolidated their influence in the community when in 1896 they actively supported the fishermen opposed to Sunday fishing after the Newlyn riot.

Figure 3 Newlyn from the air, showing the expansion of settlement to the south and west (left), the completed deep-water harbour, and the inner harbour of the 1980s. Tolcarne is top right, Street-an-Nowan middle and Newlyn Town lower left.

Figure 4 'The Ring and Thimble', Chywoone near Newlyn. John Price (1738-97), the local landowner and slave owner, put these 'follies' up. One celebrates the finding of a gold ring here in 1781 and the other is a sugar lump (chapter 9). Price's Mousehole folly – a murder site cross (chapter 6) – was removed during road-widening in the 1920s.

The discovery of Newlyn by continentally trained artists in the early 1880s and the establishment of one of Britain's most successful artists' colonies there is well known. Chapter 9 focuses on the roots of this phenomenon and the earlier fascination with natural and man-made curiosities. It also considers the reasons why artists favoured Newlyn over Mousehole, the latter being perhaps prettier but not 'primitive' enough, as well as further from the railway that linked artists with exhibition opportunities in London. The chapter also argues that artists were more integrated with the local community than is usually thought, by looking at the 1890s and 20th century rather than just the 1880s, the early experimental years of the colony.

The final chapter focuses on the 20th century, a time of great change, but also continuities. Like many old settlements, Newlyn attracted attention from bureaucrats keen to improve living conditions. Penzance had taken over local administration from Paul parish in 1934 and was keen to create a modernist Vienna or London around Mount's Bay, starting with an Art Deco swimming lido. Opposition to the slum clearances brought artists and fishermen together again, but the clearances still devastated the settlement. Developments in the town may originally have been noble in their motives, but have resulted in a Newlyn where large car parks replace the pilchard cellars and picturesque cottages. Mousehole was spared and the old networks of courts are intact, with car parks on the edge of town. How Mousehole turned from fishing to tourism, while Newlyn took steps in the 1980s to improve the natural advantages of its site to become a premier fishing port again, forms the concluding section of this book.

Chapter 1

Origins and Early Settlements

In October 1242, when Richard, earl of Cornwall, was on his way home from France, his ship nearly foundered in a storm off the coast of Cornwall and he feared for his life. In the event, his ship reached safe harbour, but Richard did not forget his narrow escape and it was to have important repercussions for the place where he landed. That place, a natural inlet in the steep cliffs of far-west Cornwall, was 'the hole of the mouse' (in the Latin used by the chronicler of the event, *pertusum muris*), which today we call Mousehole.[3]

The earl was an important man. The younger brother of King Henry III of England, he went on to marry Sanchia of Provence, sister of Henry's queen, the year after the storm, and also became the only Englishman ever to lay claim to the Holy Roman Empire. His safe landing mattered in the history of Mousehole for several reasons. It ensured that for the first time its name – unusual in west Cornwall because it derives from English – was mentioned in written sources. Secondly, in fulfilment of a vow made

Figure 5 The connections between Mount's Bay and France mapped to highlight the route of the medieval wine trade and major smuggling centres.

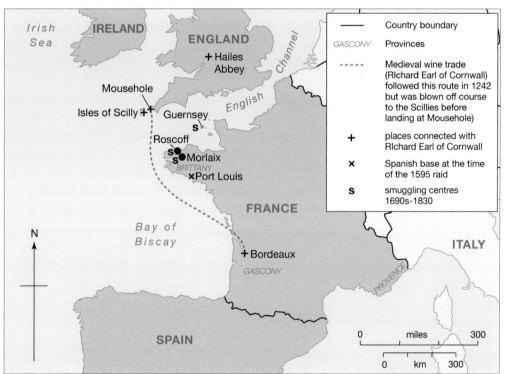

5

during the storm, in 1246 Earl Richard founded Hailes abbey in Gloucestershire. This abbey was later to have an important connection with the town, because it had the right to appoint the parish priests of Paul, prominent local figures who played a significant role in Mousehole's early development. Thirdly, the episode seems to have encouraged Richard to take a direct interest in the church at Mousehole itself. In particular his affection for St Edmund, archbishop of Canterbury (died 1240 and made a saint in 1246), was probably responsible for the dedication of one of the chapels in Mousehole. Richard had also visited the archbishop's shrine at Pontigny in France in 1250 and had given his son born in that year the name of Edmund.[4]

THE EARLIEST SETTLEMENTS

Mousehole lies on (some say just outside) the western side of Mount's Bay, which occupies the north-western corner of the seas between Land's End and the Lizard. This great stretch of water is bounded by spectacular cliffs and dominated by St Michael's Mount. Mousehole faces east (a more sheltered aspect than most Penwith ports) and is protected by an offshore island. Like its near neighbour Newlyn, it is sited on a raised beach and backed by the Penwith granite plateau. All around the land rises steeply to 200 feet – indeed to over 400 in the north-west. The Penwith plateau restricted the later growth of Mousehole and Newlyn, in contrast to Penzance which lay in more open country further round the bay.[5]

Figure 6 Cornwall *c.*1556 (300 years after earl Richard's safe landing). Mushol (Mousehole) is still the first port in the English Channel, though the Land's End road (shown as a dotted line) bypasses it.

The native names for Mousehole and Newlyn reflect the maritime focus of these settlements (Panel 1). Medieval Mousehole had two such names. By 1267 the southern part was known as Porthenys, 'port of the island', a reference to St Clement's island just offshore; later, the northern part was termed Porthengrouse, 'port

Understanding Medieval Place-Names

Many place-names have been in existence for centuries, and have altered over the ages, so it is necessary to study their earliest spellings in order to understand their meanings, rather than trusting the modern forms. Newlyn was usually spelt **Lulyn** in the Middle Ages, which makes sense as 'fleet-pool' (Cornish **lu** 'army, fleet', **lyn** 'pool'), while Mousehole was **Musehole**, showing that it does indeed contain Middle English **mus** 'mouse'. Two parts of Mousehole had the Cornish names of Porthenys and Porthengrouse, 'island harbour' and 'the cross harbour'; its English name was probably given by sailors, alluding to the smallness of this precious refuge on an exposed peninsula. The Cornish name Halwyn was originally **Helwyn** 'white hall', and does not contain Cornish **hal** 'moor'.

Most of the place-names in west Cornwall are in the Cornish language, though English ones such as Alverton and Mousehole were already being given in the Middles Ages, when Cornish was still flourishing. In either language, place-names are often composed of two parts – a general word, such as Cornish **tre** 'farmstead' roughly equivalent to English **ton**), plus a more precise, descriptive, word or phrase such as **war veneth** 'upon the hill' in Trewarveneth, or **mongleth** 'quarry' in Trungle (**Tre-vongleth**).

At all periods places have been named after people associated with them. Often nothing else is known of these people, especially those found in older place-names: Tredavoe was **Treworthavou** in 1328, and is the farm of an unknown man called **Gorthavow**, who probably lived at some time before 1100. Alverton contains the name of Alward, who held the estate in 1066. Jackford, which perhaps gave rise to Jack Lane in Newlyn, was **Jakeford** in 1278, seemingly a ford named from a man called Jack, although Middle English **jack** was also a general word for 'man'. Subsequently the reverse process has also occurred and people's surnames have arisen from the places where they lived ('By Tre, Pol and Pen, you may know Cornish men').

Some place-names do not contain any word denoting a habitation, but are taken from features of the landscape, natural or man-made. Raginnis is simply 'opposite the island', while Castallack is 'fortified place' (Cornish **castell** 'fort'). Penolva is 'lookout point', appropriately the site of a later huer's hut for spotting shoals of pilchards.

Place-names can also provide information about how the land was worked in earlier times. Gwavas (Cornish **gwaf-vos** 'winter dwelling') commemorates the practice of transhumance (seasonal movement

of livestock), and is answered by fields called **Hewas** 'summer pasture'. **Gweal** formerly meant an open (unenclosed) field divided into strips, although (like English 'field' itself) it later denoted any enclosed field. Places named with Cornish **goon** (also **woon**, **noon**) were formerly downland or open grazing. Many fields retained their Cornish names in the tithe maps of the 1840s, after the language itself had died out.

For lack of sufficient early information, many place-names remain obscure. Some, like Kemyel, look Cornish but do not correspond to any known words or names (**ke** 'hedge' is unlikely here). Others, such as Clodgy, could be either Cornish (**claf-jy** 'leper-house') or English (dialect **clodgy** 'muddy, sticky').

Oliver Padel

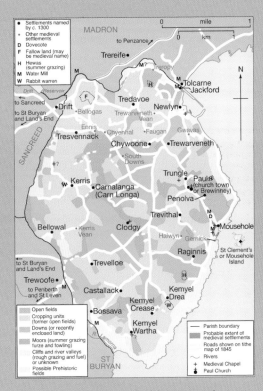

Figure A: Map of Paul parish (with hewas names).

gwavas and hewas: P.A.S. Pool, The Field-Names of West Penwith (1990), 62, and see bibliography under Cornish Names.

of the cross' (Panel 2). The earliest form of Newlyn, 'Lulyn', which occurs first in 1279, means 'pool for a fleet of boats', a reference to Gwavas Lake, the harbour by which it lay.

We cannot easily chronicle the early history of these places before they emerge as distinct settlements with names of their own. We have to consider them as part of larger units for which we do have a record, such as the ecclesiastical parish and the lord's manor. For most of their history, probably from Anglo-Saxon times, Mousehole and Newlyn have been part of the parish of Paul. Medieval Newlyn consisted of Newlyn Town (in Paul parish) and Tolcarne (in Madron parish). Jackford was part of the same settlement as Tolcarne but it lay across the river and was administratively part of Paul parish.

By the 11th century Mousehole and Newlyn also lay within the important landed estate of Alverton. Earlier still we have to draw on evidence from an even wider area – the territory around Mount's Bay as a whole. That evidence, all of it archaeological, suggests that Mousehole and Newlyn were within an area that was well populated from prehistoric times, and once stretched further eastwards out to sea, where a former forest now lies submerged in the bay. The present coastline dates from the medieval period, with occasional erosion later.[6]

Prehistoric Archaeology

In the area later occupied by Paul and its neighbouring parishes, evidence of prehistoric activity is concentrated in the upland areas away from the coast, comprising stone circles, fogous (underground passages), menhirs (large, upright standing stones) and burial mounds. At the time, extensive marshes in the central part of the land beside Mount's Bay were hostile to habitation and permanent settlement did not start in the area until Neolithic times (4000-2500 BC). Before that, the flint scatters dating from 8000-4000 BC support the theory that the Mesolithic period was one of nomadic hunting and fishing expeditions.

Finds from the neighbourhood of what later became Mousehole include a greenstone pounder from Raginnis of Neolithic date and a copper axe head from Penolva of the late Neolithic or early Bronze Age. Bronze-Age burial urns dating from between 2500 and 1400 BC were dug up in the south west of the parish at Tresvennack and Trevelloe, in the former beside a menhir. The most intriguing find, now lost, was a gold lunula (a crescent-shaped necklace) from a high status site near Penzance, while the end of a gold torque of later date was found recently at Halwyn. In the north-west of Paul parish, a hoard of 45 silver 'imitation' Greek coins dated to 200 BC could be evidence for early trading in tin.[7]

Figure 7 A gold lunula found in 'the neighbourhood of Penzance' in 1783.

Defended Iron-Age or Romano-British sites of about 150 BC-AD 400 are the first identifiable settlements in what became Paul parish. As well as a hill fort in the north of the area at Tredavoe, there are at least 14 rounds (circular defensive enclosures), housing anything from a single family to a hamlet of up to six houses. A courtyard house, like those excavated in the nearby parishes of Gulval (at Chysauster) and Sancreed (at Carn Euny), lies in the south of the parish near Castallack round and may be part of an undefended site of similar date. Interestingly, most important later farms lie close to rounds, implying a continuity of settlement.[8]

These sites are associated with a number of early signs of occupation. Part of a gold Roman bracelet was recently retrieved at Trewoofe on the Paul and St Buryan boundary. Coin hoards and part of a stone bowl of Iron-Age or Romano-British date come from Kerris and Tredavoe in the centre and north of Paul parish where there are also rounds. The hoard from Tredavoe dates to 150-100 BC (before the Romans invaded Britain) and is further evidence for trade. Anglo-Saxon pottery of sixth to seventh century date has been found at Trevelloe in the south-west of Paul parish.[9]

The Parish of Paul

Also known by the Cornish name of Brewinney, Paul is an average-sized Cornish parish of some 3,500 acres. Shaped like an almond, it is bordered by the coast to the east and inland by streams, natural features which suggest that the area of the medieval parish may have been determined by earlier land divisions. Although not recorded until 1259, the church was much earlier in origin. It seems to have been dedicated to St Paul Aurelian (in Brittany St Pol de Leon), allegedly a sixth-century Welshman who died in Brittany, where he was venerated from at least the late ninth century.[10]

Paul church was established inland, half a mile to the north-west of the later settlement of Mousehole, on a high point with a commanding view to the east over Mount's Bay. Clearly an early Christian site, it is associated with two pre-Conquest cross fragments, part of a shaft built into the north wall of the chancel and a cross head of a distinctive Cornish type built into the churchyard wall near the gate (see Panel 2). Evidence of other early Christian activity in the west of the parish is provided by a memorial stone from Kerris from around AD 600-800.[11]

The preference for siting a church inland is to be found elsewhere around Mount's Bay, but contrasts with other areas of Cornwall – such as estuaries of the rivers Fal and Fowey on the south coast and of the Hayle on the north – where churches are built by water. This may reflect the fact that in Mount's Bay,

Crossing the Landscape

Crosses are a major landscape feature in Cornwall. They are usually carved of granite, and most have round 'Celtic'-style heads. Often a cross is carved in relief by chiselling away the background rather than cutting (incising) a cross in the stone. Some crosses are more elaborate, with pierced holes and carved or incised decoration; these include churchyard crosses which often predate churches. Stone crosses also mark church paths, boundaries or chapel sites, act as memorials or grave markers and adorn market squares. Penzance's 'Market cross' was a memorial cross linked to an early Christian graveyard on the 'holy headland' there.

Paul parish had crosses of most types. The oldest cross in Paul parish is the churchyard cross head now on the churchyard wall. Dating from c.1000, this has a round head and a carved figure of the crucified Christ on the front like Sancreed and other Penwith crosses. Five bosses, or raised circles decorate the back and a shaft with interlace decoration of similar, pre-Conquest, date has been recently discovered built into the north wall of the church. It is unclear if head and shaft fit together, though they may well do so. Both show the early importance of the Paul church site.

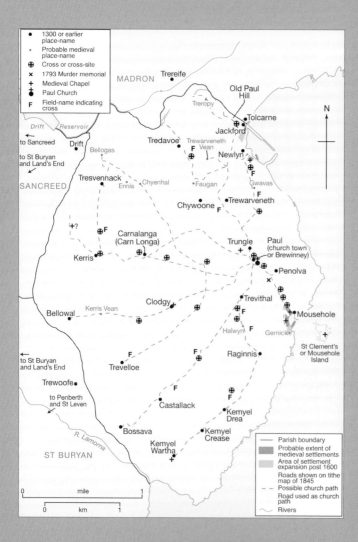

Figure A: Map of location of crosses, church paths and roads in Paul parish adapted from Cooke (see bibliography).

Figure B: Churchyard cross from Paul showing crucifixion.

Figure C: Cross shaft in north wall of Paul church.

Wayside crosses often lie at cross-roads en-route from farms and hamlets to the parish church. An unusual feature in Paul parish is that almost all have Latin cross heads rather than round heads. Latin crosses are common in Devon and are also found in St Neot and St Cleer parishes on Bodmin Moor and in the parish of Creed. The will of Reginald Mertherderwa, rector of Creed 1448, suggests that these crosses were carefully sited: 'where the bodies of the dead being carried to burial are laid down for prayers' (allowing the coffin bearers to take a rest). Field names including 'crous' or 'grouse' indicate the site of these and other lost crosses.

There was also a market cross in the northern part of Mousehole, perhaps associated with a market grant of 1300 (or 1266). Porthengrouse (port of the cross) is noted as a place-name by the 1330s. The market cross once stood outside Loon Bennett on the western side of a triangular market place (see panel 3). Given its date it is likely to have been of Latin cross form, too.

Why does Paul parish have such distinctive, and not typically Cornish, medieval wayside crosses? One reason may be that these parishes lay within the Anglo-Saxon manor of Alverton. Alternatively they could reflect the international interests of the rector of Paul, Roger of St Constantine or his successors in the mid-13th to 14th centuries.

Andrew Langdon

settlement began inland on the high plateau from which the raised coastal beaches nearer the coast were colonised from the 12th or 13th centuries. A comparison can be made with medieval South Devon. Here inland communities worked the coastal fisheries, and gradually these seasonal coastal settlements became permanent.[12]

Farms were also situated, of necessity, inland. Place-name elements indicate the once-seasonal nature of farming life in Paul parish. Thus a farm near the coast at Newlyn includes the word *gwavas*, 'winter dwelling', while there were two groups of fields called *hewas*, 'summer pasture', in the northern inland part of the parish and one on the cliffs near Mousehole.[13]

Lords and Tenants

At the time of the Norman Conquest in 1066, the sites of Mousehole and Newlyn lay within the extensive manor, or landed estate, of Alverton ('Alwareton'). This manor was based in the southern part of Madron parish and embraced the neighbouring parishes of Paul, St Buryan, Sancreed and St Levan. Alverton was then held by the Anglo-Saxon Alfward, from whom it evidently took its name.

Domesday Book, commissioned in 1086 as a basis for raising taxes, is our main source of information on resources and land ownership in England at this time. It tells us that the manor of Alverton contained enough land to support 60 plough teams, though only 15 were in use, perhaps because of the extent of moorland and rough grazing. It was originally assessed at three hides (each thought of as enough to support 'the land of one family', or a free farmer and his dependants). At Alverton, as was general in Cornwall, the assessments were low; in other words, the inhabitants of early medieval Cornwall enjoyed what we might think of as artificially low rateable values.[14]

The lord of Alverton's own direct holding, his home farm or demesne, which lay to the north of Paul, in Madron parish, was assessed at half a hide and worked by 11 slaves, using three ploughs. Horses, cattle, pigs and sheep were kept. The rest of the estate, assessed at 2½ hides, was farmed by tenants, enumerated as 35 peasant farmers (*villani*) and 25 smallholders (*bordarii*). After 1066, along with much else in Cornwall, the manor passed to the king's brother, Robert, count of Mortain in Normandy, and in 1086 it was duly recorded that since the Norman Conquest its annual value had more than doubled, rising from £8 to £20. That made it one of the most valuable of Cornish manors, and as such it was held personally by Robert of Mortain and by his royal successors as lords of Cornwall until the early 13th century when Henry III

Figure 8 The Kemyel coat of arms of three fish can be found on the early 16th-century capitals in Crowan church, as shown here, and the font at Gulval. This celebrates an earlier Kemyel-St Aubyn marriage.

granted it to the Tyes family.[15]

In common with Cornwall as a whole, Alverton became part of the earldom of Cornwall set up for Earl Richard in 1225. By then it had been let out to an important tenant family, the Tyes, from whom it passed to a succession of other aristocratic families including the Lisles, Berkeleys, Beauchamps, Beauforts, Ros and Manners. Two new manors were created out of Alverton in Paul parish. Kemyel in the south is first noted in 1185 and Fee Marshall in the north by 1202. The former passed by marriage to the St Aubyn family and the latter to the Bassets in the 14th century.[16]

Farms documented in the 12th to early 14th centuries probably descend from the holdings of the *villani* of 1086. Place-names beginning with *tre* (meaning farm or estate) identify some of them. Those still in use today allow us to find the farmstead; for instance, Trevithal near Mousehole. Place-names once containing the element *bos* or *bod* (meaning a dwelling) or *chy* (a cottage) may help us to find some smallholdings mentioned in Domesday Book. In Paul such names include Bellogas, Bellowal, Bossava, Chyenhal and Chywoone.

In the 13th century the process was already under way by which a number of estates, or sub-manors, were created. For us, one of the most significant is Porthenys, described as a manor in 1267. The name continued in use to designate southern Mousehole and eventually as the Cornish name for the town as a whole, although it was never again applied to a manor. We know that in the Middle Ages southern Mousehole continued to be the focus of a sub-manor (part of Alverton), known as Raginnis, a name which first occurs in 1201 and was still in use in 1389. It may be that the royal official who called Porthenys a manor in 1267 was simply alluding to Raginnis under another name.[17]

Other small manors or estates had been established in the parish by the early 16th century. The 'Manor House' in Trewarveneth Street (in the centre of Newlyn Town) could relate either to the sub-manor of Newlyn or be the manor office for Trewarveneth. Kerris, in the south-west of the parish, was regarded as a manor because in the 16th and early 17th centuries a major family, the Chivertons, lived there; later, however, it was only a farmstead or barton. By the late Middle Ages there were some 20 estates with property in Paul, and most had centres outside the parish. Those with Mousehole interests included sub-manors in Madron, and at least four sub-manors of Alverton – Rosmodres and Trewoofe in St Buryan, and Drift and Tregonebris in Sancreed.[18]

THE DEVELOPMENT OF MOUSEHOLE

The early development of Mousehole as a major settlement within the parish of Paul (figure 3) is difficult to reconstruct because

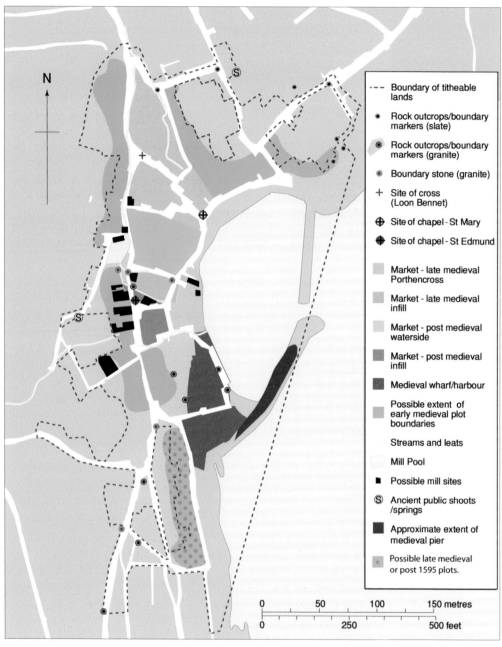

records have not survived. It looks, however, as if the crucial figure was Roger of St Constantine (*de Sancto Constantino*), one of Richard earl of Cornwall's clerks or administrators, whom Richard appointed as parish priest of Paul in 1259. The income from this post was substantial – it was put at £9 6s. 8d. in 1291 – and as Roger held it with several other such benefices until his death in 1283, he was a wealthy man. He also held the estate at Porthenys described as a manor in 1267.[19]

In 1266 Roger used his influence with the earl of Cornwall
to obtain grants to hold three-day fairs in the parishes of which
he had charge. That at Paul was said to be around the feast of
St Paulin, the patron saint of the church, commemorated on
12 March and perhaps to be understood as the local name for
St Paul Aurelian. But by then the memory of Paul Aurelian may
have been lost in Paul and he may have been confused with
Paulinus, a seventh-century bishop of York, whose feast day fell
on 10 October. A Newlyn fair was certainly later held in October.
Paul fair could have been held at Paul church town, the settlement
around the church, or in the northern half of later Mousehole,
both areas having suitable flat sites.[20]

In 1267 Roger got a further grant of a Thursday market and
a three-day fair on the feast of St Matthias (24-6 February) at
Porthenys. Together with Paul fair this furnished the inhabitants of
Mousehole with substantial trading privileges and may be taken as
marking its emergence as a town. After Roger's death, the lords of
Alverton invested in extra grants of markets and fairs. They were
responsible for a Tuesday market and a three-day fair at the feast
of St Barnabas (10-12 June) in 1300, and in 1332, Lady Lisle got a
further six-day fair at St Bartholomew's tide (24-9 August). These
were held in the north of the settlement (possibly on the site of the
1266 fair).[21]

Medieval Layout and Buildings

Such evidence, as well as that relating to the parish's manorial
structure, suggests that Mousehole originated as two distinct,
if closely related settlements. There is allusion to a dual focus
in 1338-41 when Porthengrouse (the Cornish name for north
Mousehole) was described as being next to Porthenys. The stream,
now culverted, which runs through the middle of the settlement
under Brook Street may mark the division between the two.[22]

Medieval Mousehole was laid out where the usual narrow
coastal strip widens out to form a relatively flat and broad terrace
where the Paul stream flows down its narrow valley from the
north-west. It is surrounded by steep slopes rising to the farmland
of the high plateau. The settlement also lies at a geological
junction, with blue elvan (metamorphosed slate or dolerite) to the
north and granite and blue elvan to the south.

North Street (now Church Street), Mill Pool, Chapel Street and
Duck Street were probably lined with narrow properties (burgage
plots) to make the most of access to the street or the markets.
These plots would have been formally laid out by the landowner's
surveyor as part of the framework of the new settlement. North

Street, Mill Pool and Chapel Street formed a continuous north-south line following the 15-metre contour, marking the western boundary of the settlement while Duck Street ran south-eastwards from North Street to the harbour. The plots are shorter than those of other medieval Cornish towns like Penryn, Truro and Helston, the proportion of width to length being 2:3.[23]

Between Chapel Street in the west and the harbour in the east lay the main market area, 'edged by flowing water' which assisted with cleaning after use. Originally it may have been quite large, extending from Parade Hill in the north to Keigwin Place in the south and perhaps resembling the open trading areas identified at other medieval Cornish ports such as St Mawes, Truro and East and West Looe. It was divided into roughly equal parts by a stream now under Brook Street and was perhaps originally divided between Porthenys and Porthengrouse.

A recent survey revealed the site of a medieval cross in the north of this area, at the north end of Fore Street where it joins North (now Church) Street. Perhaps this was the market cross which gave the northern settlement of Porthengrouse its name. By the 14th century the large market area seems to have been subdivided; a triangular market and fair place probably now served Porthengrouse while there was a smaller market area and quay-side in the south at Porthenys. An area of medieval infilling has been identified in central Mousehole extending north from Mill Lane to Vivian Place.[24]

The development of these features from the original open trading area may be recorded in a documentary source of 1310, which seems to describe the subdivision of a two-acre site into

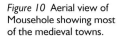
Figure 10 Aerial view of Mousehole showing most of the medieval towns.

building plots. Possibly this is the area of medieval infilling in central Mousehole noted above. Shortly afterwards we find evidence of commercial development in the record. Eight shops are recorded at Porthenys in 1324 and a *seuda* (seld or covered bazaar) in 1339. Shops were workshops where goods were made as well as sold. Surnames reflect the wide range of occupations. In 1327 people bore names such as clerk, merchant, miller, shoemaker, tailor, taverner and weaver, while baker, blacksmith, carpenter and mercer also appear.[25]

One area where medieval street plots may be detected is Keigwin and Little Keigwin, which once fronted the southern end of the market place. Archaeological evidence suggests that the medieval frontages lay further back and were probably narrower than those of the current buildings. There was clearly more pressure on space with access to the market area in the Middle Ages, when Mousehole was prospering, than in the late 16th and 17th centuries when the buildings which now occupy the site were put up.

The Mill Systems

Watermills were a significant part of the medieval manorial economy. Tenants of manors generally had to grind their corn at the manorial mills, even if this was some distance from where they lived; they paid money or toll for the service. They required a relatively large investment in an infrastructure which might include man-made mill pools and leats (feeder streams). Most larger streams had mills and there may have been as many as 3,000 in Cornwall as a whole.[26]

Mousehole's terrain, with its swift streams running down steep gradients, favoured the creation of mills. Advantage was also taken of the natural terraces (part of a raised beach) to create the necessary drop for the water wheels. In the Middle Ages there were at least four mills in Mousehole itself. Mills may have been moved and occupied a sequence of sites; there are certainly more than four sites suitable for mills within the town.

Figure 11 The 18th-century mill house and cottage on Mill Lane, Mousehole.

Mousehole's mills were divided into two systems, corresponding to the division of the town as a whole. The northern one, first recorded in the 1420s, belonged to the lords of Alverton, while the southern one, known since the early 14th century, belonged to the lords of Raginnis. In the south, the lower mill was on the shore by the site of the Lobster Pot complex, while the old mill was higher up, probably on the site of Old Mill House in Mill Lane, next to St Edmund's chapel. In the north, the higher mill was said in the 1570s to lie next to 'the long close' on Paul Lane, while the lower mill was probably at the natural drop from the 15-metre contour running along Chapel Street. A third, the middle mill, may have also lain at this contour or have been further up nearer the higher mill.[27]

This cluster of mills and the complex arrangements of pool and leats which fed them made a considerable impact on the local topography, though the former mill pool in the town may well be post-medieval. Open leats and streams were very much a feature of the street scene until the mid-20th century, and the water outfall at the harbour is still a prominent local feature.

All the inhabitants of Mousehole, unlike those of Penzance, appear to have been exempt from using the Alverton manorial mill at Tolcarne, an important concession probably related to the establishment of the borough in the 13th century. Instead they had resort to these local mills either run or let out by the manor itself.

Parish Church and Chapels

In the mid-13th century, Roger of St Constantine, the parish priest of Paul, was an important local figure. As rector or holder of the living, he was in receipt of the tithes, the dues, supposedly a tenth of their produce, including corn and fish, paid by local people to support their church. In 1291 the rectory of Paul was one of the richer livings in the area, valued at £9 6s. 8d. By then, perhaps in the 1270s, the earl of Cornwall, who had hitherto appointed the rectors, had given that right to the abbey of Hailes. By 1297, the abbey had appropriated the rectory, that is to say that it had taken direct receipt of the rector's income and appointed a vicar. He was

Figure 12 Bundle of title deeds with seals relating to Raginnis manor property in Mousehole. The first dated 1341 relates to woelas (lower) mill, probably that on the sea shore near the Lobster Pot site.

allowed much less support (indeed under a quarter) to carry out pastoral duties in the parish. Inevitably, these vicars were less grand than Roger of St Constantine.[28]

In Mousehole, although all townspeople had to go to Paul parish church on Sundays and feast days, they could go to mass in the town on other days. At a time when social life revolved round religion, they sought their own more local places of worship. Indeed, half of all known medieval chapels in Paul parish relate to Mousehole. The earliest of the four chapels to appear in records was at the leper hospital at Clodgy, a mile west of the town. This hospital was the largest in west Penwith in 1310 with about 27 inmates licensed to beg in Mousehole. That it could support such a relatively large community of the chronically sick in this way suggests that Mousehole was then a wealthy place.[29]

It is likely that Mousehole also had a town chapel – St Edmund's – by the 1300s, like St Ives and Marazion. We know of a chaplain, one John Boswran, holding property in Mousehole between 1308 and 1324 and a local man Edmund Bosvenning may have been named after this saint at about this time. St Edmund's chapel is named first in 1387 when John Poer (Pohe) was the chapel keeper. Poers of Raginnis in 1440-1 helped rebuild it. In 1488 it was said to lie just west of the old mill, evidence that it lay at the western edge of Porthenys market place; it was probably sited just off Mill Lane where a small building of appropriate size (32 feet by 18) was converted into a house in 1790.[30]

The northern chapel of St Mary at Mousehole dates to 1383-7 when Benedict Bossava (Bottesave), townsman and tax collector, and the inhabitants obtained licences for daily services there. Built in an exposed position close to where the later war memorial stands, it 'had been ruinated by the sea' by 1414. Townsmen claimed that the chapel 'had long been a useful landmark (to the saving of many lives) for vessels entering the harbour' and got ecclesiastical support to rebuild it. John Patry, vicar of St Paul, held daily services there and at St Edmund's in 1421-5. The last chapel, St Clement's, lay on the island and may have served as a lighthouse when recorded in c.1538.[31]

As well as supporting chapels and lepers, Mousehole people seem to have made Paul church one of the first complete in the late medieval, Perpendicular, style churches in Cornwall. Starting in the early 15th century, a three-hall church was built with separate gables at the east end for the chancel and both aisles, as well as a west tower. Replacing an earlier, aisled or cruciform church, it was built at the cost of townspeople, parishioners, and locally-born outsiders like John Nancothnan of Bristol. Greenstone, easier to carve than granite, was used for piers, windows and doors as

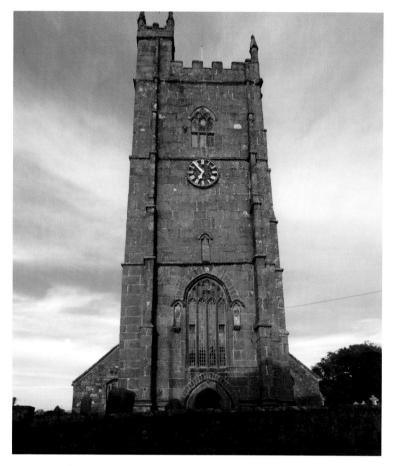

Figure 13 Paul church tower. Empty statue niches include one with a fleur de lys at its base, the symbol of the Virgin Mary. St Mary was the patron of local chapels at Mousehole and Newlyn.

surviving fragments make clear; it may have come by sea from the quarries at Polyphant in North Cornwall and was also used at St Hilary, and Lelant in Penwith. The present granite piers at Paul are of a simple type more typical of Penwith's chapels than churches, though some in the chancel area show signs of burning. If pre-1595 and not in situ, they could have been recycled from one of the Mousehole chapels after 1595.[32]

Governing Mousehole

Mousehole was a 'seigneurial' borough; that is to say it was a settlement that was granted some self-government and had its own fairs and markets, but was subject to the lords ('seigneurs') of the manor of Alverton and its off-shoot Raginnis. There is no evidence for borough courts, the inhabitants being subject to the three-weekly manor courts of their respective lords. Mousehole never became an incorporated borough, never receiving that most prized indicator of urban status, a charter to set up a governing body or corporation. In fact we know little of the way it was governed in the Middle Ages. The records suggest that by the 14th century there were two bailiffs and two chapel keepers appointed by local lords, namely the Tyes family of Alverton and the Chaunteclers or Poers of Raginnis. The bailiffs were responsible for building the quay (chapter 2) and royal commands or writs were addressed to them from 1297 until the early 15th century.[33]

Mousehole also had burgesses, local property holders, presumably men of some wealth, with a stake in the government of the town. By the early 14th century, there were at least 40 of them (half being in the manor of Alverton). By comparison, neighbouring Penzance had only 29. The number of men of substance in Mousehole may have been even greater, as there is evidence that up to 58 taxpayers may have been living there at this time.[34]

As well as the manor courts of Alverton and possibly Raginnis, other courts met at Mousehole, a reflection of its local importance. The court of the hundred of Penwith, the most important local administrative unit beneath the county, met at Mousehole and Marazion to hear local cases and claim any profits from shipwrecks in the 14th century. The maritime courts of the duchy of Cornwall met at Mousehole and Newlyn, as well as at Lostwithiel and Plymouth. Legal documents were drawn up and there may have been a prison. The local manors of Alverton, Kemyel and Fee Marshal were all tithings of the hundred of Penwith and as such each was responsible for the security and policing of their members and for presenting those suspected of misdoing at the hundred court.[35]

Population and Landholding

The Black Death, the plague which raged across England in the mid-14th century, made little impact here, although other parts of Cornwall and Penwith (Porthplement, St Ives etc), were badly affected. By 1377 Paul was the most populous parish in the area with 401 men over the age of 16, and Mousehole could have accounted for half or more. If this is correct, then Mousehole may have been of similar size to Marazion, the other most important port in the bay, with about 500 people.[36]

By the early 16th century, Mousehole's population had declined to perhaps 300 to 400 people. Tax lists give comparative population data, but achieving actual population figures is problematic. Household size in Cornwall and Devon in the 17th century was twice the national average at 9.5 because extended families lived together and poor people did not pay tax. By the 1550s, Porthenys and Porthengrouse had merged into a single settlement, no longer important or populous enough to be taxed separately from Paul parish.[37]

THE EMERGENCE OF NEWLYN

Newlyn has played little part in the story so far. That is a reflection of its relative unimportance in the Middle Ages, which saw the hey-day of its neighbour Mousehole. Newlyn's great days were still to come and we shall be talking about its growth in importance in chapter 4. Nevertheless, its origins were medieval and, like Mousehole, it began as two distinct settlements. The more important was always Newlyn Town, first mentioned in 1279. The medieval hamlet, which perhaps like other coastal villages in the South West originated as a group of fish cellars and net lofts, lay 'hard by the shore', that is at the edge of the steep sided and sheltered basin known as Gwavas Lake. From there trackways, later streets, rose steeply up the slopes to the church and farms on the surrounding plateau. Newlyn lay in the manor of Fee Marshall, and indeed as at Mousehole the manorial lord may have played a part in managing its development. Again like Mousehole, it was split between many sub-manorial estates: in 1586-7, for example, Nicholas Boson (Botesone), of Newlyn Town, built his new mansion house on land belonging to the manor of Lanyon in Madron.[38]

The smaller twin settlement of Tolcarne and Jackford lay across corn fields half a mile to the north, in the tree-lined Newlyn Coombe, on either side of the Newlyn river which here marked the parish boundary. Jackford, which lay in Paul, was first mentioned in the late 13th century, when Gilbert of Lulyn held property there comprising a messuage (building) and half an acre of land. Tolcarne, which lay in Madron, was first recorded as 'Kesteltalcarn' in 1302. The twin settlement was linked by a ford, by the 1490s superseded by a bridge, which carried the ancient routeway from the high plateau across the river to Penzance. The importance of this crossing as a route along which animals from the farmland on the plateau were driven is emphasised by the nearby Paul place-names of Street an Nowan ('street of the ox') and Fradgan (ox road).[39]

These places were very small throughout the Middle Ages and were controlled by their manorial lords. In 1327 Newlyn had fewer than eight taxpayers, and there was one more at Tolcarne. Although it had a chapel, probably dedicated to St Mary, by the early 16th century, Newlyn Town was a community of less than a dozen families. In the 1530s, Leland described Newlyn as 'an hamlet to Mousehole' and a 'poor fisher town'.[40]

Although eclipsed by its neighbour, Newlyn had potential – as is suggested by Leland's use of it as a compass point for describing the local area and by the fact that maritime courts met there in the 14th century. It had better road links than Mousehole, lying as it did, like Marazion and Penzance, on the route to Land's End. This ran north descending from the high plateau down Paul (now Chywoone) Hill and Jack Lane and crossing the Newlyn river to Tolcarne by the ancient ford and later the bridge. There was also a coastal route, across the beach at low tide and going on to Mousehole a mile and half to the south, while church paths (most notably Church Lane, now Gwavas Road) linked the settlement with Paul church, inland to the south about a mile way.

Newlyn Town also benefited from its good natural anchorage. That the Gwavas Lake was already in use in the Middle Ages is suggested by the discovery in 1839 of a medieval trading vessel 'imbedded in the beach' nearby. Although no markets or fairs are recorded at Newlyn in the Middle Ages, four shops were noted in 1320. By the 16th century mills belonging to the manor of Alverton were sited at Tolcarne, on the Newlyn river, lying within 50 yards of each other, while those of Fee Marshall probably lay across the river at Jackford or near Gwavas quay.[41]

Mount's Bay and its Ports

Chapter 2

Figure 14 Mount's Bay depicted in the mid-16th century. South is at the top so working from left to right it shows Marazion, Penzance, Newlyn and Mousehole and their quays. The Mount's square harbour is Marazion's, and there is a large open quay at Mousehole (now Gernick Street).

Mount's Bay had five ports in the 14th century and much of its later history concerns the competitive jockeying for position of these trading places. Marazion was the oldest, perhaps 11th-century in origin. Mousehole, Newlyn and Penzance first appear two centuries later, and Porthplement, now lost but then between Marazion and Penzance, soon after that.[42]

Mousehole's rise to a pre-eminent position in Mount's Bay is evident by 1297. In that year the Crown included it, along with the Mount and Marazion, among the ports to which those seeking to leave the realm had to apply for a royal licence. For the next century Mousehole was the most westerly of the Channel ports to which royal instructions were sent. The picture becomes more confused in the 15th and 16th centuries with Marazion, Penzance and Newlyn better able to protect large ships and, in the first two cases, heading for chartered borough status. Trading activities take us to the sleazier side of port life and the Spanish raid of 1595.[43]

Competitive Quay Building

Before the late 14th century the ports of Mount's Bay relied entirely upon natural harbours and anchorages. St Clement's Island gave some shelter to Mousehole, but the most sheltered area in the bay was Gwavas Lake. This area of calm sea lay east of Newlyn and south-east of Penzance, and gave these places an advantage in the long-term. Mousehole was more exposed; in the 1390s its inhabitants asserted that there had been 'no port for ships to rest securely in, whereby many have been wrecked'. In consequence, it was the first port in the bay to construct a protective pier or quay.[44]

The first move came in 1387 with the bailiffs of Mousehole leasing land on which to build their quay. Work began before 6 October 1392, when an inquiry was held to see whether this 'new made' port would damage the king's interests in Mount's Bay. The Crown was persuaded that it was 'of no value' for that 'the sea flows twice daily and nightly there' and only ships of small size were able to shelter. Thus reassured, it granted five years' quayage (payments for use of the quay) to the bailiffs and men of Mousehole on 12 February 1393. As finally constructed, the quay, much of which survives, was an extension of a natural reef at the foot of the cliffs.[45]

Quay Construction

Figure A: Photograph of north quay being built and south quay extended in 1870. This is one of the earliest photographs of Mousehole.

Figure B: Photograph showing the remains of the medieval (late 14th-century) quay. You can see the large boulders of this quay behind the boats in the foreground.

Quays are often well documented and Mousehole is no exception. Loose terminology can be a problem as terms used include quay, pier, causeway, and wharf. Piers normally refer to jetty-like structures and quays to shore-line banks or wharfs. Documents and the surviving fabric at Mousehole reveal phasing here over 600 years.

The first pier at Mousehole was built in 1387-93 as 'a defense against the sea'. Large beach boulders were used and survive as the middle section of the inside face of the south quay. Major repairs were done to this in 1435 and 1555. The Keigwin family built a low landing quay and wharf, probably in the 1630s when they improved their housing stock and this is noted in 1749. There may have been a similar landing area for fishermen at Carn Topna.

By the 18th century a new type of construction was in use, which resembled deer park hedges. Smaller stones were set on end creating a 'keystone' effect and withstanding storms – upright stones being harder to dislodge than horizontally laid ones. Work dating from 1720 is on either side of the medieval work on the inside of the pier. More major work was done in 1763-5 with the whole of the seaward side of this pier (including the parapet walkway) extended and refaced. The Wharf was probably refaced at much the same time.

The first attempt to create a more enclosed harbour in 1837-8 by building a northern pier has left only a stump below the *Ship Inn*. A slipway of Sheffield or Lamorna granite was created nearby in *c.*1855 at the expense of John Garrett, vicar of Paul. Material from the 1830s pier was recycled in 1868 to 1871 when the present harbour was created by Sir James Douglass, the great lighthouse engineer (Wolf Rock, Eddystone Tower etc.). The granite ashlar quays were the work of Freeman and Sons, a Penryn-based firm, at one time the biggest granite working and exporting business in Britain. Work began with the south quay extension in 1868 and a narrower north pier was started in 1870. Both quays are shown in an incomplete state in a photograph of 1870. Freeman's quarry was probably located just above the row of houses called Salt Ponds and a short section of raised tramway was identified there during the architectural survey.

Nick Cahill and Eric Berry

Figure C: Quay and foreshore with granite boulders. The back of the quay has a stone facing of vertically laid stones that dates to 1763-5.

Mousehole quay was copied by other Mount's Bay ports and we can infer that Penzance built its quay next. Penzance was already on the rise as a port by 1406 when Thomas Berkeley, lord of the manor of Alverton, held profitable markets and fairs there and pilgrims used it as a departure point for the shrine of the apostle James at Compostela in Spain. It was the recipient of a royal letter concerning the Channel ports in 1413 and the quay may have been built around this time, although there is no documentary evidence until 1512 when it was repaired.[46]

A square harbour, linked to the mainland at low tide by a causeway, was built at St Michael's Mount in 1427, as there was insufficient depth of water opposite at Marazion. This formed 'a handy haven for 200 ships of any tonnage'. The harbour was run by merchants and fishermen of Marazion, and the chaplain of the Mount. One more quay was added around this time to the group in Mount's Bay. The Old Quay at Newlyn (still in existence though rebuilt) had existed before 1437, when papal indulgences (reductions in punishment due for sins which had been confessed and forgiven) were offered to those who contributed to its repair. Thus established, the four man-made harbours of Mount's Bay were regarded as of sufficient importance to be shown on 16th-century maps and to be regularly repaired.[47]

The Rise of Penzance and Marazion

The process by which Mousehole was eclipsed first by Marazion and then by Penzance was a slow one. Marazion, with its links to St Michael's Mount, dominated the bay with Mousehole in the 14th century. Penzance, first noted in 1284, only became important after a new market was made in 1406. With ten inns run by foreigners in 1440, it was the 'westest market town' in c.1538. Both it and Marazion, but not Mousehole, sent ships to join the king's fleet in 1451.[48]

In the 1520s, Mousehole, a town of about 300 people, was still the largest place in west Penwith, apart from St Ives. Marazion had more than 200 people, and Penzance over 250, rising to 340 by the 1540s. By 1545, Penzance had 27 taxpayers, three more than Mousehole, although Mousehole was still the wealthier place. Thereafter Mousehole was assessed for tax with Paul parish – a sure sign of decline – and by 1595 it was thoroughly eclipsed by Penzance which had twice as many houses. Even so, it was Marazion which in 1594 because of its antiquity first became an incorporated borough, followed by Penzance in 1614.[49]

MOUNT'S BAY TRADE

Wine and above all salt were the major imports into Cornwall in the Middle Ages, grain, iron, figs, raisins, garlic and onions being more occasionally recorded. Chief exports were tin, fish, hides, and to a lesser extent cheese, cloth and horses, rather different from elsewhere in England where wool and cloth were major exports, while wine was the major import. Mousehole traded with La Rochelle, Brittany, Gascony, Spain, Ireland and Bristol amongst other places.[50]

Food and wine A key element in Mousehole's trade, as in any medieval port, was the import and export of food and drink. By the 14th century its provisioning merchants clearly included men of substance: in 1331 two of them, Benedict Noght and John the Taverner, were of sufficient importance to be implicated in the escape overseas from Cornwall of Sir John Maltravers and Sir Thomas Gurney, two of the three men convicted of murdering the English king Edward II in 1327. In this they may have been influenced by the sympathies of the Tyes family, lords of Alverton. Henry Lord Tyes had supported the rebellion against Edward II led by the earl of Lancaster in 1322 and had been executed as a result. The Mousehole merchants, who were perhaps the town bailiffs, had compounded their offence by continuing to supply the fugitives with armour, corn and other victuals. We do not know what

Figure 15 The major medieval Cornish ports.

Figure 16 Puffins were probably eaten in times of fast when fresh meat was not allowed.

happened to Noght and Taverner, but we may suspect that they escaped without serious punishment since the young Edward III, even though he had overthrown those who had ordered his father's death, does not seem to have pursued the murderers themselves with any great enthusiasm. Indeed, a Benedict Noght was still trading in Mousehole in 1342.[51]

Provisioning passing ships was a key function of Mount's Bay ports from their inception and one of the earliest activities documented. For instance, two victuallers (suppliers of provisions) were living at Mousehole by 1284. In 1444 a Portuguese ship stocked up with food and drink at Mousehole, while its broken mast was being repaired. More unusually in 1533 a consignment of puffins was sent from Mount's Bay to Lady Lisle, probably then at Calais. Supplying ships involved baking – not just bread but ships' biscuits – and we find Baker among the trade-derived surnames of Mousehole in the early 14th century. In the 16th century Mousehole's major family, the Keigwins, a merchant family who became gentry by the 17th century, were involved in this trade. They had an oven, recorded in 1577-8, which perhaps produced ships' biscuits.[52]

Another important item was wine. Although its trade was hardly on the same scale as that in and around the Fal and Fowey, Mousehole was the chief wine port in west Cornwall for a time. In 1302 Benedict the Bastard and Richard of Mousehole sold 14 casks of wine, while in 1352-3 wine and honey were purchased there. Benett of Mousehole (possibly Benedict the Bastard), a merchant vintner, operated in Bordeaux as well, supplying a ship from Normandy with 36 casks and two pipes of wine in 1320. Other Mousehole men could be found in Bristol and London in the 15th century.[53]

Mousehole had wine cellars (usually ground-floor rooms) and taverns in the Middle Ages. We have already met John the Taverner and we find another bearer of the same trade-based name, Nicholas, in the records at about the same time (*c*.1327-43). Nicholas had a cellar where presumably he stored his wine; there is record of white wine being stored for three months in a Mousehole cellar in 1342.[54]

The wine trade was dependent on imports from France, so it suffered during Edward III's wars with that country in the mid-14th century; few wine ships called into Mousehole in the troubled period between 1338 and 1356. It revived thereafter, and in the mid-1470s the customs levied on red and white wine imports for the Duchy including the Mount's Bay area totalled £24. In the 16th century, however, wine imports to Mount's Bay totalled only £5 2s. (for a mere 32 casks) and Mousehole and Newlyn had only a wine ship apiece. By the 1590s, Mousehole vessels brought in only eight casks and four hogsheads of French wine and 10½ casks of Gascon wine, Penzance by then being the principal western wine port.[55]

Figure 17 Loading wine on to Noah's ark at St Neot church in Cornwall. This shows a barrel being rolled up onto a ship (as noted in the Havener's accounts).

Other imports and exports Salt imports, used mostly for preserving fish and curing hides, greatly exceeded those of wine both in bulk and value. Salt sales at Mousehole, for example, were valued at almost £300 or 47 per cent of the Duchy of Cornwall's salt imports in the peak year of 1351-2. In 1541-2 the town imported considerable quantities of salt and Mount's Bay also had a significant share in the trade in corn. Sales are recorded at Marazion and Newlyn in the 1350s and in the later 16th century wheat and malt were imported into Mousehole from Southampton and Weymouth. Oranges were among the more exotic items in 1542, while cloth from Ireland was purchased in Newlyn in 1449-50 by the agent of the Arundell family.[56]

Exports in the 14th century included cloth; in 1364, for example, Mousehole exported 200 packs of white and russet Cornish cloth, perhaps bought at one of its fairs. It did not last: the cloth trade had declined to almost nothing by the 16th century. Another item normally sold through fairs was leather in the form of hides. Cured with salt, these are first recorded in 1342 when Benedict Noght of Mousehole paid duty on eight dickers (measures), part of the cargo of a Bristol ship. In 1349, a Mousehole ship, the *Saint Michael*, the earliest from the port known by name, was trading a cargo of wool and hides from Dungarvan in Ireland to Flanders. The leather trade continued to be important with uncured hides accounting for 16.5 per cent of Mount's Bay exports in 1541-2. In 1568-9, Ralph Nycles, John Thomas and Jenkin Teage exported salted hides from Mousehole and Barad Lovy the same from Newlyn.[57]

Tin exports from Mousehole start late, though a tin works at Lamorna in St Buryan is noted in 1390. When Peter Bevill applied to export 400 blocks of tin in 1493, Mount's Bay ports were included in his licence, and tin accounted for eight per cent of the bay's customs in the early 1540s. Various tin merchants from Mousehole are named between 1507 and 1574, including John Godolphin, Henry Stabbe, John Harry, John Keigwin, Thomas Pascoe (*Pasko*) and the four hide exporters already named above.[58]

THE FISHING INDUSTRY

Fish was the main trade of much of Cornwall in the Middle Ages and Mount's Bay ports were among those paying an annual fixed rent to the earl of Cornwall by 1300. St Ives and Mousehole were then the most productive of the earl's fisheries followed around Mount's Bay by Marazion, Newlyn, Penzance, and finally, Porthplement and Lamorna. In all, Mount's Bay yielded £9 6s. 8d. annually to the earl, of which £5 came from Mousehole. In 1541-2, the bay was still one of the major fish exporting areas of Cornwall.[59]

The main fishing ground for Mousehole and Newlyn in the medieval period was the bay itself, although from the 15th century Irish fisheries became important. Because of plentiful supplies of different types of fish, there was (as later) virtually all year round employment in the fisheries, in contrast with the more seasonal activity of eastern England. Fishing was a major contributor to the exceptional economic growth of the South West in which Mousehole and Newlyn shared in the 14th and 15th centuries.[60]

The Catch

Hake or 'dentic', a demersal or sea-bed species, normally found in coastal waters, was the major fish caught off Cornwall into the 17th century. Other sea-bed fish, including cod, whiting, ling, ray and conger, were also caught. Towards the end of the period pilchard, a pelagic fish – the kind normally found in shoals – became important. Sea-bed species were normally caught using hooked and baited hand-lines, while drift or seine nets were used for catching shoals of fish by the late 16th century (chapter 3). A more unusual fish catch in 1353-4 was the 'little whale taken in Mount's Bay'.[61]

Hake was sold at Mousehole in 1352-3. A hake fishery was recorded in Mount's Bay itself in 1427 and by the earlier 16th-century the Irish fisheries were also important providers of herring as well as hake. In 1542, the Mount's Bay fishing fleet brought in a total of 6,500 hake for re-export between 27 August and 6 September. Of this catch 5,000 hake came in on Mousehole and Newlyn vessels with Penzance boats accounting for the rest. Other fish caught then or later included pilchards, ray and conger eels, and fish accounted for three quarters of the Mount's Bay customs payments. After 1600 pilchards eclipsed hake as the major catch.[62]

Fish Processing

Fresh fish was especially highly valued, and Mousehole fishermen were compelled to supply them for the duke of Cornwall's household at Restormel Castle in 1354-5. Sales to middlemen as the catch was being landed were discouraged as this could raise the price at market.[63] Because of its perishable nature, most fish for export had to be processed quickly, either by drying, smoking or salting. Hake could be preserved for a short period by a light salting and in the longer term by drying; in 1364, for example, a licence was granted to export 30,000 dried hake from Mousehole. Pilchards were preserved by smoking ('fumadoes') or were salt-cured and pressed. Train (fish) oil was a lucrative by-product of the latter process; as early as 1595 it formed part of the Bristol-bound cargo of the *John* of Mousehole.[64]

Boats and Men In 1327, Mousehole had 16 boats, clearly a significant number although less than the fleet at St Ives, which numbered 28 before the Black Death. We next have information about fishing vessels in the 16th century. Boats, particularly seines, were managed by teams of six to nine people with four to six in the crew. By this date, too, merchant ships were employed in the fisheries, smaller boats being used for the actual fishing. The Irish hake fleet in 1542 included at least two trading vessels from Penzance, three from Newlyn and four from Mousehole. Crews were sometimes drawn from the whole of Mount's Bay: in 1556, men from Mousehole, Penzance, Ludgvan and Marazion went fishing together in the boats of James Thomas of St Hilary.[65]

Surprisingly, only one fisherman is actually named at Mousehole before 1600. Richard Newhall was typical of the wealthy fishermen-farmers who owned land (in his case at Carn Longa west of Mousehole) and shares in boats and nets. He is recorded as a fish exporter in 1519-38, and was one of the four chief men of the town in around 1540. Newhall was related by marriage to the second wealthiest man in Mousehole, William Cockes (whose will survives – the only pre-1600 will from Paul parish). Newhall's goods were worth £4 or a tenth of his father-in-law's in 1522, £10 in 1524-5 but only £6 in 1545, when he was aged about 80.[66]

Fish merchants in medieval Mousehole included local men such as John Boswens and Edmund Bosvenning (*Bosuaenon*) in 1364. Between 1498 and 1595 at least 35 men from Mousehole and seven from Newlyn were exporting fish, while others were ship masters. Foreign merchants carried most of the Mount's Bay fish to Brittany, France and Spain by the mid-16th century and one Spanish apprentice came to Penzance in 1459 to learn the art of fishing.[67]

Foreign Merchants

Foreigners are a recurring theme in Mousehole and Newlyn's history. Some, like Reginald the Gascon (a victualler in 1284), became permanent residents. In 1440, inns were run by two of the three foreigners noted in Paul parish, while 23 aliens are noted as resident in 1522. Most of the latter were servants at Mousehole, often Bretons keen to earn their marriage portions in an area with a similar language to their own. Many Frenchmen and Bretons were still living in Cornwall as late as 1545 and aliens continue to occur in Paul tax lists throughout the 16th century. By 1596, there was at least one black resident in the parish.[68]

Foreign merchants may be identified at Mousehole by their surnames, like David the Poitevin ('Peteyveyn') in 1327. Their activities are well documented; in the mid-15th century, for example, David Trembrathan of Gascony purchased fish there. By then there were also merchants from Waterford in Ireland in the town and European salt merchants at both Mousehole and Newlyn.[69]

Loges or lock-up stores were originally provided for foreign merchants at Mousehole, Newlyn and Penzance. Probably built of

stone and thatched, they provided storage for boats, nets and other
equipment or supplies and for catches of fish before export. Some
loges became hereditary and passed into local use. They also gave
their name to Loga or Logia to the south of the harbour at Newlyn,
and to Carn Lodgia or Lidgia on Mousehole Island.[70]

Seventeen loges are noted in 1327 at Mousehole and at
Penzance, on the Green near Tolcarne. An account of the manor
of Fee Marshall in 1387-8 included a rent of 3s. 4d. for two parts
of a 'logg' at Newlyn. Loges were bought and passed on at Newlyn
in 1368 and 1455 by the Tremenheere family. On the back of a
1439 deed relating to Mousehole, 'one logge' is noted which had
been held by Benedict Vyvyan, then by his daughter Isabel, then by
Joan her daughter, then by Joan's son John until it was taken from

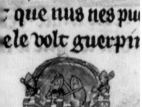

ure 19 Given the love of
acle plays in Cornwall, puppets
y well have entertained visitors
Mousehole's fairs, as this
th-century illustration shows.
ncing bears, sword dancers and
sy fortune tellers also provided
tertainment.

him in 1479-80 by Lawrence Goldsmith, bailiff of Alverton, for his lord's use. Penzance loges were used as fish stores in the 16th century and the Green was considered a suitable place to dry fish.[71]

MARITIME VIOLENCE

Sea ports are notorious for having higher levels of violence and crime than rural areas. Their exposed positions, cosmopolitan nature, fluctuating populations, easy access to drink and weapons, and good escape routes by sea may account for this. Piracy was generally tolerated as an accepted form of self-defence at exposed ports like Mousehole and Fowey. On occasion, however, English or otherwise friendly vessels were attacked. In 1318, Geoffrey Mudford, Richard the Clerk, John of Lyme, Benedict Noght and other Mousehole men took an English ship worth £20 at Hayle near St Ives on the north coast of Cornwall. In 1342 John Lyme of Mousehole and Laurence Basset carried off the goods of a Bristol merchant at Fowey. Mousehole's most outrageous exploit occurred in 1333 when a diplomatic mission from Aquitaine was attacked. Such cases were viewed much more seriously and the perpetrators were generally prosecuted.[72]

Wrecking (stealing goods from shipwrecks) was also commonplace and differed little from piracy. In 1303-4, 144 men from Mount's Bay and beyond were fined for pillaging the Spanish ship *Maudelyne* at Mousehole. Her cargo of Cordovan leather, tallow, white parchment, and 33 coffers full of valuables was taken. Mousehole men imprisoned the owner John of Spain for a year and pleaded that they were stannators (tinners not subject to English law). The thieving continued on land when a Mousehole storehouse was broken into and some of the Spanish merchant's goods turned up as far away as Kingsbridge (Devon). As duke of Cornwall, the Black Prince also brought a case against 96 men in Mount's Bay, including Mousehole men, for taking his goods in 1371.[73]

In the late 13th and 14th centuries, Mousehole appears to have been one of the most violent places around Mount's Bay. At least eight murders were recorded as linked to the town or its inhabitants. Most were not planned in advance, like the violence which erupted in 1284 when two Mousehole victuallers refused to barter with a ship from Cork. The Irish crew went back to their ship for weapons, killed the apprentice of one of the victuallers, and stole provisions. In 1310 another seafarer murdered a Mousehole man and fled, and at about the same period one Benedict the Bastard killed a chaplain from Penryn in Mousehole. On other occasions, as in 1326, both victim and murderer were Mousehole men, while in 1387 the killing of a man

Figure 20 Burnt and
recycled greenstone
pillars, Paul church.
The piers may be from
Polyphant and the niche
behind could be an
original feature, possibly
an Easter sepulchre
(where Christ's burial
and Resurrection were
re-enacted before the
Reformation).

at St Bartholomew's fair, Mousehole, led to a revenge killing five
years later. The final recorded murder occurred at sea in 1398 when
a mutinous crew, including Hobkyn of Mousehole, threw the ship's
owners overboard.[74]

The lack of local court rolls means that we know of relatively few
assaults. Enough evidence survives, however, to show that no-one
was immune. Hailes Abbey had to take out royal protection from
1327 to 1350 in order to collect its tithes in Paul parish. That was
in the wake of a mass assault and 'blood-shedding' in St Buryan
churchyard (part of a patronage dispute between the Crown and
Exeter diocese) involving John Robert of Mousehole and the
Vyvyan family who held Mousehole land. The latter family was
again embroiled with the law in 1356, when one of its members
illegally imprisoned and fined Spanish merchants at Mousehole. At
Newlyn in 1420 the Burwyk family was similarly troublesome.[75]

THE SPANISH RAID

Such events were insignificant in comparison with the violence and
destruction wrought by the Spaniards in 1595. The origins of this
affair lie in the early 1590s, when, after the failure of King Philip II
of Spain's Armada in 1588, Spanish mercenaries led by Don Carlos
of Amezola based themselves at Port Louis in southern Brittany.
Their aim was less ambitious than their king's: they sought to
launch a series of terror raids on the coasts of England and
Scotland. Two contemporary accounts of the 1595 episode survive,
one in English, the other in Spanish. In the Spanish version, the
raid was a crusade; because it was Protestant, Paul church was
deemed 'a mosque' and was to be replaced by a Catholic priory on
the hill above Newlyn.[76]

At 8 o'clock in the morning of 23 July 1595 the Spanish
appeared off Mousehole and landed to the south of the town. For
the next five hours the townsmen faced an attack by sea and land,
while a second Spanish raiding party was sent inland to destroy
Paul church, and the surrounding crops and farms. At 1 pm Sir
Francis Godolphin, deputy lieutenant of Cornwall, and Thomas
Chiverton of Kerris in Paul sent news of these events to John
Hawkins and Francis Drake, the naval commanders at Plymouth.
The Spaniards then re-boarded their ships and entered Mount's
Bay where they anchored off Newlyn, forcing a local force led
by Godolphin and Chiverton to retreat from the green between
Newlyn and Penzance to Marazion.[77] The Spaniards burnt Newlyn
and Penzance, too, and fired three ships in Penzance harbour
(including one from Mousehole), with a cargo which included the
three newly-recast bells of Paul church.[78]

Figure 21 Lewannick
church, after fire, 1890.
This photograph gives us
a good idea of what could
have survived at Paul
after the Spaniards burnt
the church. Lewannick's
Polyphant pillars on the
left are beyond repair.
Alexander the Moor was
baptised in just such a
setting at Paul in 1596.

By the time Hannibal Vyvyan wrote from 'the fort of Falmouth'
(St Mawes), later on the 23rd, the true extent of the disaster was
known. Vyvyan spoke of the 'great want of leaders', and a 'lack
of resistance', which was 'to the disgrace of the people'. A lack of
forewarning or preparation were perhaps the crucial factors, and
a request for a cannon at Mousehole in 1594 had been ignored
by the government. Jenkin Keigwin's brave stand may be a later
fabrication, but on 24 July he was the first of three known victims
'killed by the Spaniards' to be buried. Before leaving, the Spanish
held a Catholic mass on a hill above Newlyn where they had
thought to build their priory.[79]

At Paul further burials followed on 26 July 1595, but by then
the raid was being referred to as the burning of Penzance. Almost
a year later, Francis Courtenay complained that tax payments
from Penwith were down by more than two-thirds because of the
Spanish raid and hoped that a gift of fresh fish would placate his
masters in London. The church at Paul stood roofless although
services were still held there. On Sunday, 28 February 1596, it
was the scene of the baptism of 20-year-old Alexander the Moor,
the black servant of Thomas Chiverton, would-be defender of
Penzance.[80]

Chapter 3

Living off the Sea, 1600-1800

The period 1600-1800 saw significant economic growth in Cornwall and in England as a whole. In the 17th century the local gentry began to invest in trade and in fishing, as well as in mining and farming. Their control of many of Cornwall's 44 parliamentary seats meant extra protection for fishing interests. Salt taxes were successfully opposed in Cornwall until 1694, after which a 'debenture' or bounty payment was paid for all exports of fish cured with salt. In 1699 it was levied at two-fifths of the cost of each hogshead (barrel) of pilchards.[81]

Another important development in the late 17th century was the move westwards of the Cornish tin mining industry from Bodmin Moor to west Penwith. Penzance started to export tin on a major scale and in 1663 successfully petitioned for coinage town status, making it the place where tin was taken for testing or 'coining'. These developments encouraged a trade in valuable imports, and fish cellars were converted to house such items.[82]

The changes in trade at Penzance meant that fish merchants moved their businesses to Newlyn and Mousehole in the late 17th century, thus increasing the economic focus on the fishing industry in Paul parish. Most fish processing moved to these settlements after 1663. Wills, inventories and records of the Paul fish tithe disputes provide us with evidence for the organisation of the fish trade there. They show that fishing methods and pilchard curing took shape early in the 17th century and then changed little until the late 19th century.

Figure 22 Vessels at anchor in Gwavas Lake with Penzance and St Michael's Mount in the background, by Walter Tremenheere, *c.*1800. HMS *Wolf* was moored at Gwavas Lake and the two-masted lugger in the foreground is of a type used by smugglers.

The main threats to these developments were smuggling, piracy and war. Turkish piracy and smuggling, which were threats to trade in general, both emerged in the 17th century and continued into the early 19th. Smuggling became so popular that it was sometimes in danger of crowding out trade and fishing altogether, especially at Mousehole. The Revolutionary wars with France also affected trade, cutting off Mount's Bay from its traditional markets in southern Europe.

FISHING

Pilchards were now the main catch. The shoals were large – thousands of fish rather than a few hundred (as was the case with mackerel which only became important at the end of this period). Catches included herring, scad or horse mackerel, and other shoal fish, together with sea-bed species like hake, cod, ling and shellfish; lobsters were at first captured in drift nets, but willow pots are noted in the 1660s and willow trees were growing at Mousehole by 1767.[83]

Three main methods of fishing took place in Mount's Bay – hook or hand lining (the main medieval method), seining, and drifting. Sea-bed fish were usually caught with hand lines, and nets were used by the other two fisheries. Seiners needed bigger nets to encircle the shoal and these began to appear in Cornwall in the late 16th century. Smaller vertically hung drift nets snared fish from the shoal as they passed by; before the mid-17th century these were used mainly to catch bait for the hook fishery. Seining took place in the daytime in shallow water, while drifting and hand lining were both night-time activities in the deep waters off Cornwall and Ireland.

Seine boats (30 footers) were larger than drift boats. They needed a crew of 12 to 18, including a huer or seine master on the shore, and were laid up for ten months a year (the main pilchard season being about two months long). Huers were the shoal spotters and they used trumpets and semaphore to communicate with the boats. Huers' huts were sited at Penolva and Newlyn in Paul with St Michael's Mount also used in 1767.[84]

Drift boats, being smaller, needed fewer crew and were more versatile. In 1784-5, Richard Hichens of Newlyn's drift fishing boat carried a mackerel seine (much smaller than a pilchard seine) in the spring, pilchard drift nets in summer and autumn, and in winter caught cod, ling and other hook fish with hand lines. Boats like Hichens' worked for ten months or more a year and were only laid up for about six weeks in December and January for repairs.[85]

As Hichens' practice shows, drifters caught pilchards in season but also herring, mackerel and other fish at other times of the year. For the part-time seiners, pilchards were the only catch. In

Figure 23 Seine fishing in St Austell Bay, from John Norden's map of West hundred, c.1600. Two seine nets of great length are being manouvred by the crews of small boats so that they encircle a pilchard shoal. A huer, or shoal spotter, signals instructions from the shore and on a nearby hill a fishwife waits with her basket on her head.

addition, the pilchard season was short – six to eight weeks only – and unpredictable. In the 17th century pilchard shoals could arrive at any time between late July and the end of September, but by the 18th century they came in October or later. Shoal size could also vary. In 1649 and 1762 there were good pilchard catches, but the 1750s were poor years. The shortness of the season led to intense competition. Seiners complained that the drifters broke up the shoals before they came near the shore, although in reality many wealthy fishermen had an interest in both kinds of fishing. From the mid-17th century, drifting was the main fishery in Paul parish, partly because of the fish tithe dispute (Panel 5) and partly because of a lack of sandy beaches of the type favoured by seiners for landing the catch on the western side of Mount's Bay.[86]

Fishermen and Mariners

A maritime survey of 1626 shows that over 10 per cent of Cornish fishermen and mariners lived in Mount's Bay, many of them in Penzance, Marazion, Mousehole and Newlyn. There were 29 fishermen and mariners at Penzance, 34 at Marazion, 38 (including three shipwrights) at Mousehole and 45 at Newlyn; at the same time there were 76 fishermen and mariners on the north coast at St Ives. Newlyn and St Ives had 43 and 47 fishermen respectively, while Mousehole had 28 (more than Marazion and Penzance). These men were probably employed in the hook and drift fisheries. Newlyn and Mousehole's dominance of the fishery increased after 1663, when Penzance turned increasingly towards tin, and the luxury goods trade. There were at least 160 drift fishermen in Paul parish by 1679, equal to half the adult male population.[87]

As early as 1626, the maritime survey included a group of surnames (Cotton, Crankan, Keigwin, Kelynack, Pentreath, Tonkin, Wills and Yeoman) which, together with Downing, Leah, Mann or Wright, represent the key fishing families identified in the Paul parish marriage registers from 1754 to 1792 (the only period when occupations are given). At this time almost half of all Paul bridegrooms were fishermen. Over 70 per cent were able to sign their names (almost the average for Paul parish). The Pentreaths of Mousehole were the principal family. There were 24 Pentreath fishermen-bridegrooms and 19 Pentreath brides marrying fishermen (almost half of partners being from other key families) in the second half of the 18th century, and the surname was so common in the 19th century that it could be divided into eight 'tribes'. In Newlyn, fishing attracted Huguenot refugees; in the 18th century, William Rouffignac, a net-owning fisherman, was grandson of a Huguenot pastor, while in the 1690s the Gruziliers, a

Figure 24 Drift fishing from John Norden's map of Penwith hundred, c.1600. A small sailing vessel uses a vertical net to catch bait.

family of coopers, probably had a similar background. Both names are known in Newlyn to the present day.[88]

Organisation and Ownership

Fishing was the major employer in both Newlyn and Mousehole throughout this period. Almost 30 per cent of 17th-century inventories and 38 per cent of 18th-century ones mention fishing or maritime activity. Boat ownership, or partial ownership, was common among wealthier fishermen. About half of all fishing wills and inventories include a boat or boat-share, and more than half record nets.

The Drift Fishery Most Paul wills and inventories relate to the drift fishery, as we would expect. Thomas Boson of Newlyn was one of the wealthiest fishermen in Mount's Bay. He 'provided a [good] deal of employment in Newlyn and Paul', with a fleet of possibly 10 to 15 boats, before his death in 1633. In reality he was a merchant and his descendants were leaders of the Cornish language movement or revival (chapter 5). More typical of a drift fisherman working on his own account was Thomas Hutchens of Mousehole. He had two old pilchard drift nets and a boat called *Content* with masts, sails, ropes and oars, among goods worth over £27 in 1628-9. John Richards, alias Hew, was typical of the men who provided nets; he had two fish lines and a 'pilcher' net among goods at Mousehole worth under £5 in 1622.[89]

Drift fisheries were usually family or neighbourhood concerns with shares divided between the boat owner, the net providers, and the crew. In 1728 there were at least 119 drift fishermen in Paul parish and 17 per cent (the wealthiest) owned boats and nets. Of the rest, 42 per cent had boats or shares in boats, 31 per cent nets only, and 10 per cent were just crew. Wives and girlfriends were a key part of the fishing economy as they could increase a man's earning power by making nets for him.[90]

The Seine Fishery Seine concerns offered opportunities for capitalist investment all over Cornwall. Expensive to fit out and not in use for most of the year, they tended to be in the hands of merchants and dealers. A good example is Thomas Richards, a huer or seine master, who died in 1660 and whose inventory shows that he owned a quarter of three seines and six boats valued at £20 (half the total value of his goods), besides fish cellar equipment. His house, probably at Newlyn, contained only a few luxury items – a cloak and hat, one pewter dish and a table carpet.[91]

By the 18th century, shares in seines, as in mines, were generally divided into 64 parts. In 1753, Thomas Tregurtha of Newlyn had such a share in the *Endeavour*, *Newlyn Content* and *Mount Content* (the last based at St Michael's Mount) and a 32nd part of the *St Peter* seine. Mousehole then had four or five named seines and Newlyn seven to eight including the *Cabbage Net*.[92]

Processing and Marketing

Pilchard Processing Before 1600 pilchards were usually smoked, when they were known as fumathoes or fair-maids, or pickled in brine; Honor Fryer, for instance, had '2,500 pickle pilchards' in her Newlyn cellar in 1627. In Mount's Bay, these processes were being superseded by pressing in the late 1620s when pilchard cellars with 'lean-tos' and pressing poles first appear. The lever pressing process used until the late 19th century, extended the 'sell by date' of pilchards. Only the scale varied with much larger cellars and work forces associated with the seine fisheries. Pressing produced a valuable by-product in the form of train (fish) oil and sales of this to tanners and others could cover the processing costs. After Penzance became a coinage town in 1663, most fish processing in Mount's Bay moved to Newlyn and Mousehole.[93]

Many casual shore workers were required for the harvest of the sea. Women carried pilchards up from the beach on their backs and a 'cawell' (cowel or carrying basket) is noted among 13 baskets worth three shilling in the Mousehole inventory of Elizabeth Noye in 1677. In 1711 two old baskets and two old cowels were worth 1s. 1d. Wooden gurries (four-handled trays) and barrows were also used, mostly by men. Poor fishermen were given damaged fish, and, at Newlyn, 'Bucca' (the sea spirit) got his share, too.[94]

The fish were cured in bulks (walls), built by women working in pairs with a thick salt mortar (Panel 8). The same salt could be used up to three times in the curing process. In 1740, for example, Elias Crankan had new French salt, as well as once- and twice-used salt. Cellar equipment is mentioned in over a fifth of 17th-century local probate records, but in only about a tenth of 18th-century ones, by which time inventories become rare. Half a dozen poles, bucklers and a dozen pressing stones occur in the 1691 inventory of Richard Standly, a Newlyn fisherman, whose goods were worth only £5 16s. 4d.[95]

Female fish-curers included Elizabeth Noye of Mousehole (a Keigwin by birth) whose 1677 inventory included 16 bucklers, 14 pressing poles and 21 pressing stones. Lydia Tonkin was her Newlyn equivalent in the late 1690s-1700s (Panel 4). An idea of the number of women employed by the seine fishery comes from the accounts of lay rectors of Paul. The Veale and Carlyon family employed eight women in their Newlyn tithe cellar and six at Mousehole in 1759 including Orchard Crankan and Dorcas Wills.

Figure 25 Pilchard cellar on St Peter's Hill, possibly Colmear's or Coleman's Court, demolished in the slum clearance of 1951. Families often lived in first-floor accommodation, over the ground-floor fish-processing cellar. Two 'palaces' for curing pilchards are noted in Newlyn Town in 1659; the term 'palace' being more commonly used in east Cornwall.

Assuming these 14 women dealt with a tenth of fish (the tithe) caught by Paul fishermen, this could imply a labour force of at least 140 women for the two-month pilchard season.[96]

Half the Newlyn women and two-thirds of the Mousehole women working in the tithe cellars were from key fishing families. Thefts of salt were blamed on non-cellar-women in 1762 and, when the cellar-women threatened to strike for more pay in 1766, the tithe owners considered recruiting women from Penberth Cove in the neighbouring parish of St Buryan instead. The situation was still tense in 1767, when Newlyn cellar women were given 'a very great rattle' by Mr Veale, because of the slowness of their work.[97]

Marketing The main market for pilchards remained southern Europe, particularly Italy and Spain. What changed after 1663 was Newlyn and Mousehole's market share, as Penzance turned to tin exports and other types of trade. In 1759-65, pilchards went

Letters from Lydia

Letters are among the most personal of records, but relatively few survive from before the 19th century. Many civilisations have produced great letter writers and books of instruction for letter writing survive in England from the 13th century. Women's letters are rare, and often written for them by male scribes (as in the case of Margaret Paston). Cornwall is important in later postal history as from 1689 to the 1840s Falmouth in Cornwall was the centre of a worldwide letter distribution service known as the Packet service.

Family archives and company records include many letters. In the Arundell archive at the Cornwall Record Office are 15 letters written by Lydia Tonkin of Newlyn in 1702-18. Most were sent to her 'cousin' George Bere, a gentleman of St Ervan, owner of Newlyn Manor and steward of the Arundells. Lydia kept Bere informed about his Newlyn tenants and one of the earliest letters (15 July 1705) refers to the royal touch widely believed to cure scrofula (a swelling of the neck). Although Lydia's handwriting is sometimes hard to decipher and her spelling erratic, the letters reveal her as a good business-woman and mother.

Born Lydia Hicks at Kerris in Paul parish in 1659, she was a gentleman's daughter. In 1691 Lydia married Nowell Tonkin, a Newlyn merchant, and had two children by him – Henry baptised in 1694 and young Lydia, 1697. When Nowell died in 1697 Lydia took over the family pilchard business and in 1699 sold 65 hogsheads of pilchards to a Falmouth merchant. This was the fourth largest amount from any Newlyn merchant. Not surprisingly, pilchards are often mentioned in letters. For example, after a fever on 18 October 1702 Lydia was just able to 'creep abroad against ye pilchards'. On 4 August of the following year she wrote that 'pilchards begin to come now'. A fuller picture is given in 1704 when Lydia had to get home from Plymouth before the fishing season started. On 30 August she was expecting 'my little pilchard cousins' and by 19 September was 'busy about my fish'.

Lydia's letters reveal much about life in Newlyn. Her children caused her worry, especially her daughter who was lame. On 24 April 1706 she wrote of young Liddy's 'weak limb', which did not reach the ground and in an earlier letter agonised about whether to have the bone reset. Doting on her son Henry, Lydia soon came to regret his excesses. In 1714 he went on a fish-sponsored 'Grand Tour' of France, but by 1718 was married and had 'taken up with scroungers'. Lydia was then supporting her son Henry, his 'meek' wife and two sisters, a daughter of Mr Allen's and 'many guests he brings in sometimes without the least notice'. 'God almighty arm me with patience', was almost the last thing she wrote to cousin Bere. Despite frequent illnesses (fever, cholic etc.), Lydia lived to be 84 and died at Newlyn in 1743.

Figure A: The courtyard of the 17th-century house at Kerris Barton where Lydia was born.

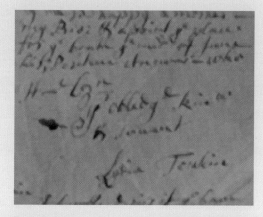

Figure B: An extract from a letter written by Lydia Tonkin.

Letters:
AR 10/158, 169, 206, 223-4, 226, 259, 267, 274, 282, 424-5, 450, 665;
George Bere:
L. McCann, *Introduction to the Arundell Archive* (1996), 8.
Business and landholding interests:
TNA, C 7/761/5; CRO, BRA/833/241-3.

Figure 26 Dolly Pentreath engraved by Richard Scaddan, 1781. Dolly wears the traditional fishwives costume with black beaver hat and the illustration also shows her pair of clay pipes and pouch of tobacco. Other versions show a cowel or carrying basket, and a jug of ale.

Figure 27 Harvesters making merry in fields near Madron church with Mount's Bay behind, by Henry Pendarves Tremenheere, c.1800. The merrymakers include a man, perhaps an ex-sailor, with a wooden leg, and two gentlemen.

to Alicante and Valencia in Spain, and Genoa in Italy, but also to Roscoff in Brittany (a smuggling centre) and Falmouth. Falmouth was a distribution port. In a legal case brought in the Court of Chancery in 1699 George Richards of Penzance was reported as having bought 432 hogsheads of pilchards from Newlyn for Robert Corker, a Falmouth merchant. The total value, including the salt bounty, was £2,155. Eight Newlyn merchants, including James Keigwin and Lydia Tonkin, were partly paid in cash, salt and cork, but Richards died before the bounty money was paid.[98]

There was also an important local market served by fishwives carrying fish in cowels on their back and bags of salt in their pockets. They tramped for miles around the Penwith peninsula, went to Penzance market, and included Dolly Pentreath of Mousehole. Even in old age, Dolly's route still took in Castle Horneck, near Madron, a six-mile round trip. Martha Blewett was another who provided fish and salt to country people. Sadly, she was murdered less than a mile from Mousehole in 1792.[99]

Fishermen-Farmers

Fishing or farming interests are noted in over 70 per cent of probate records made between 1600 and 1799 for parishioners of Paul. Some 31 per cent of these inventories concern fishermen of whom 10 per cent were fishermen-farmers. Paul parish was an area of mixed farming like the rest of Penwith, with an emphasis on horse and cattle raising. Sheep, pigs, geese, ducks and poultry were also kept and two farmers had goats. Wheat and barley were the most common crops with oats, rye, hemp and peas grown, too. Marriage cycles were determined at first by the harvest, like the rest of Penwith. A new pattern of winter marriages in Paul parish after 1700 related to the sea harvest, and showed the increasing importance of fishing in the local economy.[100]

Fishermen-farmers were the wealthiest group, and the average value of their goods at death rose from £20 in 1600-49 to £70 in 1700-99, while the goods of farmers more than doubled from £17 to £45. Fishermen's goods rose from £15 to £25, less than the Cornish average. Richard Sampson of Newlyn, who described himself as a yeoman, is a good example of a fisherman-farmer. He had one boat and half shares in three others, half a seine, and 15 pilchard nets 'good and bad' as well as a cow and four pigs in 1680. Rather than investing in new consumer goods, fishermen-farmers took an active part in the land market of west Penwith. Subletting at high rents became profitable with leases noted in inventories as chattels.[101]

THE ROYAL NAVY

The Royal Navy was the main alternative to fishing by the 18th century and 87 mariners' wills survive for Paul parish. Although these are among the least detailed of any wills, they provide occasional glimpses of naval life. In 1740 Alexander Hosking, a seaman on HMS *Montague*, left his wages to his father, clothes to his 'messmate' Thomas Purefoy and books to his brother William Hosking; Purefoy was to see that the books were not 'sold to the mess'. By then, mariners were mostly young men without family commitments, unlike their counterparts in 1626.[102]

At the end of the Seven Years War (a war in Germany involving all of the major European powers of the period) in 1763 Mousehole was 'a nursery of seamen' (a common claim). 'No less than sixty are now in his Majesty's [service] and more than the like number in the last war voluntarily served in the Royal Navy'. Service was not always voluntary and impressment or compulsory recruitment to the Royal Navy was widespread as foreign warfare became endemic. In 1652, a compromise was reached: only one or two men would be taken from each fishing boat. In the next century, 'seamen in port claim to be customs men to avoid impressment'. Richard Pentreath of Mousehole, a witness in a customs case, was mistakenly taken by the press gang to the *Active* frigate in 1762.[103]

Dealing with Piracy

Policing the sea was a naval responsibility, but not an easy one in west Cornwall after 1625, when Turkish raids affected trade and fishing. 'Turks' might be of many nationalities, including disgruntled Europeans. They made the north coast of Africa their base in 1598 with ports at Algiers, Tunis, Tripoli and Salee. Christian prisoners were sold into slavery in north Africa and ransoms had to be paid for their release. On 16 June 1640, in one of the worst raids, 60 people were taken from five fishing boats and four other vessels near Mousehole. Stories that men, women and children were taken from their beds by the Turks were widely believed, though probably unfounded. There were also Spanish (Biscayners), French (Dunkirkers), Dutch and local pirates, too. Bristol wanted additional ships to be stationed off Land's End to protect trade, while Penzance asked for eight cannons and £600. In 1626 government hopes of resisting the 'Turks' rested on the trained bands of militia at Fowey, Looe and Penzance.[104]

SMUGGLING

The greatest period of smuggling coincided with wars from 1689 to 1815. Starting as a response to a salt tax in the 1680s, by the 1690s many other imports were heavily taxed to fund war. In 1695 the first smuggling case was reported in the port of Penzance when six gallons of brandy were found in a small fishing boat. By the early 18th century the 'free trade' was a major sideline in Mount's Bay. Roscoff in Brittany and Guernsey in the Channel Islands were the main suppliers of smuggled goods. In addition to brandy, gin and rum, contraband also included tea, sugar, vinegar and velvets (this last found in 1780 on the *Hampden*, a Falmouth packet – a fast vessel that carried letters and bullion to the Mediterranean and the Americas).[105]

Smuggling cases involving Mousehole or Newlyn people occur in most of the surviving customs books for the port of Penzance in the period 1738-1800. Two-thirds of the 70 named smugglers came from Mousehole and the rest from Newlyn. About a third were fishermen, eight (including one fisherman) were boat owners, and a further eight, crewmen. Nine of the 12 key fishing families are represented. In 1749, eight young fishermen of Mousehole were arrested for such activity, and in the next year three Newlyn fishermen were charged with rum-running on the *Polly*. A typical smuggling voyage began on New Year's Day 1773 at Newlyn pier. With a cargo of potatoes, a sloop belonging to John Leah of Paul and captained by his son John sailed for Brittany. At Roscoff (Roscrou) they loaded tea and 12 ankers or casks of brandy. They then sailed to Morlaix and returned to Mousehole on Saturday 30 January, by which time the crew had consumed two casks of cargo.[106]

Customs officers were not usually local. One candidate for the Penzance customs service in 1789 had been baptised in a dissenting meeting-house in Truro. Officers lived among the smugglers and were expected to set a good example. But in 1767 Edward Rowling was reprimanded for keeping company with known smugglers at Mousehole, while John Richards reputedly cursed and abused

'Smuggling is carried on to a great height and in a most barefaced and impudent manner on this coast, and sometimes even under our noses in the Harbour'

Comment in Penzance customs' book for 23 November 1761.

Figure 28 The view from Mousehole Island, looking toward Mousehole, H.P. Tremenheere, published as an engraving in 1804. This was the setting for an attack on a customs officer in 1789.

'persons of honour and distinction' at Newlyn on May Day 1739. Charges of accepting bribes were common.[107]

Customs officers were regularly assaulted. In 1769 soldiers had to be stationed in the Mount's Bay area after the murder of William Odgers, an officer at Porthleven. In the 1760s and '70s, the *Wolf* sloop assisted officers in some anti-smuggling operations and brought new blood into the area; Paul parish registers in 1766 and 1770-6 record 15 marriages between the *Wolf*'s crew and local girls. The crew were also involved in the unexplained death of John Pentreath in early January 1771.[108]

A new phase in smuggling began in the late 18th century. In 1783 it was reported that, while in the past 'small vessels and open boats' had been used, now there were 'vessels of great force some carrying from twenty to thirty guns'. It was claimed that these luggers and cutters were built at Folkestone, Dover and Cowes. The Carter family of Prussia Cove in Breage parish had extended their activities to Mount's Bay and set up a gun battery. Violence increased on both sides and culminated in a pitched battle in Prussia Cove in 1794 in which smugglers came into conflict with Mousehole and Newlyn customs officers.

A case from Mousehole in 1789, involving John Pentreath (alias St Alban) and William Badcock (alias Cat), illustrates the rise in violence. Pentreath's boat was spotted by a customs officer as it rounded Mousehole island. When a guinea bribe was refused, the officer was struck over the head with his own stick and was abused by five or six smugglers (including Badcock) who uttered 'horrid oaths' and threatened to throw him into the sea. Another smuggler of this period, Henry Rickard of Newlyn, appears to have been equally lawless, being described variously as sergeant in the militia, deserter, privateer, tinner and fisherman.[109]

Searches of houses, fish cellars, outbuildings and even the parish church were more common in this later period, and could also involve violence, especially since receivers who hid smuggled goods were punished as severely as the smugglers themselves. When a posse of officers arrived to search the house of William Trewavas at Mousehole in 1786, they found themselves staring down the barrels of the loaded pistols of William Trewavas the younger and John Trewavas; William the younger may have been exceptionally dangerous. He was probably the murderer of Martha Blewett, for which he was hanged at Bodmin in 1793 at the age of 26.[110]

Smuggling had complex and unexpected effects on local society. In 1788 a man, wrongfully arrested for smuggling, spent five months in Bodmin gaol, while in the following year a churchwarden of Paul parish told the customs officer, William Carey, that it would be better to have a single family (namely Carey's) on the poor rate rather than seven families of smugglers. Such attitudes were prevalent at the end of the 18th century, perhaps because there was a lot at stake, especially from the 1790s when the wars with revolutionary France drove up taxes. When, after the return of peace in 1815, taxes were lowered, smugglers were less inclined to resort to violence.[111]

Figure 29 Paul church interior looking south by H.P. Tremenheere, *c*.1800. William Carey, a Mousehole customs officer, searched for smuggled goods here in 1788, and accidentally fired his pistol in the tower. This area of the church was also the scene of major pew disputes in the 1790s.

Chapter 4

The Expansion of Newlyn, 1600-1800

MOUNT'S BAY AFTER THE SPANISH RAID

The Spanish raid of 1595 with which we ended chapter 2 was followed by changes in all of the Mount's Bay towns. After 1595 Mousehole shrank; Newlyn doubled in area and population, and Penzance joined Marazion as a charter town in 1614. Although in the year after the raid money was collected from as far away as Hampshire and London for the communities which had suffered, bad harvests in 1596-7 led to a fall in population and more died of hunger than in the raid itself. Homeless former residents of Mousehole, Newlyn and Penzance were among the starving. It was a national crisis reflected locally in the fact that more deaths than births were recorded in parish registers. By the time it was over in 1601 some families had left the area permanently.[112]

Already in the mid-16th century it had looked briefly as if Newlyn would become the chief town in the bay. Although it failed to catch up with Penzance or St Ives, it went on after 1595 to overtake Mousehole and Marazion in importance. The town's rise, the main subject of this chapter, is linked with the development of the pilchard fishing industry, of which the impact upon the townscapes of Newlyn and Mousehole forms a secondary theme.

Local Government

Around 1600 local government came to be based on the parish rather than the manorial court. The important body was the parish meeting, which was known from the place where it was held as the vestry, and which included the minister, churchwardens and local parishioners. At Paul, a poor rate was being collected by 1613, probably by the churchwardens of the day. A constable is named in about 1623 and constables' staffs of 1828 and 1838 are still kept in the church. Poor Law overseers, also answerable to the vestry, raised rates to support local paupers and their presence is implied in the records of neighbouring parishes. Paul parish way wardens are recorded in 1793.[113]

How Paul was governed is largely conjectural because, apart from parish registers, there are no parish records before the 19th century. The churchwardens' accounts, vestry minutes, constables' or highway accounts, and Poor Law records are all missing. Nor are there any early Cornish quarter session records to show the workings of local government at county level.

Fish Tithes

One tenth of all crops and young animals went to support each local church which had a resident clergyman or rector in the Middle Ages. These payments in kind were known as tithes and can be traced back to the ninth century. Richard earl of Cornwall appointed the clergy at Paul in the early 13th century, but gave this right to Hailes abbey in 1259. Sometime between 1291 and 1308, Hailes abbey appropriated the rectory and appointed a vicar (or deputy) to serve the parish. From then on the tithes were split between the rector and the vicar. Hailes got the great tithes (crops) as rector until 1539, when the Crown became the lay rector, and the vicar got the small tithes (young animals). The great tithes included fish, and in the 17th century these were worth £120 a year, less costs.

Local people leased the rectorial tithes in the 16th and early 17th centuries – Godolphins of Trewarveneth in Paul parish c.1539-40, Chivertons c.1604-29 and then Hicks of Kerris. In 1640 John Gwavas of Sithney bought the rectory from Charles Cokayne (who had bought it from the Crown in 1629). William Gwavas, John's brother inherited it in 1642 and this family held it until 1741. Veales and Carlyons then inherited by marriage and held the rectory jointly until 1828-9 when William Hitchens of St Ives became the last tithe owner.

Figure A: Newlyn Quay, by Walter Tremenheere, c.1800. Men unload fish by wading out to boats while merchants wait on shore. Fishwives in black beaver bonnets are busy sorting the fish on the sand and a cart and horse wait to carry the fish away.

There were always problems collecting Paul tithes. In the 13th century Hailes abbey had to take out a royal protection, and in the early 17th century Justice Chiverton objected that the fishermen 'threw out' the smallest fish as the tenth or tithe fish at Newlyn pier. James Loase, tithe farmer of William Gwavas I, brought the first legal case against the drift fishermen in 1653, but by 1679-80 tithe evasion had reached such serious proportions that 160 Paul fishermen faced trial. The fishermen claimed unsuccessfully that drift nets were a new method of fishing and so were exempt from tithe.

The fish tithe dispute flared up again in 1724 when William Gwavas III brought a case against 119 drift fishermen in Paul parish. John Tregurtha and John James had been defendants in 1679-80, but had 'conceived the decree to be hard; and therefore not binding on them'. The fishermen brought their own case against Gwavas in 1728, but this was defeated.

The final phase of the dispute began in 1828, when 53 fishermen in Paul parish agreed to pay a guinea a year instead of tithes, but the new owner tried to double this rate in 1829. On Christmas Eve 1830 the women of Mousehole and Newlyn pelted his bailiff with fish offal. Placards reading: 'It is better to die than to starve – No tithe – One and All' were put up. No further fish tithe payments were made in Paul parish though the Hitchens were still trying to extract money as late as 1842.

tithe background: 'VCH Penwith', 52; T. Pawlyn, 'Cornish pilchard fishery', JRIC (1998), 77-80.
Chiverton interest: TNA, PROB 11/155, ff.296-v; TNA, E134/31&32Chas2/Hil12.
1640 sale: CRO, CN 951.
1653 case: CRO, CN 1628.
Hicks interest: BL, Add 813, ff.3-6.
1679-80 dispute: TNA, E134/31&32Chas2/Hil12.
1720s-30s: see chapter 5.

Figure 30 Tolcarne, engraving from drawing by H.P. Tremenheere, 1804. This shows the still extant medieval bridge with Street-an-Nowan to the left and Tolcarne on the right. Half the houses were still thatched then and Tolcarne rock was not yet obscured by trees.

Other parishes in Mount's Bay, such as adjacent Madron, which included the Tolcarne part of Newlyn, are much better documented. They illustrate the kind of activities which must also have gone on in Paul. Madron churchwarden accounts start in 1762 and vestry minutes begin in 1829. In addition, overseers of the poor for Madron are noted as far back as 1742 and detailed poor rates and accounts survive from 1757. As well as collecting rates and distributing clothing, shoes, spectacles and the occasional wooden leg, the overseers kept the poorhouse and workhouse repaired and prosecuted other parish overseers who tried to unload their poor on to Madron.[114]

Paul parish had a poorhouse noted in the burial registers in the late 18th century. There were also private almshouses at Paul known as the Hutchens Gift House, which housed six poor men and six poor women of the parish. Founded in the early 18th century they still stand below the parish church. The Madron overseers had dealings with some Paul families in the period 1758-87, as well as with the residents of Tolcarne, the only part of Newlyn for which they were legally responsible. Thus we know that William Verran and his bed were removed to Madron poorhouse from Newlyn in Paul parish in 1779-80.[115]

One other important figure in Paul's affairs was the lay rector. With the dissolution of the monasteries Paul rectory, which had belonged to Hailes Abbey until 1539, became the property of the Crown. It was generally leased out to laymen, who often had local connections. In the later 17th and 18th centuries they included

Willam Gwavas (1638-84) and his son, also called William (1676-1741), who played an important part in local life and culture. The lay rectors were presumably responsible for the upkeep of the chancel, although the right to appoint the vicar seems to have remained vested in the Crown. From the local point of view, their most important entitlement was to collect the great tithes, including those levied on fish landed at Newlyn and Mousehole. The exercise of this right was not popular with the local inhabitants and in the early 1680s and again in the 1720s the Gwavases became involved in prolonged disputes with local fishermen (Panel 5).[116]

Growing populations

Cornwall's population increased by one-fifth in the 17th century from around 100,000 to about 120,000. The population of west Penwith grew more rapidly than this, rising by almost half between 1600 and 1649 – nearly double the rate of growth recorded for the country at this time. In the period 1650-1701, when the population of England fell by 3.3 per cent, that of west Penwith rose by 44 per cent, as the tin industry moved west from its medieval roots on Bodmin moor. Although the major growth in Penwith was in mining parishes like St Just, Paul's population rose by just over a third in 1650-99. In all, between 1600 and 1699 it rose from about 600 to almost 1,300.[117]

We do not know definitively how many of these people lived in Newlyn and Mousehole, but records of the 1664 hearth tax (a tax on fireplaces) provide a good indication. They list 91 households for Paul, of which seven were too poor to pay and have been excluded from any calculations. Of the remaining 84 more than half were in the towns – 17 at Mousehole and 27 in Newlyn. Using a multiplier of 12.3 (based on a parish population of about 1,032) we arrive at 209 people in Mousehole, and 332 in Newlyn (or more than 350 if Tolcarne in Madron is included). There were also some 491 inhabitants in the rural area. Marazion, Penzance and St Ives were larger towns, containing about 600, 1,000 and 1,500 people, respectively.[118]

Some Leading Families

In the Paul protestation roll (or oath of loyalty to Charles I) of 1641 the first two names in the list are William Boson and John Keigwin. These men headed two of the leading families in the parish. Among only 18 per cent of parishioners in Paul able to sign their own name, they and their families were in the forefront of the Late Cornish language movement of the later 17th century (opposite). The Keigwin dynasty derived its name from its origins at Keigwin in St Just, while the Bosons may have acquired theirs from the occupation of boatswain. Both surnames first occur in Paul parish records in the early 16th century. While the Keigwins put down their main roots in Mousehole, by the mid-century Newlyn was the Bosons' base. All were involved in the trade of Mount's Bay, held large estates, and gave local leadership. One Keigwin was mayor of Penzance in 1663.[119]

Keigwins and Bosons were among the major exporters of 'cured' pilchards in Mount's Bay. For example, Barthram, younger brother of Thomas Boson, merchant and Cornish writer, was master of six different Penzance vessels in 1675-87. Both families also included gentry and all three sons of Richard Keigwin, a Mousehole merchant, married into gentry families in the early 17th century. Although later legend refers to Richard's father Jenkin as 'Squire Keigwin' it was Richard's grandson William who was the first esquire in the family. This William Keigwin bought the manor of Alverton in 1663.[120]

Figure 31 Simplified Boson and Keigwin family tree. The abbreviation fl. comes from the Latin verb *floruit* meaning 'he flourished'.

More literate than most of their neighbours, members of the main branch of Keigwins went to university. Keigwins and Bosons witnessed many wills and valued almost a third of Paul inventories in 1600-49. Several Bosons also acted as attorneys while the eldest

Boson and Keigwin Family Tree

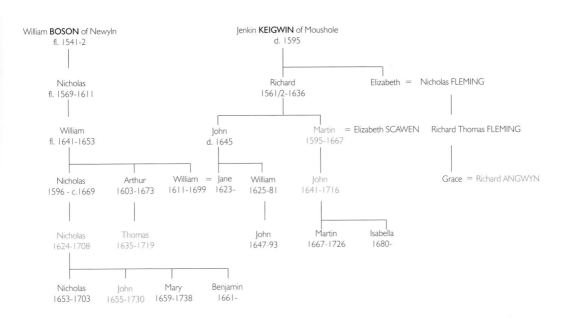

Language writers are shown in colour.

Sources: J. Vivian's **Visitations of Cornwall** with supplementary information from Ledbury, MS. and Matthew Spriggs.

Figure 32 William Gwavas
(1676-1741).

son of Nicholas Boson (1624-1708) became a 'grasping' lawyer. Closer ties between Bosons and Keigwins included a ship, a marriage, and land-holding. Nicholas Boson (c.1569-1611) took over as captain of the *John* of Mousehole from Richard Keigwin of Mousehole in 1595; in 1642, Jane Keigwin married William Boson the younger; and in 1585-1664 Bosons owned Keigwin ancestral lands in St Just.[121]

The Gwavases, owners of the fish tithes from 1640, were another important local family. Originating from Sithney, near Helston, they had strong connections with the Middle Temple in London where at least three were barristers. The most distinguished member of the family was William, born in Suffolk in 1676 and a pupil of John Boson of Newlyn in the early 18th century. After inheriting the fish tithes from his father, he retired to Penzance and Newlyn in 1717 and played there an important part in the Cornish language movement until his death in 1741.[122]

Much grander than any of these were the Godolphins, established in Breage at Godolphin House since at least the late 13th century. By the 16th century they were one of the county's leading families, deriving much wealth from the exploitation of their tin mines. As we have seen, their then head, Sir Francis (d.1608), took a leading role in the Spanish Raid. Another branch of the family was actually based in the parish of Paul at Trewarventh manor on the outskirts of Newlyn in the 16th and 17th centuries. Owners of the mills at Tolcarne, they also briefly leased the fish tithes from the Crown in the mid-16th century.

The Rebuilding of Paul Church

Fund-raising to rebuild Paul church began soon after the Spanish raid. The old arcades (chapter 2) were made of Polyphant (or a

Figure 33 Trewarveneth manor house, by H.P. Tremenheere, c.1800. The distinctive gable of the Godolphin's mid-17th-century house is still there though most of the window openings are blocked.

similar greenstone), which does not stand up to fire, and were described as 'utterly ruined' in 1595. Only a few pieces of burnt stone were recycled in the present building. Although the shell survived, especially the tower and the west and north sides, Paul church today is mostly a 17th century and later creation.[123]

The rebuilt church retained its characteristic Cornish design. It had three aisles of equal length and height, with a barrel vault, later plastered (figure 20). There was no clerestory. The only distinction between the eastern sanctuaries and the naves is a step marking the point at which the rood screen ran across the whole church. The contrast of the pointed arches on the south side of the nave with the round ones on the north suggests that at least the form of the medieval arcades had been preserved. The new piers were a simple type used previously in Penwith's poorest churches – Zennor, Gwithian, St Levan, Sennen and Towednack. On the north side, three bays from the east, a clumsy reconstruction of calcined materials salvaged from the medieval church includes moulded jambs with attached columns and capitals of unusual design like Mawgan in Pydar or Padstow. They perhaps came from a chantry within the 15th-century church. The two piers to the east of this bodged rebuilding also look scorched. Possibly they were survivors from the fire or had been reused from a Mousehole chapel?

The rebuilding of the parish church seems to have been undertaken by the parish as a whole. Both the lay rector and the parish vestry, which seems to have been in existence by then, might

Figure 34 Street an Nowan, by Walter Tremenheere, *c.*1800. The view shows the new settlement and Gwavas Quay, with North Corner slip and fish cellars behind. Belle Vue is shown above with Boase Castle being the seaward-facing house. Much of the foreground where the artist sits painting was washed away with the road in the great storm of 1880.

have been expected to be involved in this, but the absence of parish records makes it difficult to assess the role of the latter.

The lay rector, Thomas Chiverton of Kerris, left £13 6s. 8d. in his will of 1604 for the 'finishing of Paul church'. Nicholas Boson of Newlyn, a wealthy fisherman, lent the parish money to buy lead for the roofs in 1608. Both he and Chiverton gave money to the repair of the tower and Richard Denys left £2 'towards the making and casting anew of the bells' in 1608. The medieval bells, recast at Bristol as recently as June 1595, had been destroyed soon after their return. An inscription: 'the Spanyers burnt this church in 1595', was put up when the church was finished.[124]

NEWLYN IN THE ASCENDANT

Newlyn's rise was associated with the development of its fishing industry. Changes in pilchard fishing and methods of curing (chapter 3) were accompanied by increased investment and new building. In particular, the new settlement of Street an Nowan grew up in the earlier 17th century on open fields in the triangle between the beach, Paul Hill and Newlyn Town, linking Newlyn with Tolcarne and Jackford. This development doubled the size of Newlyn, and brought a considerable increase in population. Already in 1623 Newlyn had more fishermen and mariners than Mousehole, and by 1664 it had almost twice as many inhabitants. By 1687 it probably housed one of the two inns in Paul parish.[125]

The fishing industry also had an impact on the built environment in both Newlyn and Mousehole. Its domestic scale gave rise to characteristic houses with living accommodation on

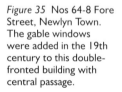

Figure 35 Nos 64-8 Fore Street, Newlyn Town. The gable windows were added in the 19th century to this double-fronted building with central passage.

Figure 36 Old Manor House, Trewarveneth Street, Newlyn. Early 17th-century, possibly the manor house for Newlyn manor.

the first floor, approached by external steps, and with ground-floor cellars in which the pilchards were pressed. Behind these buildings were courtyards, where the fish were salted in 'baulks' before the pressing process, and around which were pentices or 'lean-tos' where pressing might also take place. An early example, recorded in 1629 as belonging to 'widow Boson' and probably in Newlyn, comprised a 'cellar with one little court and lean-tos round it'.[126]

Newlyn Town

Newlyn Town (medieval Newlyn) recovered quickly from the Spanish raid, in comparison to Mousehole; at least one building – the Bosons' mansion house, near the old quay – probably survived the attack, but was demolished in the early 20th century (Panel 7). Rebuilding began before 1615 when the fish merchant Nowel Tonkin constructed a 'new house or hall' with a kitchen next to it. Stone houses with slate roofs were built for Newlyn merchants near the harbour and the old quay and at the point where trackways led off up the hillside. The best surviving example from the early 17th century is the so-called Old Manor House which lay near the lower end of Trewarveneth Street, the road to Trewarveneth Farm and ultimately to Paul church. Another, more altered three-storey house, lies at the bottom of the same street on the south side. More typical of the homes of fishermen is the one-and-a-half storey, four-room house at 64-8 Fore Street.

In the same period Newlyn Town grew southwards over Withen Gwavas field towards the Bowjey. Space was less of a problem here so houses were built with their longer frontage rather than gable end to the street. Trewarveneth manor house now part of the south-west outskirts of Newlyn was rebuilt for the Godolphin family shortly before 1664 (figure 33).[127]

Street an Nowan

The place name Street an Awan, or 'street of the oxen' (now Street an Nowan) is first found in Thomas Chiverton's will of 1604 when the area was still farmland. However, a new settlement was evidently developing here, between the areas left ruined by the Spanish raid. By 1615 Nowel Tonkin had a 'little new cellar and a courtlege [courtyard] and cellar' on Chiverton's land. It could only be approached directly from Newlyn Town across the beach at low tide; otherwise, it was necessary to take the tracks which climbed up the hill behind. Based on the fishing industry, its main focus was the beach, where the catch was landed at low tide, and Breton merchants dried their fish. Tithe cellars belonging to the lay rector of Paul were also sited here and there was a quay, later known as

Figure 37 Higher mill at Tolcarne, *c.*1800. This is the smallest mill of the five then in operation at Tolcarne.

Gwavas Quay after the fish tithe owner. Today the quayside of Street an Nowan is cut off from the water by the harbour road.[128]

Tolcarne

In 1600 the third settlement that made up 17th-century Newlyn, Tolcarne with Jackford, was already a place of some antiquity, with its focus on the ancient route from Newlyn and Paul to Penzance. By the late 1630s there were at least four or five households, besides a fisherman or two, and a glover. Tolcarne's activities were dominated by the ancient manorial mills. Householders included two millers, a mill loader, and a baker with the unusual name Haleknight Stephen. The mill loader ran a door to door service for Penzance – taking corn and returning with flour. Mills and a bakehouse lay further up the Coombe to the west of the coastal settlement.[129]

Before 1614, two mills were in use at Tolcarne. They were served by the same leat (watercourse) so that 'the water fleeted and ran from one of the said mills to the other'. The higher mill ground 'clean corn' and the lower one 'oatmeal and malt'. The enterprise was extended after an agreement in 1614 between the miller Bennet Benettowe and the owner Nicholas Godolphin of Trewarveneth. Bennettowe was to build a new leat at Tolcarne, which was to carry water at a higher level using wooden launders (gutters). A third mill was then added to the gable-end of the lower mill around 1618.[130]

In the 1630s, the Godolphins employed Lewis Penkevil to oversee their milling business (then worth £20-£30 a year). When the lower mill gable fell down in 1655 it was rebuilt and two more mills were added by John Williams between the higher and lower mills in about 1660. An enormous tree found buried in sand further down the Coombe was brought by 'a great number of people' as the foundation for the new mills. By this date the upper mill was the malt mill with four lower mills grinding corn and occasionally 'skinning oats'.[131]

The Godolphins' monopoly, derived from the rights of the lords of Alverton, was both profitable and controversial; the ambivalent attitude of the Cornish in general to such arrangements is reflected in their proverb, 'a miller has a golden thumb'. The inhabitants of Penzance resented having to grind their corn in the mills of Tolcarne; they wanted to use mills closer to their town and claimed that those at Tolcarne could not grind all the grain they needed. They also complained of 'ill dealing' at Tolcarne, which allegedly included adding sand to their malt, and supplying underweight bread to the town. This dispute continued into the early 18th century. [132]

MOUSEHOLE IN DECLINE

Survival and Reconstruction

After 1595 the population of Mousehole seems to have fallen to
fewer than 200 people. Indeed, there were still only about 220
residents in the town in 1664. Mousehole had no deep water
harbour or sheltered anchorage and was not on a main road. To
get to Penzance over land its inhabitants had either to go along the
coastal route through Newlyn, only operable at low tide, or to go
up the hill to Paul churchtown across the high plateau and down
to the bridge across the Newlyn river at Tolcarne. As Newlyn and
Penzance began to grow, Mousehole stagnated and some parts
were never rebuilt. As late as the 1680s the Spanish were still being
blamed for old ruined walls in Mousehole and an uninhabited
vicarage (half a mile up the hill at Paul churchtown). The
stagnation continued well into the 18th century: 'old walls here and
there that the people call chapels' were characteristic of Mousehole
140 years after the Spanish raid.[133]

A few buildings survived the attack, although they were almost
certainly re-roofed. By tradition, the only house not to be destroyed
was Keigwin (now Keigwin and Little Keigwin), probably built only
a few years before, but recent research has shown that at least three
other buildings in Mousehole also probably survived (Panel 7).
Another early house behind the Old Standard, and alongside the
quay, was later rebuilt. The long survival of these early buildings
in Mousehole may in part be due to their acquiring iconic status
through having escaped destruction in the raid.[134]

Rebuilding at Mousehole after 1595 was slower and more partial
than elsewhere. When Mousehole Quay needed repair in 1610 there
was a Cornwall-wide collection, and dendro-dating suggests that
Keigwin was re-roofed and the Old Standard built around 1612-13.
Gernick Street in the south of the town may not have been laid
out until after the Spanish raid. Like Street an Nowan in Newlyn,
it does not appear to have been a built-up area in the Middle Ages
and may still have been an open space at the time of the raid.
Documentary evidence for new building occurs in the 1632 will of
the merchant Richard Keigwin. This mentions a 'convenient and
competent house' at Mousehole, 'to be built at the common cost of
the [Keigwin] trading stock', probably for Richard's two younger
sons but which may never have been built. A ruined hall at Keigwin
itself, mentioned in 1632, may have been rebuilt then, but 'decayed
walls and a garden' belonging to Richard's widow Elizabeth were
not rebuilt in 1638-9 and could be the garden behind Keigwin
known as Mulberry Square.[135]

Surveying Keigwin

The common belief in Mousehole is that only Keigwins, the subject of the architectural survey, survived the Spanish raid of 1595. Survey work and documentary research (which suggest that two or three other substantial buildings in the town also survived) and dendrochronology, or tree ring dating, were used to test this theory.

Unfortunately, later remodelling of Keigwins has removed clear evidence of 16th-century fabric – most of the surviving early decorative detail could as easily post-date 1595, while the roof timbers were felled as late as c.1612-13.

However, an original late 16th-century build-date is possible; the building has a cross passage of a type associated with the hall-house plan then still common in Cornwall, and an oven noted in 1578 lies at the back of the Little Keigwin part of the house. Other contemporary merchant families were building mansion houses in Mousehole and Newlyn.

An earlier date is unlikely. Keigwins and its early 17th-century neighbour, the Old Standard, occupy a square footprint fronting and overlying medieval house plots, their long sides facing a former market place.

Older footings were found partly underlying one of the back ranges to the south and old photographs show that another ancient range lay alongside the quay behind the Old Standard, suggesting that the medieval frontages lay further back, probably with narrower gable-ended street frontages competing for space on the market frontage.

Today the main visible features on both buildings are largely 17th-century – the mullions and central door on the Old Standard and the moulded stone doors and ceiling in Keigwins mark the beginnings of Classical symmetry and detail; the great porch on Keigwins dates from c.1700 (when a series of grand upper rooms was created with plastered barrel ceilings).

These were houses of substantial gentleman-merchants – ten hearths are noted for Keigwins in 1664 (see plan) and six at the Old Standard.

In the late 18th century, after the Keigwin family moved out, both houses became inns known as the *Keigwin Arms* and the *Standard*, and Keigwin later became a tearoom.

Eric Berry and Nick Cahill

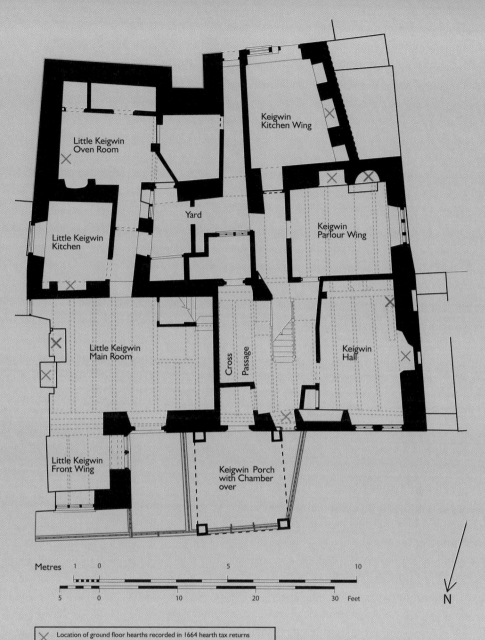

Little Keigwin
Oven Room

Keigwin
Kitchen Wing

Yard

Keigwin
Parlour Wing

Little Keigwin
Kitchen

Little Keigwin
Main Room

Cross Passage

Keigwin
Hall

Little Keigwin
Front Wing

Keigwin Porch
with Chamber
over

Metres 1 0   5   10

5   0   10   20   30   Feet

N

✕ Location of ground floor hearths recorded in 1664 hearth tax returns

✕ Relational location of first floor hearths recorded in 1664 hearth tax returns

Figure A: *Keigwin with the Old Standard to
the left of the second gable (from cover of
Arch. Rep. A).*

Figure B: *Ground-floor plan with 1664
hearths marked (Arch. Rep. A).*

Sources
Arch. Rep. A; Stoate Hearth Tax, 88; J.J. Maclean,
History of Trigg Major (1876), ii, 140 (Tretawne).

Figure 38 Mousehole quayside, *c.*1880, showing an early house (far left), no longer standing, and the gable end of the Old Standard to its right.

Civil War and Gear Rout As well as being the victims of foreign attack, Mousehole and Newlyn residents were drawn into national events, participating in the 1640s in the civil war between king and parliament. Cornwall was strongly Royalist in the generally Parliamentarian South West, partly because its rights and privileges were tied up with the royal Duchy and Stannaries. The Cornish indeed saw the civil war as much a fight between England and Cornwall as between king and parliament. Local notables joined the Cornish Royalists led by Ralph Hopton, first Baron Hopton, as early as 1642 and his army did not surrender to the Parliamentarians until 1646. Later, during the Gear Rout, a Cornish insurrection of 1648, a group of rebels again fought the Parliamentarian forces but they were defeated and 70 Cornish Royalists were killed at Penzance.

The Keigwins joined the Royalists in 1642, and John Keigwin, eldest son of Richard, built a fort at Penolva in 1644. John's younger brother Richard, then a Penzance merchant, tried to supply the Royalists at Pendennis Castle when they were under siege in 1646. Then on 16 May 1648, the West Cornish rose under the leadership of John's son William and other royalists in support of the king. During this brief resumption of the Civil War, they re-took West Penwith from the Parliamentarians. Royalist numbers rose to 500 at Penzance, and 300 on the Lizard and the lord of the manor of Alverton, the Parliamentarian, Alexander Daniel of Larrigan in Madron, was put under house arrest.[136]

Penzance was recaptured by Colonel Bennett, the Parliamentarian leader, on 22 May 1648 and the Lizard rising ended in defeat at Gear in St Martin in Meneage. Penzance was thoroughly plundered (as was Keigwin) and triumphant Parliamentarian soldiers marched east via Penryn in June 1648, some dressed in Penzance aldermen's gowns. They had with them 40 prisoners and horses laden with feather beds and household goods. The procession was led by three soldiers with hurling balls (chapter 5) on the points of their swords giving the whole episode a distinct 'ethnic undertow'.[137]

Rebuilding resumes

Keigwin was remodelled for the main branch of the Keigwin family in the late 17th or early 18th century when plaster ceilings were inserted. William became esquire by the 1670s, and had a country house in St Kew parish in North Cornwall – he had benefited from their Royalist connections in the Civil War. In 1670-89 Thomas Hutchings agreed to rebuild a plot, thereby tripling the value of the site. Another rebuild, probably in North Street, was due to start in 1668, but was delayed until the start of the 18th century. With so

Figure 39 18th-century thatched farmhouse at Raginnis near Mousehole, site of continuous settlement from prehistoric times.

little demand for houses in Mousehole, ruined walls came to act as surrounds for garden plots.[138]

PAUL'S POPULATION AND OCCUPATIONS, 1664-1801

The population of Paul parish grew rapidly from about 1,100 in the mid-1660s to 2,937 in 1801 (the first census) in line with the rest of Penwith, which was an industrial area at this time; Paul church had to enlarge its burial ground in 1786. By 1805 much of the population appears to have been concentrated in Mousehole, which had about 100 families, and Newlyn, which had about 200 families. Parish registers from 1793 to 1800 show an urban-rural ratio of two to one. Deducting about 1,000 for the rural population allows us to estimate the population at the main settlements by the time of the first census in 1801. We can put the number of Newlyn's inhabitants at 1,360 (about 100 of these being at Tolcarne) and of Mousehole at 680, which represents a threefold increase since the 1660s. Newlyn grew a little faster than Mousehole and overtook Marazion during the 18th century but failed to catch up with St Ives or Penzance. In 1801 Marazion's population peaked at just over 1,000, while St Ives parish as a whole had 2,714 inhabitants and Penzance 3,382.[139]

One way to measure the importance of a town is to count the number of distinct terms for employment. There were at least 36 different occupations in Paul parish in the 18th century, compared with about half this total in the 17th century. About a quarter of jobs were maritime or maritime-related – fishermen, mariners and seamen, customs officers, coopers, sailmakers, shipwrights and ropemakers (chapter 3). Newlyn was also home to a surgeon in 1769 and a peruke (wig) maker in 1787, and potters worked on either side of the Coombe river. A pewterer in 1729 had property at Trungle above Mousehole, but goldsmiths and silversmiths were based in Penzance. In 1718, there was at least one black servant – Peregrine Cornwall – in the wealthy Hutchens household in the parish (chapter 5).[140]

In the later 18th century, from the 1750s to the 1780s, the parish registers record the occupations of local bridegrooms. More than half were fishermen, and if maritime or maritime-related jobs are included then the total rises to almost two-thirds. By comparison, only a fifth were farmers, mainly living in the rural areas of Paul parish. Of the rest, most were building workers including masons and a thatcher, shoemakers, or involved in the food and drink trade. Only two per cent were tinners with one being a smelter. As we shall see, this pattern remained typical of the parish in the 19th century.

'The inhabitants are near 2,000 and everyone (except two or three barbers, shoemakers and tailors) maintained by fishing, and in the season of their curing the Pilchards, I guess it is the most stinking place in ye whole world'.

C.T. Gooch, 1754.

18TH-CENTURY NEWLYN

Continuing Investment

The medieval quay at Newlyn Town, noted as 'lately blown down' in 1732, was rebuilt by William Arundell of Trengwainton, who owned property in Newlyn Town. Old quay was extended on new foundations at a cost of £300. Then described as 'a broad hedge' (stone parallel walls with earth infill), this new quay was built of vertically set stones rather than huge boulders as in the medieval period. To prevent the quay from falling again, it was agreed that sand could only be dug up for ballast at the head of the pier. Two local fishermen came to an agreement with Arundell in 1744 to keep the new quay in repair in return for low quay dues.[141]

There was also a quay or wharf at Street an Nowan where the tithe cellars were; it was rebuilt at a cost of £80 or more in 1772-3. In 1795, a plan by William Harris of Kenegie in Gulval and inhabitants and fish curers of Newlyn to build a new pier or public quay at Green Rocks, south of Newlyn's medieval quay, was opposed by Penzance and nothing came of it. Some investment in sea defences was at a very local level; in 1796, for example, Mary Jaco, a widow of Newlyn, built 'a buttress or fence against the sea' next to and below her dwelling house at the Fradgan.[142]

Near the wharfs, fish cellars were built for lay rectors and seine companies. The Great and Little [Tithe] cellars were near Gwavas Quay in Street an Nowan, and the lay rector also owned Middle,

Figure 40 Gwavas Quay, early 19th century. Newlyn and Mousehole were described in 1754 as 'little more than two single lines of houses built within twelve or 15 feet of a cliff more than 20 feet high on the edge of which is no wall or rail so that nothing can be more dangerous than to walk twenty yards in the narrow street in the dark'. After three accidental deaths here in a three-month period in 1799-1800, rails were put up.

Brick and Green cellars at Newlyn Town, south of the old quay. Brick Cellar may be the new cellar for which five tons of brick were needed in 1762. There were also seven or eight of the larger and more substantial seine cellars, including the Fradgan cellars of Richard Richards and Edward Downing, built in 1757. In his will of 1760 Downing left boats, nets and seines. Other cellars owned by seine companies may have been in the St Peter's Hill area of Newlyn Town (figure 25).[143]

New Streets and Buildings

The 18th century was an important period in the development of Newlyn; most buildings in the town today date from then or later. The open spaces within the early area of settlement were infilled with both grand merchant houses and humbler cottages, to be found across the town. In Newlyn Town itself, John Boson began to build a new classical-style house overlooking the harbour late in 1705. Other gentry or merchant houses of a similar period in this part of town included no. 1 Church Street, and to the south towards the Bowjey, the former Balconey on Newlyn Green, also known as the Green House or *Navy Inn*. The Balconey (with its two-storey porch which looked a little like that at Keigwin in Mousehole) was perhaps the town house of William Gwavas or home to another Cornish writer (chapter 5). A letter of December 1798 suggests that the original balcony may have been an open loggia with views across Mount's Bay.[144]

Figure 41 Pembroke Lodge with its imposing granite ashlar façade, fan light and views. In 1800, the first owner left furniture, books, pictures, plate, linen and china to his widow Rachel Reichenberg. Later it was home to the artist Walter Langley.

Figure 42 Whitehall, Mousehole – a classical house with wings, 1790s. 'Blue elvan' boundary stones mark out its garden, once the edge of the settlement.

The infilling of empty plots continued throughout the 18th century. The stable and rear of Boson's mansion in the centre of Newlyn Town became a fish cellar, of which square socket holes for the ends of the pressing poles remain. The lower half of what is now the Rosebud Memorial Garden was filled up with new houses in the 1750s. Care was taken to leave space for hemp plots, furze-drying ricks and dung heaps where possible. Minor streets in Newlyn Town begin to be named about this time, too. Tonkin's Street, mentioned in 1710, could be Church Street or the Narrows while Street Sheeta was the name given to Trewarveneth Street in 1740.[145]

Already by the early 18th century meadows and orchards were giving way to building on the outskirts of Newlyn Town and Street an Nowan. In 1716, for instance, John Thomas built two properties (messuages) on Trewarveneth orchard to the south-west of the town, while in 1717 a house to be built nearby at Redes meadow was to have two under-rooms and two chambers each 12 foot square.[146]

A major area of expansion was to the south, including the Bowjey and, beyond, Cliff Castle and (by 1799) Pembroke Lodge, smart houses on the cliff overlooking the bay attracted some newcomers. In Belle Vue on the hillside above and to the west of the town, larger houses were scattered among small thatched cottages, often dependent on the nearby farms; the new buildings included Myrtle Cottage, a grand brick house of 1745, Orchard Cottage (by 1773) and Boase Castle House (1780). The area remained physically separate from historic Newlyn Town until the 19th century.[147]

There was also building in Street an Nowan. In Fradgan, which lay to the north of Newlyn Town near the harbour and mainly housed fishermen, building began in 1730 on 'Park an Fradgian

Identifying Older Buildings

At first sight this would seem to be an impossible task in towns like Mousehole where so much has been continually rebuilt. As well as being burnt by the Spaniards in 1595, Mousehole underwent major rebuilding in the Victorian period. Despite this, as the architectural survey shows, older buildings (18th-century and earlier) are still easily identifiable. Criteria used here can equally well be applied to other towns. A key example is the two- or three-unit medieval plan form – service end, hall, parlour end. This can be easily 'read' from the outside of a building: front and rear doors align forming a cross passage often with a wooden partition on one side, a lack of symmetry on facades, and large areas of blank walls towards the ends of the main elevations to give room for large interior inglenook fireplaces.

Older buildings are often gable-end to street frontages. They may also be one-and-a-half storeys in height, often with small windows just under their eaves;

many were heightened later. Key examples of older work can be seen in Keigwin, the Old Standard and the *Ship Inn*, with fragments elsewhere (chamfered window or door lintels for instance). Steeper roof pitches, and stone chimney stacks (brick being common after 1800) may help identify some other older buildings; steep roofs were once covered with thatch or large slates which pre-date railway imported Welsh slate (but beware of tall 'Gothick' roofs). Finally, evidence that a building has gone through several phases of work can suggest an older house, as at Keigwin, though this can be deceptive – the much altered houses around Mill Pool only date back 140 years or so.

Geology is also a useful guide, as is the way stone is laid. Many of Mousehole's older buildings include blue elvan or the brownish local granite or moorstone (a type of weathered granite taken from surface outcrops). Walls, even of high status buildings like Keigwin, are often of rubble construction or of roughly shaped

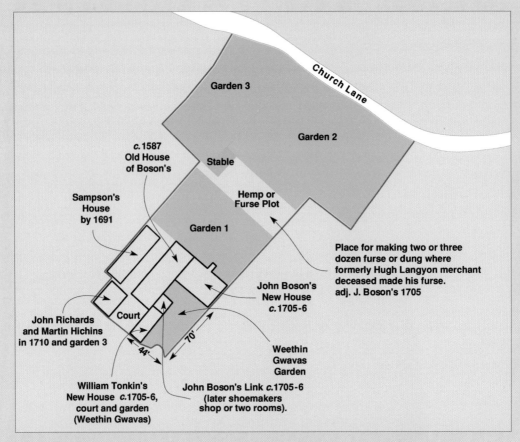

Figure A: *Map of Boson lands in Newlyn Town, based on c.1744 plan (CRO, X573 4/2). This shows site of 1587 house in Primrose Court. Only John Boson's new house survives today.*

and square stones, laid to course (*Ship Inn* has some blue elvan laid in this way). The blue elvan was clearly quarried from around the present boundary stones as houses near to these include more of this material than those further away. Lintels and quoins of older buildings are roughly shaped not sawn or squared with some being of wood (recycled ships' timbers at Keigwin). Fake voussoirs (keystones) scratched over windows are typical of the 18th century. Locally quarried granite from Sheffield and Lamorna was produced commercially from the mid-19th century; it is of lighter grey, large-crystalled type, and architectural details and clear drill marks show the late date.

Some puzzles remain including the half house (semi-detached houses or rows with shared doorway recesses). This type is generally considered 19th-century, perhaps very late 18th-century, and an industrial housing type, but they could be adaptations of earlier wide doorway (i.e. fish-processing) buildings. Brick, too, can be found before the 19th century – the fine walls to the rear of Carmania, The Parade need investigating, as do two hipped brick buildings in Fore Street and North Cliff (see Chapel Street, Penzance). These reflect a wider interest in brick in mid-18th-century Cornwall – much of it associated with Thomas Edwards of Greenwich – the Truro mine magnates' favourite architect. Unsuitable for the damp Cornish climate, the brick house was the ultimate show house of 18th-century Cornwall.

Eric Berry and Nick Cahill

Figure B: The Mousehole

Figure C: Houses next to Keigwin

meadow'. On the hillside, Chywoone Hill was probably laid out in its present form at this period, somewhat to the south of the earlier track; cottages there and at Old Paul Hill may go back to the 18th century. Tolcarne (and Jackford) also expanded a little way up the Coombe (Vine Cottage dates from this time).[148]

Landlords invested heavily in Newlyn property. In 1759 William Arundell's 17 houses were worth £2,009. Building was accompanied by commercial development. At least two shops are recorded in the mid- to late 18th century: one on the cliff, near Church Street and a shoemaker's shop in the front garden of Boson's house (now Cliff Manor House) opposite. There were then six or more inns in Newlyn including the *Tolcarne Inn* and probably the *Wheatsheaf* at Tolcarne, and the *Fisherman's Arms* and *Red Lion* at Newlyn Town. By 1775 the old mansion house of the Bosons had also become a tavern.[149]

Industrial Suburbs and Tin Mining Tolcarne continued to be the industrial suburb of Newlyn with 20 houses, a brewery and a smith's shop by the early 1800s. The mills, rented by the Boase family from the mid-1780s, continued in operation. Boat-building went on at the mouth of the Newlyn River and also south of Newlyn Town where there was a ropeworks by the early 18th century. Vessels were often beach-built for ease of launching and a lime kiln is noted there in 1789.[150]

Tin was found in the cliffs at Newlyn Town in 1759 near Gascoyn's garden and St Peter's Hill and at Street an Nowan in 1794. In the latter case a large area from north of Gwavas Quay to the Coombe was leased to prospectors. But although there was some tin-working in Paul parish, it was never as important as in other Penwith parishes such as Madron or St Just.[151]

18TH-CENTURY MOUSEHOLE

Mousehole buildings mostly date from the late 18th and 19th centuries, but unlike Newlyn, the town has retained its pattern of courts and lanes. Nevertheless, there were some changes in the housing stock and Chapel Street may have been rebuilt in the 18th century and Whitehall, a classical-style mansion, was built on the northern edge of Mousehole by Edward Biddulph, gentleman and captain of the Mousehole volunteers, in about 1795. Perhaps rather more important were the changes to the milling systems. By then they had become one, with a mill pool in central Mousehole, above the main thoroughfare on the 15-metre contour, which may have been created at this time. The pool was fed by a leat which can still be traced opposite Regent Terrace.[152]

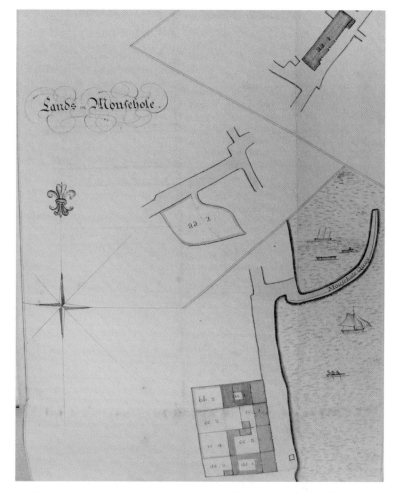

Figure 43 Detail of Alexander Law's survey of Mousehole 1789. This, the only pre-1785 map of Mousehole shows only Tregonebris manor holdings in Church Street, Fore Street and Gernick Street, (CRO, WH 4475). For another version see CRO, BU 1176.

Further developments took place at the quay and wharf, which belonged to the Keigwin family, by the 1730s. As early as 1733 William Gwavas, who owned the rectory of Paul and with it the disputed fish tithes of Mousehole and Newlyn, had offered to rebuild the quay as a conciliatory gesture, but a major scheme began here only in 1762 after the wharf had been repaired. Attempts to employ John Smeaton (engineer of the Eddystone lighthouse) or his assistant Thomas Richardson seem to have failed, and a local man, Thomas Read, took on the work. On 10 March 1763, Thomas Carlyon, a joint lay rector, asked for a proper plan to be made as it is 'not like the wall of a house that you can build up and take down at pleasure'. Outlays were large – over £500 in the first year and the quay was finished only in 1768.[153]

A significant social change was the abandonment of Keigwin by the Keigwin family in the middle of the 18th century, probably due to financial problems. The house then became the

Keigwin Arms Inn. John Wills, the innkeeper, had been a servant of the Keigwins from childhood. He purchased the property 'from a motive of respect to that family' and his sister Susanna was landlady of the *Standard* next door. By 1751 there was at least one shop at Mousehole, run by Thomas Furse; among the new fangled items sold there were blue and white window curtains. In 1796, during the French Revolutionary War when salt was in short supply, Mr Halse of St Ives experimented with salt-making at Salt Ponds, at the bottom of Gernick Street. The site marked the southern extent of the town in 1800.[154]

The Mayoress of Mousehole's Girdle Mousehole continued to nurse pretensions to borough status and in the later 18th century memorials of Mousehole's glorious past were collected at the *Keigwin Arms*. These included the cannon balls and the musket ball that reputedly killed Jenkin Keigwin in 1595 and his sword. Other curious items included a surviving green and white waistcoat (the Keigwin colours) and an 'old court dress – a coat of light colour richly embroidered with red braiding'.[155]

Another Keigwin treasure was noted in the 1750s by William Borlase, antiquarian rector of Ludgvan. This was the girdle, allegedly worn by the mayoress of Mousehole and claimed as proof that Mousehole had once been a charter town like Marazion and Penzance. The girdle was of 'leather and studded with silver plates or bosses'. The metal was melted down sometime between the 1750s and 1807. Girdles were highly prized articles of clothing and Olive Badcock's silver girdle was worth 26s. 8d. or a quarter of the value of all her goods in Paul parish in 1602. Margaret Peres, widow of Mousehole, had two girdles worth a little less than £4 in 1616. 'The best silver girdle with the buckles and tycles on it and a cow named Gracious' was given to her son. But Mousehole never had a mayor, or a charter, and their 'mayoress's girdle' is more likely to have been worn at Plymouth or Penzance where Keigwins had once been mayors.[156]

Chapter 5

Speaking Cornish in Mount's Bay

On 22 May 1724 a group of gentlemen, including John Boson, the last of the Cornish writers of Newlyn, and William Gwavas, holder of the Paul fish tithes, met at Marazion bowling club. As well as choosing Cornish mottoes for a pair of bowling balls they also chose a Cornish motto for the bowling-green house itself. One motto translates as 'end well with friendship' an apt epitaph for the Cornish language they were struggling to keep alive.[157]

If we accept, as this chapter will argue, that Newlyn and Mousehole were central to Cornish language survival then there appear to be two possible explanations. First, both places were home to wealthy inhabitants with the interest and leisure time to pursue their Cornish language studies; there is ample evidence for this because the activities of the Bosons of Newlyn and Keigwins of Mousehole are well documented. The second possible explanation concerns socio-economic circumstances, but this is harder to demonstrate.

Fishing, like mining, created an occupational community well suited to sustaining a language, with few network ties to other communities. The location of Mousehole and Newlyn in the far west of Cornwall was also a factor, most Cornish language writers in both places, except William Gwavas, being home-grown. We can only glimpse the community aspect at Newlyn and Mousehole in the early to mid-18th century when Cornish stopped being a community language.

THE CORNISH LANGUAGE

Close to Welsh and Breton, Cornish was a distinct Brittonic language. As Carew noted in 1602 Cornish was more like English 'more easy to be pronounced, and not so unpleasing in sound, with throat letters, as the Welsh'. The development of the Cornish language is divided into three phases: Old, Middle and Late Cornish. Middle Cornish was the language of medieval Cornwall with Late Cornish in use after 1600.[158]

Before the Civil War

In the later Middle Ages (c.1300-1540), the Cornish language became restricted to the western half of Cornwall beyond Bodmin. It was here that a literature emerged in what was arguably the language's finest period. A cycle of three Biblical plays known as

Figure 44 Hell from the 2000 *Ordinalia* production at St Just in Penwith plain an gwarry. Richard Pendarves of Camborne may have taken part in a similar play.

the *Ordinalia*, two saints' plays – *Beunans Meriasek* and *Beunans Ke* (the latter a recent rediscovery) – and the poem *Pascon agan Arluth* may well have been written at Glasney College near Penryn. The plays were written to be performed in open air 'plain-an-gwaries' or circular playing places, such as exist at St Just and Perranzabuloe. They were originally staged in order to spread the teachings of the church to a Cornish-speaking population.

In 1538 the Lord's Prayer and Creed were translated into English for use in England and east Cornwall, and probably into Cornish for west Cornwall. This lasted until the Prayer Book rebellion of 1549, when an English Prayer Book replaced the Latin mass. After Mary came to the throne, some Catholic homilies and up-to-date religious materials were translated into Cornish. There were no Cornish equivalents of the Welsh prayer book of 1567 or Welsh Bible of 1588 because the local gentry unlike the Welsh did not patronise such activity.[159]

The Chiverton family from Kerris in Paul parish were later reputed to have had a Cornish Bible in their library, but this is unlikely. More probably it was a copy of John Trevisa's English translation of the Bible or perhaps another version of the *Ordinalia*. *The Creation of the World* was reputedly written by William Jordan, a Wendron gentleman in 1611. This last Cornish play is based on *Origo Mundi*, the first play of the *Ordinalia* and, if written in the early 17th century, would suggest that Old Testament subjects were still acceptable for public performance. There is also a reference to a Camborne play with devils at this time.[160]

By the late 16th century the extinction of the Cornish language was already seen as inevitable. The antiquarian John Norden predicted 'that in few years the Cornish language will be by little and little abandoned.' He noted, too, that although Cornish was still used in Penwith and Kerrier by respectable families, all were able to talk to strangers in English.[161]

The Civil Wars and Language Decline

During the first Civil War (1642-6) the Cornish language could be heard at Pendennis Castle (Falmouth). This was because the Royalists who held the castle recruited heavily in west Cornwall (296 men from Kerrier and Penwith were in Slanning's regiment at this time, including six men from Paul parish). They also used the Cornish language as an instrument of war; to persuade Royalist deserters to become Royalists again.[162]

After the Gear Rout of 1648 and second Civil War (1649-51) came the period of greatest iconoclasm in Cornwall, when most of the objects associated with the old (Catholic) religion were destroyed. When John Ellis, a gentleman and Quaker of Sennen, tried to remove a wayside cross in 1656 he was told by a bystander in Cornish 'that it was a holy cross and if it were good before it is good now'; for us, the significant point here is that a gentleman, living in a parish west of Paul, could still understand Cornish.[163]

Visits by the naturalist John Ray to Cornwall just after the Restoration of the monarchy may give too pessimistic a view of the state of the Cornish language. In 1662 he claimed to have met with 'none here but what could speak English; few of the children could speak Cornish'. Ray's contemporary, Nicholas Boson of Newlyn (1624-1708) noted that after the English Civil War Cornish had 'no Place but about the Cliff and Sea' in Penwith and Kerrier. Nevertheless, in 1700 Cornish could still be heard 'all along the sea shore' from Land's End to St Keverne on the Lizard and in 13 parishes of west Penwith including Paul but not St Hilary. This was the view of Edward Lhuyd, the Welsh linguist and nationalist, who visited Cornwall in that year. He included Cornish in his word lists and published a Cornish grammar in 1707. The common language of Penzance (and presumably Marazion) was still Cornish at this time.[164]

Monoglots The presence or absence of monoglot speakers – Cornish speakers who understood no English – is the best indicator of a language's health. By the late 17th century, Nicholas Boson claimed there were 'scarce any but both understand and speak English'. Cheston Marchant of Gwithian who died in 1676 may have been the last monoglot. Cornish sermons at Feock and Landewednack, and possibly St Ives, Marazion and Penzance show that older people in these places were still more at home with Cornish than English as late as *c.*1670-80. The significance of monoglot speakers is clear from Brittany, where there is evidence that when monoglot Breton speakers had bilingual children, their children's children became French monoglots. In such an environment, Breton could disappear within three generations or 60 years. By this reckoning the Cornish language should have died out in 1730-40 (which is indeed when it did as a community language).[165]

The Last Native Scholars   Cornish was not just an oral language, as the medieval miracle plays show. The language continued to be written down after the Civil War, but in 1695 it was noted that 'tis a good while since that only two men could write it, and one of them no Scholar or Grammarian and then blind with age'. The blind scholar was Richard Angwyn (Dickan Gwyn) of St Just in Penwith, who was distantly related to the Keigwins and died in 1675. In 1667, John Ray visited Angwyn at St Just and collected Cornish words from him, but Angwyn's manuscript of part of the Old Testament to the Book of Numbers was burned by his wife.

The other can be identified as Richard Pendarves (*c.*1596-1674), gentleman of Camborne, part of a nexus of Cornish speakers and actors there.[166]

There were a few other native scholars around including university-educated clergy like William Oliver, a Presbyterian minister, 'who could say and do much' in Cornish. He was at Camborne in the early 1650s and might have known Pendarves, but then moved to Launceston where he died in 1681. Joseph Sherwood, vicar of St Hilary, may have written Cornish sermons for his parishioners as late as 1680.[167]

The Late Cornish Language Movement

Launched in 1678 in the unlikely setting of the judge's chamber at Launceston, this was both a language movement and a revival. According to an account given later by William Scawen, gentleman of St Germans, Lord North, the circuit judge, was concerned about the loss of the Cornish language and:

> blaming us all then present, enquiring also whether there were anything written in it now remaining. To which a Minister of good Learning, and one who was the greatest pretender to the knowledge of it, (he being born and bred up fitly for it) made answer there was none, for which I told him he was too bold in his negation, saying there may be such which you have not seen, and tis your own fault you have not seen an old piece thereof long in my keeping.[168]

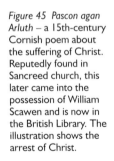

Figure 45 Pascon agan Arluth – a 15th-century Cornish poem about the suffering of Christ. Reputedly found in Sancreed church, this later came into the possession of William Scawen and is now in the British Library. The illustration shows the arrest of Christ.

Figure 46 Little Keigwin first-floor barrel-vaulted room with late 17th- or early 18th-century panelling. In towns, the poshest rooms were always upstairs. This ceiling and the two similar ones at Keigwin would have had ornamental plaster work like Prideaux Place or Lanhydrock. Over the fireplace is a modern copy of the Keigwin green and white coat of arms – the three white dogs are a mistranslation of the Cornish name, which actually means white hedge.

The minister may have been William Oliver who was certainly in the right place at the right time. Reputedly found in Sancreed church, Scawen's old piece was the early 15th-century poem about the Passion of Christ, *Pascon agan Arluth* (figure 45).[169]

William Scawen and the Cornish Language   William Scawen of Molenick in the East Cornwall parish of St Germans was born in 1600 and educated at Oxford. His close links with west Cornwall began when his sister Elizabeth married Martin Keigwin of Mousehole in 1639. Briefly an MP, Scawen became a Royalist and fought alongside Cornish speakers. This, and his sister's marriage, may be how his interest in the old language started. Rewards came Scawen's way in the 1660s: he became the vice-warden of the Stannaries (tin mines) and was proposed as a member of the Order of the Royal Oak. As early as 1660-3 Scawen talked about Cornish place-names with Launceston Assize court judges and by 1678, as the extract above shows, took a serious interest in the language itself. The first translation of his *Pascon agan Arluth* (passion poem) in 1679-80 was so 'execrable' that he turned to his nephew John Keigwin of Mousehole for a better version in 1682. The work was begun for Lord North, but never presented because Scawen became infirm and house-bound.[170]

The project evolved instead into Scawen's tract on the Cornish language, *Antiquities Cornu-Brittanic: … [or] Memorials of … the Primitive Speech of Cornwall*. In this work Scawen came up with 16 reasons for the decline of the Cornish language. These included the loss of contact with Brittany (after the Reformation), the end of miracle play performances, the loss of records in the Civil War, the absence of a Cornish Bible, gentry antipathy to the language, and the proximity of English-speaking Devon. Scawen's nephew John Keigwin at Mousehole, Keigwin's 'neighbour' Mr Boson at Newlyn and the Quaker, John Read, helped with various versions of this manuscript. Scawen also encouraged Cornish gentry to write letters to each other in Cornish.[171]

LATE CORNISH AT MOUSEHOLE AND NEWLYN

Translation in Mousehole and writing in Newlyn

Martin Keigwin of Mousehole, brother-in-law of William Scawen, was born in 1595 and spent time in both Wales and Brittany. He was the second son of Richard Keigwin, merchant, and founded a second gentry branch of this family. Martin was a native speaker of Cornish and it was later claimed that Martin and his son John 'sucked in the broken dialect' of Cornish with their milk. Martin had an interest in how Cornish related to Welsh and Breton speech and talked about this and place-names with his brother-in-law William Scawen. It is possible that he also translated some Cornish place-names into English before his death in 1666.[172]

John Keigwin, 'a great master of ye Cornish tongue', was Martin's oldest son. He spoke Cornish, English, Greek, Latin, Hebrew and French. Born in 1642, probably at the Old Standard in Mousehole, there is no evidence that he went to university (though his son Martin did). In 1692, John Keigwin was living in the 'higher house' (probably Keigwin and Little Keigwin) in Mousehole. Later, when William Gwavas knew him, he lived at the 'lower house' (Old Standard).[173]

Figure 47 Old Standard and Keigwin, Mousehole, by H.P. Tremenheere (1800).

Figure 48 'The Creation of the World' translated by John Keigwin and transcribed by John Moore for Bishop Trelawney in 1693.

Figure 49 Richard Pearce of Kerris's silver and apple-wood hurling ball, 1705. Its Cornish motto means 'fair play is good play'. Hurling was Cornwall's national sport and resembles rugby played with a cricket ball.

From the 1680s until 1716, Mousehole (and perhaps Sancreed) were the places to go for translations. Beginning in 1682, John Keigwin translated all the major Middle Cornish works then known to exist into English – *Pascon agan Arluth*, Jordan's 'Creation of the World' and the three-part *Ordinalia*. According to his son Martin, John also collected several Cornish proverbs and worked on the meanings of Cornish place-names. Among the more remarkable of his commissions was a Cornish translation of King Charles I's 1643 letter of thanks to his Cornish supporters (still a feature of many Cornish churches). John Aubrey certainly thought John Keigwin the right man to make the first Cornish dictionary in 1692, but nothing came of this project.[174]

John Keigwin's first translation from Cornish – Scawen's Passion poem – was finished in 1682. From 1691 until 1693 he was working on the 'Creation' and his final and most ambitious project was begun in 1693. This was the translation of the *Ordinalia* – three plays covering the Book of Genesis (Creation), Passion and Resurrection of Christ – and his daughter Isabella may have helped him with this work. John normally worked directly from original manuscripts, but in the case of the *Ordinalia* had only imperfect transcripts and omitted the humorous sub-play, 'The Death of Pilate', altogether.[175]

Keigwin's patrons included his uncle William Scawen, Jonathan Trelawney, bishop of Exeter, then collecting material for another edition of Camden's *Britannia* – the first local history best-seller – and William Gwavas. Perhaps Trelawney also saw this translation work as part of his duty of responsibility to a diocese that still included some Cornish speakers. In 1702 Keigwin sent work to Sidney Godolphin the Lord Treasurer, who was a Cornishman.[176]

Although not a native speaker and from the next generation, Nicholas Boson of Newlyn (1624-1708) knew Richard Angwyn, the native scholar, well. All references below are to Nicholas Boson the Cornish language writer, unless otherwise stated. Some of Nicholas's Cornish writing predates the growing interest in the Cornish language in 1678. His own view was that 'if any attempt be made about preserving the Cornish, it must be by such as are perfect natives, and good scholars, scarce to be found; for they are but few'.[177]

Nicholas Boson was born at Newlyn in 1624. As he tells us himself, he only learned Cornish, a language which he came to love, as an adult. This was because his mother did not allow 'the servants and neighbours to talk to me otherwise than in English'. At six he was sent away to school and finished his education in France. By 1657, Nicholas Boson held 26 messuages and 216 acres of land and lived in an old house overlooking Newlyn quay. He later moved to Gwavas Farm, just to the south of Newlyn.[178]

Nicholas Boson's first known work, 'The Duchess of Cornwall's Progress to See the Land's End and to Visit the Mount', was written mainly in English. Generally dated to 1660-70, it may have been written to teach Boson's children Nicholas (1653-1708), John, Mary and Benjamin some Cornish. It featured Harry, a wizard hermit, witchcraft, fairies and the Cornish sport of hurling and included 'educational' facts like the amounts paid to the duchy havener for port rents (chapter 2).[179]

Nicholas is credited with two other works, entirely in Cornish. The first of these, *Nebbaz Gerriau Dro Tho Carnoack* or 'A Few Words about Cornish' is partly autobiographical. It is likely to date from after 1678, but could have been written in Newlyn at any time up to his death in 1708. The other work, 'John of Chyanhor', is a version of an international popular tale known to modern scholars as 'The Servant's Good Counsels'. The basis for this may be 'a very old Cornish Screef written about Lands end' which Nicholas owned in 1700. John of Chyanhor, by taking heed of his master's advice, avoids three bad things – a highway robbery, a false accusation of murder, and the manslaughter of his own child. The original manuscript was only half a sheet long and closely written, and it is possible that John Boson, Nicholas's son, adapted it. In Nicholas Boson's letter to Lhuyd in 1700 we get a rare insight into a Cornish gentleman's library – several boxes of 'stitched' (bound) books and scraps of manuscript, with other books out on loan. Books worth £10 are mentioned in his eldest son's inventory of 1704.[180]

Figure 50 In 1705 John Boson, a member of one of Newlyn's wealthiest merchant families, began to build a new classical-style house overlooking Newlyn harbour. Named Cliff (Manor) House, the property has recently been extensively and sensitively restored.

Figure 51 Stephen Hutchens' monument in Paul church. The Cornish translates as 'Life without end is the reward of your charity to the poor people of Paul and our church'. Hutchens founded an almshouse in 1709 which still stands below the church.

William Gwavas and the Bosons

'You have found out the mystery of our lost language', John Boson wrote to his friend and pupil William Gwavas (figure 33) in the early 18th century. Boson came from a family which played a significant role in the Cornish language movement. His father's cousin, Thomas Boson, who was born in Newlyn in 1635 and died there in 1719, worked in partnership with other Cornish writers like Oliver Pender and the Keigwin family. His only known Cornish work is an inscription for William Gwavas's hurling ball in 1705. The son of Arthur Boson, he had married Ursula the daughter of Anthony Gubbs, Parliamentarian leader of Penzance and, in the last 20 years of the 18th century, imported salt for Newlyn's fisheries on the *Grace* of Penzance and exported pilchards and other fish on ships of London, Milford and Southampton.[181]

John Boson himself was more central to this later phase of the language movement. Born in Newlyn in 1655, Oliver Pender may have been his schoolmaster. John was also at some time a servant of William Harris of Kenegie in Gulval parish and used 'John of Chyanhor' to teach Cornish to William Gwavas. In 1705-6 John began to build a classical mansion near Newlyn Quay, an expense which caused him financial problems by 1714. He never married and with his death in 1730 the Boson line came to an end in Newlyn.[182]

John's own literary output included a pilchard curing rhyme in Cornish – still one of the best descriptions of Newlyn's main trade (Panel 8). He also wrote Cornish epitaphs for tombs, including John Keigwin's at Paul church in 1716, and died at Newlyn in 1730.[183]

The Cornish culture of 'Bleau Pawle' The Cornish writers of Newlyn, Mousehole and the surrounding district formed a neighbourly club, collecting songs and poems for Gwavas and writing mottoes. As well as Keigwins and Bosons they included Oliver Pender and Martin Bodinar of Newlyn, Edward Chirgwin of St Buryan and James Jenkins of Alverton in Madron. All were closely linked. For example, Pender was a Newlyn merchant who married Margaret Keigwin, and his ship-masters were neighbours of John Boson. Bodinar, another Newlyn merchant, leased land from John Boson and died in London in 1727 (Gwavas wrote a Cornish 'pilot's motto' for Bodinar's widow). James Jenkins the younger was Boson's executor and Chirgwin a close friend of Nicholas Boson (1653-1703). With the help of this group, Gwavas diligently preserved manuscripts and used Cornish in everyday life – even his garden door had a Cornish motto on it.[184]

The Community Divided

But then in the 1720s Gwavas split the Cornish language community by reviving the fish tithe dispute (Panel 5). John Boson sided with the fishermen and acted as a witness for them in London in 1728, while Gwavas wrote in Cornish about the dispute. Even after the case was resolved in Gwavas's favour, bad feeling continued. For instance, in April 1732, when Newlyn quay needed rebuilding after a storm, Gwavas offered to send his workmen to help. Local fishermen refused because 'they and you [Gwavas] are not yet hearty friends'.[185]

Gwavas turned to other correspondents like Thomas Tonkin, gentleman scholar of St Agnes and Gorran, and William Borlase, rector of Ludgvan and antiquarian, for consolation. Borlase was another member of the Marazion bowling club with which this chapter began. Tonkin and Borlase continued to use informants from Paul parish. When in 1790 William Pryce published the first complete book about the Cornish language, it was simply an abridgement of Tonkin's manuscript which included much from Gwavas.[186]

The Last Native Speakers

Far less is known of the fishermen and market women of Paul who still spoke Cornish. In about 1730, William Bodinar of Mousehole (perhaps a distant relation of Martin) learnt Cornish from the old fishermen with whom he went to sea. Shortly after this in 1746, Samuel Barrington was amazed to find that one of his sailors from Mount's Bay could converse with Bretons. It is possible that this man was called Martin Keigwin. The episode prompted the 1768 visit to Mousehole of Samuel's brother Daines Barrington, ten years after William Borlase had pronounced the language dead.[187]

Daines at first set out for Sennen to find the last Cornish speaker, but was re-directed to Mousehole. Here he found Dolly Pentreath at her house opposite the Old Standard (possibly the Mousehole holding rented for 15s. a year in 1743-52 in her 'married' name of Dorothy Jefferey). Dolly Pentreath became famous as a result of this visit, though none of her speech was recorded; and her portrait was painted by John Opie RA. So the woman who claimed to be the last fluent native Cornish speaker became the first Cornish fishwife to be immortalised in paint.[188]

'When wee talke Cornish and are with other[s], it is not without such an intermixture of English as renders it very ridiculous to ourselves; and discernible to others'.

Nicholas Boson to Edward Lhuyd, 1700.

Figure 52 Portrait of Dolly Pentreath by John Opie, 1770s. Dolly was later recalled as 'a filthy discoursed old woman'.

Chapter 6

Growth and Development 1800-1914

In the early 19th century Newlyn had 'one principal street, nearly half a mile in length with three or four small streets branching out from it', while Mousehole was still divided into two parts, first at Brook Street, which was culverted in the mid-20th century, and later at Duck Street after the 1860s. The period between the 1870s and 1914 created the two settlements we see today. Before then, structural change was minimal – a few villas in both places and a new church at Newlyn (chapter 8). Early population growth was largely contained within existing boundaries by infilling. From the 1870s hillside terraces were built and thatch was replaced by slate, transforming the look of each place. New harbours, roads and industrial buildings had a similar effect at sea level. These changes were happening just as a colony of artists began to make Newlyn their home (chapter 9).[189]

By the late 19th century these developments had given rise to a distinctive topographical terminology, which was part of local dialect and varied subtly in the two places. Newlyn's inhabitants went 'up-long' (inland), 'down-long' (towards the sea-front), 'in-long' (towards the town centre') and 'out-long' (away from the centre). The focal point on which all these directions were based was North Corner. A visitor to Newlyn in 1895 noted that 'one's progress in going up or down-long is sometimes considerably facilitated by an alarmingly quick slide to an unexpected destination caused by fish guts on cobbled streets.'

Figure 53 Newlyn Town from Tolcarne, by Walter Tremenheere, *c*.1800. Looking over the top of the Tolcarne rocks and roofs of Street an Nowan, this view focuses on the 1730s quay and density of settlement. Houses tumble down Green Rocks, and Pembroke House and Cliff Castle are indicated beyond. Fishing boats shelter in Gwavas Lake.

At Mousehole one could simply go 'up-town' or 'down-town', while at both places one went 'in-town' to Penzance. The term 'down-long' was also used at other sea-faring places like St Ives and Clovelly. Such terms helped inhabitants to navigate their towns, acknowledging their relative complexity. Although Mousehole was by this time more recognisably one settlement, Newlyn was often seen as four – Tolcarne, Street an Nowan, Newlyn Town and Belle Vue.[190]

POPULATION

Censuses were held every ten years country-wide starting in 1801. From 1841 detailed house listings should survive, but there are some problems in using them for Newlyn and Mousehole. First, some enumeration sheets are missing including the whole of Tolcarne in 1841. Secondly, crews of ships were sometimes included as in 1851 and 1901. In the earlier case this means that 741 fishermen are listed with their boats rather than with their families. Thirdly, the 1841 census was taken in June, after the fishermen's seasonal migration had begun. Later censuses taken in late March or early April pick up the fishermen but hide the fact that women headed many households in these coastal communities for four to five months a year. Finally, the kinds of information recorded and routes taken by census takers varied from one census to the next.

In 1801 Newlyn (including Newlyn Town, Street an Nowan, Belle Vue in Paul parish and Tolcarne in the adjacent parish of Madron) had about 1,360 people and Mousehole 680 out of a total parish population of nearly 3,000 (chapter 4). By 1841 Newlyn's population nearly doubled to over 2,500 with Mousehole more than doubling to 1,461. The population of both places continued to grow, though less rapidly – Newlyn's by a third and Mousehole's by just over a fifth. The population gap between the towns had widened by 1901; Newlyn then having 3,750 people and Mousehole 1,655. Four out of five Paul parishioners were now urban dwellers. Of the other west Penwith towns, Penzance grew fastest, more than doubling from 3,382 in 1801 to over 8,500 people in 1841 and then increasing by a third (like Newlyn) to more than 13,000 by 1901. The pattern at St Ives was more like that at Mousehole – a doubling of population from 2,714 to 5,666 in 1801-41 and then slower growth (15 per cent) to 6,700 in 1901. Marazion's population rose from just over 1,000 to 1,680 and then fell to 1,250 people, less than that of Mousehole in 1901.[191]

Emigration Fishing and trading communities were relatively stable and west Penwith towns, with the notable exception of

Marazion, prospered. In contrast with other parts of Cornwall, where emigration was a major depopulator during the 19th and early 20th centuries, few people left Mount's Bay for uncertain futures in the Americas, South Africa, Australia or other parts of Britain. Cornishmen in general were seven times more likely to emigrate than men from Paul parish. A few did, naturally enough, choose to leave. In 1857-1914 wills from Paul parish show nine people in Australia, six in South Africa, three in America (including Henry Giles of Raginnis) and two in New Zealand. Most of the 261 emigrants from the parish to America in the period 1801-1940 left after 1900. Would-be Australian emigrants included some Kelynacks of Newlyn in the 1850s. A few went as Methodist missionaries, including the three Mousehole fishermen who died at Tierra del Fuego in South America in 1851. Migration levels from Paul parish to other parts of the British Isles were also low.[192]

DEVELOPMENT

Tithe records, drawn up after tithes were commuted by Act of Parliament in 1836, form a starting point for studying a settlement because they provide the names of owners and occupiers of each property. In Paul parish, the tithe map of 1843 omits the urban areas where tithes had already been converted to money payments. The blank areas are labelled 'houses and sand of no value' and the only detailed coverage is for Tolcarne in Madron parish. What the Paul tithe map does show are settlement boundaries for Mousehole, and for Newlyn within Paul parish.

Newlyn

The 19th century saw very mixed development in Newlyn. New housing for working men and their families was built down by the harbour, and for the middle classes higher up on the hillside. Most artists (there were around 17 living in the area at the time of the 1891 census) had their homes and studios in Newlyn Town and Belle Vue to start with (chapter 9). There was also considerable commercial and industrial development, especially in the late 19th century in the north of Newlyn at Coombe, the area at the seaward end of the Newlyn river, and also in Street an Nowan, around the Fradgan and Gwavas Quay.[193]

The main settlement at Newlyn Town had almost reached its maximum southern extent along the coast by the 1840s (Penlee Quarry curtailing further expansion there later on). To the north and west expansion had barely begun and it still remained distinct. Fields, orchards and a beach divided the Town from Street an Nowan and Belle Vue lay separate to the west. Indeed, Street an

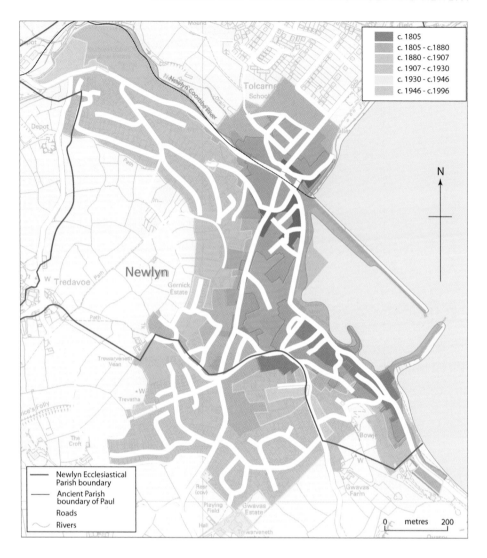

━━━ Newlyn Ecclesiastical
Parish boundary
━━━ Ancient Parish
boundary of Paul
Roads
〜 Rivers

Figure 54 Development
of Newlyn since 1800.
The 1805 Ordnance
Survey plans suggests that
only the south side of
Trewarveneth Street, and
the lower parts of this
street, Boase and Church
Street were then built up,
with Belle Vue a separate
settlement.

Nowan still to a degree remained distinct from Newlyn Town until
the new road known as the Strand was built alongside the harbour
in 1908. To the north development had engulfed Jackford, the area
immediately to the south of the Newlyn river. Further north still,
on the other side of the river, Tolcarne developed a rather different
character, especially after the creation of the new coast road from
Newlyn to Penzance in the early 1880s. Newlyn as a whole had nine
inns along its coast road by 1830: the *Tolcarne Inn* at Tolcarne, then
the *Dolphin*, *Star* and *Union* at Street an Nowan, and the *Three Tuns*,
Red Lion, *Prince Regent*, *Fisherman's Arms*, and *Navy Inn* at Newlyn
Town. The *Prince Regent* had gone by 1841, but another inn, the
Duke of Cornwall, was there in 1856 (perhaps giving its name to
Duke Street). By comparison, there were about 22 inns at Penzance,

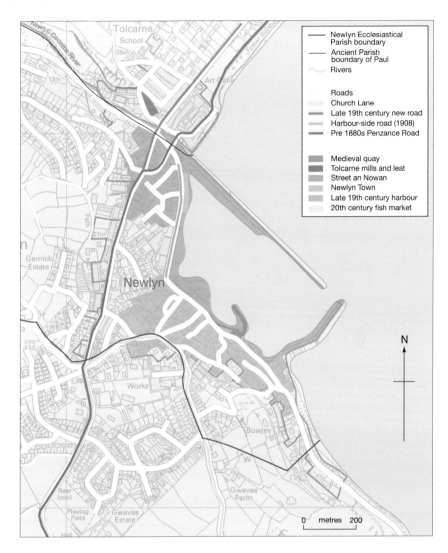

Figure 55 Newlyn in the medieval period was Newlyn Town but from the 17th century Street an Nowan linked the original settlement with Tolcarne.

five at Marazion, three at St Michael's Mount in 1830 and probably only two at Mousehole. The number of inns at Mousehole is low in relation to its population, but this could have been due to Methodist disapproval, and successful teetotal campaigns.[194]

At Newlyn, despite the rise in population, the number of inns declined, partly presumably because of the growth of Methodism in the area. By 1914 three inns had closed in Newlyn Town, now the least commercial part of the town. The *Duke of Cornwall* and *Navy Inn* closed in the late 19th century, and by 1914 the *Three Tuns* on the corner of Fore Street and Boase Street had also gone. On the other hand, the *Star Inn* at Street an Nowan was rebuilt in 1907. Unionist and Liberal clubs were founded in that part of Newlyn and the settlements contained eight communal bakehouses by 1902.[195]

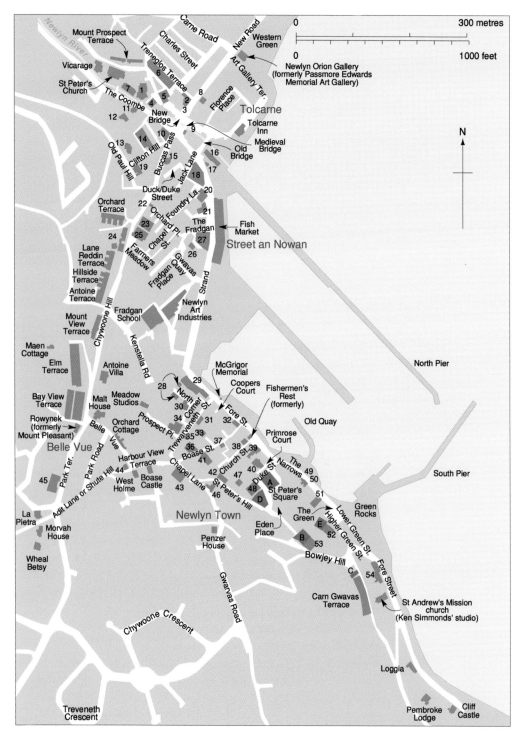

Figure 56 Key places
of historic interest in
Newlyn.

Surviving Buildings

1	Gaiety Cinema (now Meadery)	28	Dod Procter's house and studio
2	Jelberts Ice Cream Shop	29	Fish stores-Hunkin and Cippolina at Norard Slip
3	Herbert Villa	30	Old Mullion Cellar (former)
4	Pilchard Works (formerly 1874 ice store)	31	The Old Manor House
5	Tolcarne Mill (formerly)	32	Three Tuns (former public house)
6	West Terrace	33	Olive Villa
7	Parish Hall	34	Infant's School
8	Trevorrow House	35	Trewarveneth Street Studio (site) and Rue des Beaux Arts
9	Barclays Bank	36	Roseland
10	Buccas Pass store	37	House at entrance to High Mountains
11	Vine Cottage	38	Church Street no 1
12	Vivian House	39	Red Lion Inn
13	Chypons	40	Cliff Manor House (formerly Cliff House)
14	Clifton Terrace	41	Ebenezer Chapel
15	Kenilworth House	42	Cairn William Terrace
16	Ship Institute (RMDSF,	43	Centenary Chapel
	formerly National School and Newlyn Institute site)	44	Mount Vernon
17	War memorial	45	Newlyn Hill Board School
18	Union Inn (now Swordfish)		(former, now Stevensons fishing museum)
19	Chypons Terrace	46	Myrtle Cottage (the Myrtage)
20	Dolphin Inn	47	Jacob's Well
21	Star Inn	48	Rosebud Gardens (formerly houses)
22	Ope	49	Vaccination Court (now Dolphin Court)
23	Trinity Sunday School (now Community Centre)	50	64-8 Fore Street
24	Trellis Cottages	51	Fisherman's Arms
25	Trinity Methodist Chapel	52	Navy Inn Court
26	Langley's Studio (former site)	53	Bowjey Court
27	Ice Works	54	Gwavas House/Terrace

Lost Sites

A	Colmears or Coleman's Court
B	Factory Row/Sambo's Row
C	Foxell's Chapel
D	Gascoyn's garden
E	Navy Inn

A recent study identified five types of housing of various dates in the settlements which comprised 19th-century Newlyn: larger houses (including Cliff Manor House and the Old Manor House in Trewarventh Street), double-fronted houses, terraces or rows, houses epitomising the fishing community of Newlyn, and shops and 'government' buildings. Most houses were now two-storey but small, with two-thirds (and rather more in Newlyn Town) being of four rooms or less in 1891, parents sleeping in one room and children in the other. By the standard of other fishing towns this was not overcrowding.[196]

Newlyn Harbour

Newlyn, hampered by rivalry with Penzance, lagged behind Mousehole in its harbour developments. A new harbour had been built at Penzance in 1845-55 and in 1865 Penzance again opposed Newlyn's plans to build a south pier. Without this Newlyn's fishing boats were exposed to south-east winds, and Gwavas Quay was undermined by storms. But the primitive conditions attracted artists (chapter 9).[197]

Figure 57 North
Pier, Newlyn. In the
foreground are the
remains of the old coast
road destroyed in the
storm of 1880.

The south and north piers at Newlyn were finally built in the
1880s and early 1890s. The south pier was originally intended for
fishing and its foundation stone was laid in 1885. Progress was
hindered by the death later in the year of the clerk of works, who
fell from the working platform. It opened on 15 July 1886 and was
visited by the Penzance Natural History and Antiquarian Society
on 7 September. Some members went up the lighthouse on the pier
end 'to examine the revolving light'. The south pier soon became
the Penlee Quarry stone pier with a narrow gauge railway link to
the quarry and was later extended and a new lighthouse built. A
light railway from Newlyn to St Just was planned in 1898 but never
built.[198]

Work on a north pier for fishing boats began in 1888, and this
pier was extended into deep water in 1891-4. To the relief of the
urban district council it stood up well to a storm on 12 January
1895 and became the chief landing place and (for a short time) the
market for Newlyn's fish. An admiralty boat house (now the post
office) was built alongside the fish market c.1901.[199]

As early as 1903, a new harbour road was planned at Street an
Nowan, with the support of 119 rate payers. Costing £7,000, of
which Paul Urban District Council paid £2,000, it was finished in
1908, and known as the Strand. The 30-foot roadway ran from
North Corner Slip northwards to admiralty boat house, thus
providing a crucial link between Fore Street and a new bridge and
road at Tolcarne. Raised above high tide level on a causeway or
viaduct, it cut Gwavas Quay off from the sea. Already in 1907 the
fishmarket had been moved from the new north pier to its present
site at the northern end of the Strand, while at the southern,

North Corner, end new fish stores were built in 1906 by merchants including the Italian Virgilio Cippolina. The crown of the harbour improvements was the Arts and Crafts style Royal National Mission to Deep Sea fishermen (Ship Institute) of 1911 designed by Edward Prioleau Warren. Built by the north pier, it had a locally made weather-vane in the shape of a galleon.[200]

Private enterprise created a 'curtain wall' of industrial buildings that gives Newlyn its present character, and cuts off the old town of Street an Nowan from the sea. Dunn and Son of Mevagissey built a new fish store in the Fradgan area in 1901 while the Bazeleys had their fish store there and another up the Coombe in 1903-5. R. Richard Bath's fish store was built further up the Coombe in 1904 and he also built the landmark Ice Works building at Fradgan in 1907. Old cottages demolished to make room reputedly included the old Post Office at Fradgan. Shopping was also transformed in the Edwardian period with the Buccas Pass Stores in 1904. Barclay's

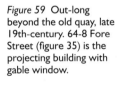

Figure 58 Eden Terrace, Newlyn in 2008.

Bank next to the new bridge dates from 1910.[201]

Newlyn Town In 1841 Newlyn Town remained the largest and most populous settlement with a population of over 1,400 people (or 55 per cent of Newlyn's total). The core area along the shore from North Corner to the Bowjey had already been established before 1800. During the 19th century there was some extension to the south, mostly complete by 1840, except for a few detached residences added in the late 19th and 20th centuries (below). There was also extension to the north, around North Corner and in the west towards Belle Vue, with the Ebenezer chapel being built on Boase Street by 1835. By 1901 Newlyn Town had more than 1,700 inhabitants or 45 per cent of Newlyn's residents overall.

Newlyn Town was the main working-class area of Newlyn with comparatively few grand new buildings. Its heart lay in a dense grid

Figure 59 Out-long beyond the old quay, late 19th-century. 64-8 Fore Street (figure 35) is the projecting building with gable window.

Figure 60 View of artist's studios (in the foreground) taken from Boase Castle, on Harbour View Terrace. Belle Vue rises above the studio on the left with Orchard Cottage immediately behind.

of streets near the Old Quay, rising westwards from the harbourside roadway known variously as Fore Street and the Narrows. At the southern end of the Narrows lay Lower and Higher (or Upper) Green Street, the latter the site of a 17th-century building (*Navy Inn*) superficially similar to Keigwin. An inn between 1813 and 1871, later it became the notoriously overcrowded Navy Inn Court. To the north of this, off Fore Street, lay Church Street, Boase Street and Trewarveneth Street, and between, set back from the northern end of the Narrows, lay the crowded courts and fish cellars around St Peter's Square, perhaps including Colmears Court. Most of the houses in this central area were small – four rooms or fewer – and 64 were still thatched in the 1860s. In 1871, 45 of the 48 houses in Church Street had less than four rooms, and a windowless attic was wall-papered and used as living space in Boase Street at this time. While the area contained much pre- and early 19th-century housing, there was some later building, most notably in 1884 and *c.*1899 near St Peter's Square at Eden Terrace and Eden Place, with back-to-back granite terraces, and, further to the south and east, at Navy Inn (Higher Green) Street.[202]

Building was also going on in Church Street in 1905 with Carrisbrooke (*sic*) Cottages having a date stone of 1910. Among the larger houses in the area, Olive Villa and Roseland House (home of the upwardly mobile Stevenson family) were built between Boase Street and Trewarveneth Street in about 1889 and 1900,

respectively, while just outside the Newlyn parish boundary, at
Cross Field, Penzer House was built *c*.1893.[203]

Some artists' studios were also sited here as well as at Belle
Vue. Net lofts were converted to this use and passed from artist
to artist, or were shared by them. Glass studios were first built in
1889 in Benjamin Bateman's Meadow off Trewarveneth Street.
Frank Bramley's new studio was 'a lovely glasshouse [or] magnified
conservatory not lumbered with plants and water pots', a contrast
to his earlier cob and thatch net loft in Trewarveneth Street.[204]

Belle Vue   At the start of this period, Belle Vue was already a genteel
suburb on the hill above Newlyn Town; it had 87 residents in 1841,
mostly professional people rather than fishermen, and three artists
were still lodging there in 1891. Orchard Cottage was the original
focus of the area. By 1883 John Weeks, a local builder, lived in
Westholme, one of the first new detached houses to be built there.
Mount Vernon is recorded in 1889 and the census of 1891 records a
Royal Navy pensioner, Richard Cock, living there, while after 1889
the Malthouse was enlarged for the Newlyn artists, the Gotches.
West of Chywoone Hill, only half of Elm Terrace was finished in
time to be included on the 1906 Ordnance Survey map.[205]

Homes fit for Royal Academicians were also built to the
west of Chywoone Hill for those Newlyn artists who stayed on
after the majority had moved away during the late 1880s and
1890s (chapter 9). La Pietra was the earliest, begun in 1895 for

Figure 61 Wheal Betsy,
Newlyn's only Arts and
Crafts house, designed
for the Gotch family by
Arnold Mitchell, 1910.

Lionel Birch. This was followed by Higher Faugan, Stanhope and Elizabeth Forbes' granite 'Jacobethan-style' house, in 1903-4. A new road was made there from Chywoone Hill and, when a man fell over stones left here by careless workmen, questions were raised about whether Forbes was liable. Arts and Crafts influences came into Newlyn in 1910. Plans for Wheal Betsy, the Gotches' new house, were passed on 3 November 1909; bricks came by sea, and the house was finished by Edward Pidwell, a local builder, in 1910. The last of these grand houses, Morvah House at Lower Faugan, was begun on 8 July 1914 for Reginald Dick.[206]

Terraces with gables and bay windows continued to be built in the Belle Vue area. Park Terrace and Villas (part of the Park Sheeta estate at the top of Chywoone Hill) were finished in 1909-10, their early residents including an undertaker and Primitive Methodist minister. By 1914 Elm Terrace, and Bay View Terrace on the opposite side of the hill, were also inhabited. Most of these houses were known by name rather than number, individual house names being painted on glass panels above the front door.[207]

Street an Nowan   Street an Nowan's continuing expansion in the early 19th century is marked by the construction of Trinity chapel on Chwyoone Hill in 1832; Trellis Cottages nearby on the west side of the street also probably date from about this time. By 1841 the area, which by then included Jackford, was the second most populous part of Newlyn with 945 people. Expansion continued throughout the century and the area contained more than 1,230 people by 1901.

It was in Street an Nowan that villas and terraces were built first for the new middle classes. Villa development started here in the 1850s, with Chypons, later home to Josiah Pawlyn, fish merchant. Built as an Australian-style bungalow it had a galvanised veranda roof. Vivian House was built in 1860 and 10 years later had a dining room, study and small kitchen, with a drawing room and three bedrooms above. The grandest of all the villas, Antoine Villa higher up Chywoone Hill, was built in neo-classical style with a granite ashlar front for Christopher Bodinar Foster, gentleman, who put his own oversize initials and the date 1863 on its granite façade.[208]

On the hillside, the earliest terrace built on any scale seems to have been in the 1860s. Unlike Truro and other Cornish towns, which started in valleys, Street an Nowan's terrace development was not a steady progression from below, but rather fluctuated up or down as meadows and orchards were bought up for building. Chypons Terrace and Clifton Terrace in the Coombe and Antoine Terrace and Mount's Bay View Terrace on the west side of

Figure 62 View from Tolcarne *c.*1868 showing Vivian House above the roof of the unfinished Newlyn church (the arches for the north aisle are shown). Clifton Terrace or 'Upstarts Terrace' stands out in the middle of the view with Newlyn Town behind.

Chywoone Hill are all noted first in the 1871 census. Speculative building attracted the upwardly mobile and Clifton Terrace was soon nicknamed 'Upstarts' or 'Captains' Row. A master mariner, sailor, two coopers, a fish merchant, a Wesleyan minister, and a fisherman were among the first residents. Before the building of large fish stores at the Coombe, there were good views out to sea and one house had a lookout.[209]

Eventually, terraces were built up and down Chywoone Hill on 'raised, engineered platforms on the steep hillside'. Hillside Terrace had been constructed below Antoine Terrace by 1901, and building continued downhill with Lane Reddin Terrace *c.*1910, and Orchard Terrace, built at right-angles to the hill below this, in the period 1909-15. One important change to the layout of the area was made in the late 1880s with the building of Buccas Pass to link New Road, Tolcarne, with Chywoone Hill. That involved the demolition of some cottages, and the building of Kenilworth House on the new road alignment before 1910.[210]

Figure 63 Photograph showing the building of Carne Road and Charles Street *c.*1893. Alexandra Terrace (in the middle ground) was included in the new 1848 Newlyn parish, but the flour mill and serpentine works at Wherrytown were just outside. Penzance is in the background.

Rebuilding was also going on in the heart of Street an Nowan. In the Fradgan a dense network of narrow lanes and alleys were built just down from Chywoone Hill around Orchard Place (formerly an orchard) in the early to mid-19th century. They comprised rows of small cottages, two bays wide and two storeys high, opening directly on to the street (and so were quite different from Newlyn Town's small fishing cellars built around their courts). There was also some later activity here, generated by local artists and incomers. At Gwavas Quay, for example, Ocean Cottage, home to a retired farmer in 1871, bears a date stone of 1863, while Langley's cottage studio at Keel Alley in the Fradgan acquired a glass front in 1896. Seven artists lodged in the Street an Nowan area in 1891.[211]

Tolcarne This area suffered a major change in 1817 when erosion took away its side of the river bank, where all the Newlyn boats were drawn up for the winter. Newlyn gardener and botanist, William Curnow, later recalled 'a good-sized garden and a small meadow near the Newlyn River, where it is now all beach'. The development of the settlement can be traced in detail from the 1840s, unlike other areas of Newlyn. In 1851 Tolcarne, which no longer included Jackford, was the least densely populated part of the town with 132 people housed in 24 dwellings (1841 figures would have been similar). By 1861 its population had increased by only seven, but then it rose to 298 in 1891 (including one artist), more than doubling again to 654 in 1901 (against the local trend).[212]

Tolcarne remained Newlyn's industrial suburb and there were only a few fishermen's cottages near the seashore. In 1843 the Madron tithe map shows a cooper's and a carpenter's shop, two smithies, a timber yard and 'cellar' at Tolcarne, as well as

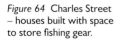

Figure 64 Charles Street – houses built with space to store fishing gear.

Figure 65 Plague stone at Mousehole (in foreground) where money and goods may have been left during the quarantine imposed in 1832 (like Eyam in Derbyshire during the Great Plague of 1666). Cholera was the plague here and Richard Mann, a wealthy bachelor of Newlyn, one of the victims. We know about this because Richard made two wills which later led to a dispute. On the second occasion his Penzance solicitor was too afraid to attend.

the brewery, inn, and two mills. The settlement is well served by communications; between 1806 and 1808 some 300 yards of new road was made across Western Green and a new bridge (that nearest the sea) was built.[213]

The area continued to be mainly industrial until the late 19th century. In 1874 a three-storey ice works, taller than the surrounding buildings, was constructed in the Coombe (the former Pilchard Works), while in 1875 plans were made for a railway (in fact never built) from Penzance to Tolcarne via Newlyn Coombe. Tolcarne mills stopped grinding corn in the early 1880s but continued to function in the later '80s and '90s, crushing stone from Penlee Quarry for the new coast road.[214]

It was the creation of this new road, replacing the old Penzance to Newlyn coast road, washed away in the storm of 1880 that opened Tolcarne up for speculative building development in the 1890s. When rebuilt further inland in 1882-3, New Road, Tolcarne, started with detached houses like Herbert Villa and Trevorrow House. Terrace houses with bay windows and pocket handkerchief-sized front gardens soon followed. A new bridge – the present road bridge – was also made, and Paul Urban District Council agreed to take over the medieval (middle) bridge as a footbridge to prevent its demolition in 1904.[215]

West of New Road, in the area known as Park Saundry, a three-street development was laid out in the early 1890s. Work began at the top of Carne Road and bottom of Charles Street and Treneglos (or West) Terrace was finished last. At the Penzance end of New Road the Passmore Edwards Gallery opened for the exhibition of Newlyn and St Ives paintings on 22 October 1895.[216]

Mousehole

Mousehole's boundary stones of blue elvan and granite mostly coincide with the town limits in 1843. The largest blue elvan stone at the junction of Duck Street and North Street is still known as the plague stone and may record 'unneighbourly' quarantine arrangement during the 1832 cholera outbreak when 88 Newlyners and 66 Penzance people died. Cholera started in Sunderland (County Durham) in 1832, and Newlyn and Penzance were the Cornish towns worst affected, possibly exacerbated by coal trade links. Victims were buried in the Cholera Ground at Paul church town; significantly, they included no one from Mousehole.[217]

Mousehole may have had as many as five inns at one time (appropriate to its growing population) but by 1841, in part because of the growth of local Methodism, there remained only the *Ship*. In 1902 the town also had six communal bakehouses. In the centre of Mousehole houses were in poor condition with

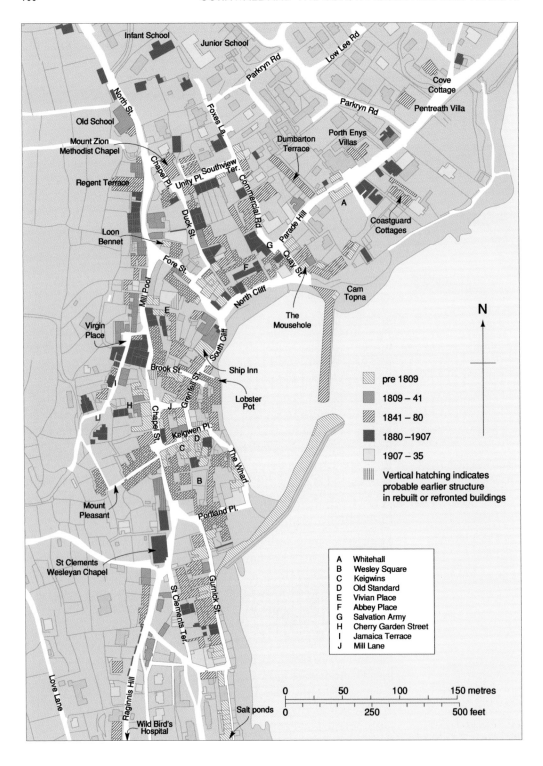

Infant School
Junior School
Low Lee Rd
Parkryn Rd
Cove Cottage
North St.
Parkryn Rd
Pentreath Villa
Old School
Foxes La.
Dumbarton Terrace
Porth Enys Villas
Mount Zion Methodist Chapel
Chapel Pl.
Unity Pl.
Southview Ter.
Regent Terrace
Commercial Rd
A
Loon Bennet
Duck St.
Parade Hill
Coastguard Cottages
Fore St.
G
Quay St.
Mill Pool
F
Cam Topna
E
North Cliff
The Mousehole
Virgin Place
South Cliff
Brook St.
Ship Inn
Grenfell St.
Lobster Pot
H
Chapel St.
J
Keigwen Pl.
D
C
B
Mount Pleasant
Portland Pl.
St Clements Wesleyan Chapel
Gurnick St.
St. Clements Ter.
Love Lane
Raginnis Hill
Salt ponds
Wild Bird's Hospital

N

pre 1809
1809 – 41
1841 – 80
1880 –1907
1907 – 35

Vertical hatching indicates
probable earlier structure
in rebuilt or refronted buildings

A   Whitehall
B   Wesley Square
C   Keigwins
D   Old Standard
E   Vivian Place
F   Abbey Place
G   Salvation Army
H   Cherry Garden Street
I   Jamaica Terrace
J   Mill Lane

0   50   100   150 metres
0   250   500 feet

Figure 66 Map of Modern Mousehole.

thatch and cob common. In all, 18 houses were unoccupied in 1881 (compared with 22 in Newlyn), while eight more were 'being built'. Mousehole's predominantly Victorian townscape today reflects the intense building activity of the late 19th century paid for from the proceeds of fishing around Britain. Older fabric survives, if at all, at ground-floor level.[218]

Houses were built at Salt Ponds in 1838 (though not shown on George Wolfe's painting of 1860, figure 92), but the main areas of 19th-century expansion were Raginnis Hill, Paul Hill and the coastal road towards Newlyn. Cove Cottage, the most northerly villa, was built by 1861, while nearby on the Parade Dumbarton House, Pentreath House, and Porthenys Villa could also date from the 1860s or early 1870s. In 1875, the expansion towards Paul Churchtown included Lynwood, a gentry-house set in its own grounds, with 18 rooms, coach house and stables, and, by 1903, a museum (gone in 1905). To the south of the town, the most important villa was Clifton House, probably built in the 1860s.[219]

Figure 67 Ship Inn, Mousehole as seen from the harbour. The steps were moved after the 1838 quay was removed.

Figure 68 Fradgan industrial buildings with an early 19th-century pair of houses with quoins and string course in the background.

Mousehole Harbour

Like that at Newlyn, the quay at Mousehole started to land salt in 1833. A new quay, constructed below the Lobster Pot in 1838 at a cost of £1,400, created a more sheltered, though 'far too small', harbour in southern Mousehole. Traces of this lost 1838 quay can still be seen in the harbour wall below the *Ship Inn*.[220]

As it appears today, Mousehole's harbour was created in 1868-71 at a cost of £5,400. The harbour area was now two to three acres or double its 1838 size and the gap between the two quays could be closed by wooden baulks in stormy weather, so that boats could 'lie as snugly as in a duck pond'. Larger boats were expected to pay £3 5s. a year in harbour dues. In 1884, slate for the church roof was landed there.[221]

Water and Other Problems

All this building work needed an infrastructure of improved water supplies and sewers. While that was relatively easy to achieve for new buildings on the edges of the town, in heavily built up central areas it was more problematic. Duck Street in Street an Nowan acquired water pipes in 1898, while North Corner in Newlyn Town had to wait until 1906. Standpipes became a feature of Newlyn from 1902, despite opposition from householders who feared leaks and overuse by fishermen cleaning their oilskins.[222]

Although the link between poor refuse disposal and disease was understood, diphtheria and typhoid were far from eliminated. John Vibert, vicar of Newlyn, died of diphtheria in 1873, and between 1900 and 1914 there were at least five deaths from typhoid and seven from diphtheria in the two towns. Links with the rural hinterland stayed strong – typhoid came into the town via a farm dairy in 1890 and Newlyn's narrow streets posed problems for fat cattle in 1913. Other nuisances at Newlyn at this time included tall bean plants and fishing nets, both of which blocked light from houses.[223]

By 1914, a number of favourite artistic locations were disappearing, and there were claims that the Baths, Bazeleys and Dunns had ruined Newlyn with their monster fish stores. Greenhouses and glass studios were also thought to spoil the look of the town, though market gardening and art were by now mainstays of the local economy. At Mousehole, too, cob and thatch cottages were being lost in a wave of Victorian rebuilding. Yet compared to what was about to happen to Newlyn, these losses were minor.[224]

Chapter 7

Earning a Living, 1800-1914

The century from 1815 to 1914 was overwhelmingly one of peace and legitimate trade, both in Cornwall and country wide, which saw major changes in the economy including more investment from outside. Newlyn and Mousehole prospered from developing the pilchard industry and – less respectably – from smuggling in the 18th century, and they still shared urban functions with Penzance. But, unlike Penzance, which by now was much larger than either, they failed to diversify or invest to any great extent in the new consumer culture; both places stayed as fishing ports and took part in seasonal fishing migration around Britain. Railways reached Penzance mid-century and thereafter fresh fish, early potatoes and flowers from this area went to London. By the late 19th century Newlyn fishermen, especially, faced outside competition in their home waters as East Coast drift boats followed them home from the North Sea but, until industrial quarrying began at the end of this period, the two settlements really had no major occupational alternatives to fishing.

The French Wars

War with France broke out in 1793 and except for a brief period of peace in 1802-3, continued until the decisive battle of Waterloo in 1815. Around 1800 gun batteries were set up to counter a possible French invasion in Mount's Bay as elsewhere along the south coast. In Paul parish there were batteries at Gwavas, Tavis Vor and Merlin's Rock and volunteer brigades were formed to man them. The Mount's Bay volunteers, described as 'a very indifferent corps', wore red uniforms and 'stuck well on their little cat-like horses' when charging over rough ground in 1805-6. Press gang activity was intense, with the *Navy Inn* at Newlyn a 'sort of naval HQ'. William Lovett, the Chartist social reformer from Newlyn, witnessed Honor Hitchens, a deaf fishwife, attacking a press officer with a dogfish in the early 1800s; the unfortunate officer had tried to seize Honor's 60-year-old father to work in the navy.[225]

The war had a considerable impact on the people of Mount's Bay. The Emperor Napoleon, in particular, was vilified locally. Penzance celebrated the temporary peace of 1814 by carrying an effigy of Napoleon through the town, and the mayor, the gentlemen and the effigy then embarked in several boats 'and proceeded to Mousehole Island, since called Elba [the island to

Figure 69 Tolcarne from Newlyn Battery, by Walter Tremenheere, c.1800. Green rocks (later the site of the South pier) screens Newlyn Town and part of Street an Nowan, but masts of ships taking shelter within the old quay can be seen. Tolcarne is to the right with Madron church and Larigan House beyond. Buildings on the sea-wall include the *Tolcarne Inn*.

Hail favourite Mousehole! Once the pride of Paul, Ere haughty Dons Did meditate its fall.

Extract from 'On the Burning of Mousehole by the Spaniards' in R. Treffry, *Memoirs of Richard Trewavas, jun. of Mousehole* (1815), 165.

which Napoleon was banished in 1814]'. Yet as late as 1850 pictures of Napoleon 'in impossible costume … crossing impossible Alps on an impossible charger' could be seen hanging on the walls of superior cottages in Mount's Bay. Fear of invasion, allied to the finding of charred timber in Paul church porch roof in 1807, a topical reminder of the earlier Spanish Raid, meant there was plenty of scope for celebration when the war finally came to an end in 1815. At Newlyn, two newly-built fishing boats, the *Victory* and the *Peace*, commemorated the end of hostilities. A new fishing vessel at Penzance was named the *Lord Nelson*, after the great naval victor of the Nile and Trafalgar.[226]

The End of Smuggling

Even before the peace of 1815 led directly to a lowering of taxes and hence a reduction in the motive for smuggling, more effective measures had been put in place for its control. In 1801, the first preventative station to counter smuggling in Cornwall had been established at Polperro, and it was followed by Penzance, Porthleven and, in 1808, Mousehole. It took ten years to build the customs boathouse at Mousehole, because of local obstruction; indeed the first site was sold secretly to someone else after work had already started. Finally finished in 1818, the boathouse measured 36 feet by 18, the boat being stored in a loft six feet above the ground. Newlyn, by contrast, was less ambitious and customs officers rented a boathouse and storage space as needed.[227]

Newlyn and Mousehole people continued to smuggle goods. In 1800, it was reported that Mary Tonkin of Newlyn had been a smuggler and a spy for the English government in France. In 1813,

Figure 70 Newlyn c.1830 by Anna Margareta Scobell of Poltair, showing the effects of unemployment as smuggling was coming to an end.

Nicholas Kelynack, a customs officer at Newlyn was asked to 'wink at and not discover smuggling', while in the autumn of the following year 81 casks of brandy were seized at Newlyn, brought from France in the *Two Johns* of Mousehole. A little later in 1819 John Blewett, a fisherman of Mousehole, who had lost a leg in the Napoleonic Wars, supplemented his navy pension of £12 with smuggling.[228]

The abolition of salt duties in the 1820s led to a dramatic decline in customs seizures. Only one large run of smuggled goods was noted in the bay in the six months up to 12 October 1826 and not much after that. Most smugglers had taken up 'more honest employment', like the Mousehole fisherman licensed in 1829 to land his catch at Guernsey, once a notorious smuggling base. The last customs case from Mousehole was noted on 2 May 1833 when the *William* of Newlyn tried to land Roscoff brandy there.[229]

In this final phase, the character of smuggling changed, in part, because of Methodism. The convicted smuggler, William Richards of Mousehole, 'conducted himself with great decorum at Bodmin' in 1817 and helped in 'correcting fellow prisoners for swearing and profane language'. Violent attacks on customs officers were rare and smugglers ran away under cover of darkness. Coastguards replaced customs officers, but the nickname 'Keggers', meaning smugglers (as well as designating Keigwins) was used at Mousehole well into the 20th century.[230]

Finally, whatever threat there still was piracy ended in 1816, when Edward Pellew, a Cornishman, crushed the last of the Turkish pirates from Algiers.[231]

Mount's Bay Trade in the Mid-19th Century

The war with France had an adverse impact on trade, particularly in cutting off the Italian markets. Sea salt could no longer be imported from Brittany and Spain and local fish processors were obliged to use less suitable rock salt from inland areas of Cheshire to cure their

Figure 71 Gwavas Quay, Newlyn – a wide landing area with a former fish cellar with wide entrance (one of the tithe cellars, perhaps) to the right.

pilchards. This salt came by sea from Liverpool to Newlyn and local fish curers claimed damages for salt lost on the voyage.[232]

Between 1830 and 1866 the men of Mousehole and Newlyn invested in at least 18 trading schooners (a two- or three-masted trading vessel), a brigantine and a brig that sailed from the port of Penzance. Mount's Bay schooners traded with Ireland, the Mediterranean and the Azores taking out bulk goods, like tin, copper and fish, and returning with groceries and oranges for Christmas. As was common practice, shares in each vessel were divided into parts (as was the case with mines and seines), to spread the risk. Usually 64 separate parts were identified, with up to seven owners. William Tonkin, a Newlyn merchant, had shares in the *Lady of the Lake*, the *Dolphin* and the *Fame* in the 1830s and 1840s, as well as investing in the Newlyn fishing fleet. In Mousehole shipowning families such as the Wrights, Penders and Trewavases also had shares in more than one schooner.[233]

THE FISHERIES

In the 19th century fishing in Cornwall became a highly organised business, mostly run by two families, the Bolithos of Penzance and the Foxes of Falmouth. At Newlyn, change was already apparent early on: between 1798 and 1815 fish merchants and curers at Newlyn included John Batten, the Cunnacks, William Chenalls, Thomas Reed, Michael Davy, Edward Tregurtha and William Colenso, none of whom were from the key fishing families or old merchant dynasties. But fishing remained extremely important both there and at Mousehole with offices of the Shipwrecked

Fishermen and Mariners' Royal Benevolent Society in both villages
following the charity's foundation in 1839. At least two-thirds of
the men of Mousehole and half those of Newlyn in 1851 earned
their living from the fisheries, while 30 per cent of the female
population were fishermen's wives, and daughters or were in
the closely related occupation of net making. In the 1891 census
fishermen and fish dealers accounted for almost 50 per cent of
male workers in Newlyn and over 60 per cent in Mousehole,
respectively. This may underestimate the number of fishermen,
since an 1896 report suggested that fishing actually employed up to
77 per cent of Mousehole men and boys.[234]

Initially, the activities of these men continued to include seining
as well as drift fishing. St Ives with its sandy beaches was the centre
for pilchard seining by 1835 with no fewer than 132 of Cornwall's
200 pilchard seines based there. Mousehole and Newlyn remained
peripheral with only ten to 12 pilchard seines between them,
although Newlyn had several seines at this time, including *Success*,
Happy Return and *Speedwell*. Later in the century seining all but
disappeared.[235]

Unlike seining, the Cornish drift fishery was centred on Mount's
Bay, although some boats were based at the Scilly Islands for part
of each year. The local drift fleet fished for pilchards and mackerel.
Mackerel fishing became more important as pilchards began their
slow decline. By 1849 drift boats cost between £120 and £180, with
a complete drift net costing the same as a small boat. Profits were
divided as follows: one-seventh to the boat, three-sevenths to the
nets, and the rest divided among the crew. This made owners of
boats and nets 'the capitalists of their calling' distinguishable from

Figure 72 Newlyn fishing
fleet and old pier *c.*1880.
This shows Mount's Bay
luggers and the fish sale
on the beach.

the rest by their 'generally healthy look, and the superior style of his house, family and dress'.[236]

After the Napoleonic Wars seasonal migration began, involving only the larger drifters from St Ives and from Mount's Bay. Like the *Nancy* of Newlyn in 1820, they joined the Irish fleet fishing for herring and mackerel in the Irish Sea in June and July; by the 1850s, if not earlier, however, some of the larger boats went on from there to join the North Sea herring fishery in the late summer and autumn via the Caledonian Canal. They then returned for the winter and spring fishing in Mount's Bay (and later fished off Plymouth). This annual circumnavigation of Britain remained important until 1914.[237]

Curing and Marketing

Catholic countries of Southern Europe were still the main markets for preserved pilchards and a common toast in Cornwall at this time was: 'Long life to the Pope: Death to our best friends [the pilchards]: And may our streets run with blood.' Italian merchants now wanted half hogsheads and quarter casks, which were easier to handle, rather than full hogsheads. This demand may have led by the 1830s to a new invention – the continuous jetty or reversed ledge. In older cellar walls holes had been generally spaced one hogshead apart and so were less versatile than the continuous jetties, which allowed barrels to be put closer together (Panel 8). Some drift-net caught pilchards were sold fresh, but only for local consumption, and the rest, together with all those caught by seine, were salt-cured and pressed.[238]

Mackerel was usually sold fresh from the beach, or from the backs of local fishwives, but some were also sent to the London market. At first, the trade also used fast pilot cutters and trawlers and 'swift paddle steamers', but from 1841, with the completion of the London to Bristol line, the railways began to make an impact. In 1851 a line from Penzance went to Hayle, from where by sea and rail (via Bristol) it took 16 hours for the fish to reach London. In 1859 all this changed with the coming of the through line from London to Penzance.[239]

The Role of Women

Fishwives sold fish all round the Penwith countryside, often travelling round the locality on foot. In the 1840s, for example, one Mousehole fishwife went to nine parishes with half a cowel of fish on her back and 20 pounds of salt in her pockets. Early engravings of Mount's Bay fishwives focus on their costume – black beaver hat and red cloak – rather than their work. A smaller number,

Figure 73 Mary Kelynack, the elderly Newlyn fishwife who walked to London to see the Great Exhibition in 1851.

including Sally Berryman of Newlyn, 'queen of the fisherwomen', had a regular pitch at Penzance market from the 1830s. In 1862, 80 of the 200 fisherwomen belonging to Newlyn, including Sally, worked 16-hour day shifts in the market at Penzance, in companies of eight or ten which shared profits.[240]

The central role of women in the Newlyn fishing industry in the late 19th century is apparent in *The Widow Woman,* a novel written by Charles Lee, who stayed in the town in 1893-4. This closely-observed fictional account shows that women handled the money, making sure that 'the boat gets one share, the captain one, those who put nets aboard one each, and the rest, who give only their services, half a share'. At the end of the week any profit was 'set out in heaps on the kitchen mantelpiece' for the crew to 'drop in' and collect. When asked why wage disputes were rare, a Mount's Bay fisherman replied: 'We leave all that to the women.'[241]

Traditional Fishing

'Any method of fishery at all periods of the year in the same boats' was still Newlyn's motto, but by the end of the 19th century, its sole pilchard seine was rarely used. The home fishery now extended from the Lizard to Godrevy (beyond St Ives). Seasonal migration to the Irish and North Seas continued, while the Western mackerel fishery was attracting unwelcome outside competition. A report into the state of the fisheries in 1896 noted optimistically that 'the balance was still in favour of the local fisherman', but the violent destruction, in that year, of fish caught by foreign boats suggested otherwise (chapter 8).[242]

Fishing was at a peak all over Britain in 1881, the year of the only census in which fishermen in Paul parish exceeded one tousand. Crew lists, which survive for eight boats from Mousehole

Figure 74 Mrs Pollard's admirers are Billy Jenkins, a Newlyn fisherman and Mr Jones, a Yarmouth fish buyer (C. Lee, *The Widow Woman*, 1899).

Figure 75 Breadwinners by Walter Langley. Unlike earlier depictions of Cornish fishwives, Langley's painting shows the hard labour involved.

How to Cure Pilchards

Pilchards were salt-cured in pilchard cellars of two types – large commercial cellars or palaces (a term commonly used in east Cornwall) or small domestic premises, usually under the dwelling houses of the fishermen and often indicated by external stone steps. Commercial pilchard cellars had big stone paved open courts with lofts supported by tall granite pillars over part. In the walls about four or five feet above the cobbled pavement were 'square apertures to accommodate the ends of long beams, or "pressing-poles".' Cobbled floors or 'causes' drained into wooden gutters, which led to the 'train-pit' (where fish oil collected – a valuable by-product).

Here 'in incessant confusion and noise' women and girls worked in pairs to build bulks or walls of fish. A glass of brandy and a piece of bread and cheese was provided for each worker every six hours. Cellar workers first laid down a thick layer of salt, then a layer of fish, then another layer of salt and another of fish, and so on. A large bulk was about four foot (or four or five fish) in width (as far as two women could easily reach when working from both sides). When the wall got to chest height, or when a fresh catch came in, a new bulk would be started (under cover as far as possible). Pilchards were left in bulk for about a month to allow the fish to 'take the salt'.

The bulk was then 'broken out' with great care by the women, and men then washed and drained the fish (a 'tray for washing pilchards' occurs in Elias Crankan's inventory of 1740) leaving bright clean fish fit for packing. Packing was women's work. Each packer would pick up a fan-shaped handful of fish, and lay them in the hogsheads (barrels) heads outwards and backs downwards. More and more handfuls were added building up the contents in circular layers of fish. Men then laid a stout false barrelhead or 'buckler' on the top of the fish, setting a few square blocks of timber on this to act as a fulcrum. Above this, bearing on the fulcrum blocks, they placed a substantial 12-foot 'pressing pole', with its heel set in the pressing niche. The pressing pole lay square across the head of the cask, bearing on the fulcrum blocks about two feet off the wall, with the free end projecting out into the central square. Rope strops were hung from the free end of the poles and, with the aid of a whip (a stout timber pole with an iron hook at its central point), two cellar men would lift one or more heavy pressing-stones and suspend them from the rope strops. Care had to be taken in applying these weights so as not to damage the fish being pressed.

The cellar men attended the presses several times a day, adding more weights as necessary, and throughout the pressing process valuable train-oil was expressed. More fish were added every two to three hours and a further repacking occurred after 24 hours. The final 'back-laying' was done after two days with the backs of the fish now uppermost – giving the contents an identical appearance irrespective of which end was viewed. Each cask now weighed four cwt. and contained 2,000-3,000 'fairmaids'. The whole had a last pressing before the cooper came to 'head-in' the cask'. Merchants or agents observed the curing process at different stages and so only a few sample hogsheads needed to be opened and checked for quality. Full hogsheads were branded or stencilled with the curers' names, the quantity and weight and sometimes the destination, or 'British Fish.'

Tony Pawlyn

Poem by John Boson

(English translation by Oliver Padel):

My song is about Pilchards with boat and net
taken in the Bay of the Grey Rock in the Wood.
When the boats are come home
from the sea, the harbour folk cry 'tithe, tithe'
and every woman with her behind near
with a creel and three hundred pilchards on her
back,
to make bulks in every house
with many a voice, 'Pilchards, pilchards – more salt.'
When they are well salted, one month altogether
it is time to break (them) up and pull (them) away.
After that, washing clean in salt water;
It will give a good name to all girls.
Put (them) bright in a barrel, head to tail;
they are a profit and a great thing for smart
merchants.
Look you for a log, thirteen feet long;
put on that stones, of five hundred weight;
three times in a day look you to it.
For half a month oil will fall from it.
This it the true way to prepare pilchards;
in the market they will sell best.
Year upon year let boats come
and full with pilchards go from Gwavas Lake.
At last let a north-easterly wind blow afar,
for the people of hot-land to eat (them) all.
There is wealth of pilchards alike of all the world –
more of poor people than of great people.

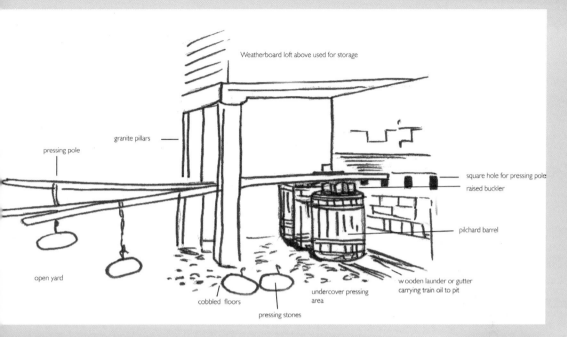

Weatherboard loft above used for storage

granite pillars

pressing pole

square hole for pressing pole

raised buckler

pilchard barrel

open yard

wooden launder or gutter
carrying train oil to pit

cobbled floors

undercover pressing
area

pressing stones

Figure A: *Sketch of pilchard pressing process.*

Figure B: *Example of continuous corbel or jetty in Mousehole garage. This allowed barrels of different sizes to be used with the heels of the pressing poles going under the overhang instead of into square holes.*

and 15 from Newlyn between 1868 and 1913, show that crews comprised five or six men and a boy, with most of the key fishing families still represented. Crews could be drawn from the same neighbourhood as the owner. Thus in 1890 the acting master of the *Pride of the Sea* lived in Church Street, Newlyn, just round the corner from the ship's owner Julia Stibbs, landlady of the *Red Lion*, the only female owner named in these lists.[243]

The local focus of the fishing industry was already being challenged by the 1880s when the Newlyn fleet was joined by 68 East Coast boats. Local fishermen at Newlyn grumbled that they were building a harbour for strangers. By 1896, there had been similar developments at Mousehole, which then had 123 fishing boats compared with 138 at Newlyn. In 1901 there were 83 non-local boats in Newlyn harbour. Half were from the east coast, mostly drifters from Lowestoft; just over a third were trawlers from Brixham in Devon, which had previously fished off Dover; and there was also a Norwegian ship. Alongside this went a decline in traditional skills, although withy pots were still used for crabs at Mousehole in preference to galvanised ones. Only a few older fishermen were aware of the importance of changes in temperature – 'when the nets feel warm we know we shall have a good catch' – or counted their mackerel in the Cornish language.[244]

Marketing and Processing

Beach auctions were the prime means of disposing of fresh fish at Newlyn until the 1890s when the first fish market was built. Mousehole fishermen employed 'yawlers', young boys in rowing boats, to get their fish to Newlyn market. From there it was sent to Penzance railway station and arrived in London only 12 hours later. Railway rates in 1896 were £3 per ton for fish, twice the rate for vegetables and meat. A saving of £1 a ton could be made in summer, by sending fish by weekly steamboat from Cornwall to Billingsgate (a four-day voyage, weather permitting). Early canning of fish was not successful and local fishermen were encouraged to consider making 'dog biscuit', oil, and glue from surplus fish.[245]

Pilchards were still salt-cured and pressed, but the process was changing. By the late 19th century, tanks of brine were used for the pilchard catches. On 7 September 1888, Penzance Natural History and Antiquarian Society visited Mr Toman's fish cellar at Newlyn and saw 'the new process of preservation in brine, and the new mode of pressure by screws in place of the old lever' or pressing pole. The screws (of three inches or more in diameter) were fixed to the underside of a wooden beam and the barrels put directly below. Production became more industrialised, especially at Newlyn, and many domestic cellars were converted to other uses.

Use of tanks certainly speeded up the process, but the end product was thought to be inferior (see Panel 8).[246]

In 1896 there were six pilchard curing houses at Mousehole and 20 at Newlyn (employing 50 people and 150-200, respectively). About 600 additional people were employed in the 'cartage' of cured pilchards at Newlyn. Italian steamers first arrived at Newlyn in the 1860s and there was a regular steamer service by the 1880s. Destinations were stencilled on the lids and the Cippolinas were the first Italian firm with a base in Newlyn.[247]

Fishing Superstitions and Taboos

Newlyn and Mousehole naturally shared in the superstitions and taboos common to fishing communities around the British Isles. This process was no doubt encouraged by the annual migration of the drift fleet. In the early 1890s, making a 'chalk drawing of a cat or a dog on a Newlyn boat when building it' would 'make the men pull it to pieces again'. Carrying a hare's foot was also unlucky and if found would cause a boat to turn back for port. Mention of clergy or churches was avoided as this could foretell a funeral. Fish offerings were made to the Buccaboo or storm devil at Newlyn (the nickname Newlyn Buccas derives from this spirit).[248]

'when there's a wind they wussn't go, an when there's a calm they cussn't go'.

An old Newlyn woman.

Fishermen had a love-hate relationship with the sea and houses at Mousehole harbour turned their backs on it (windows tended to look inland). Mr Simons, a Newlyn fishermen, had a dream 'to live inland among the trees out of sight of the sea for ever' rather than in Lower Green Street next to the south pier. Losses of fishing boats remained rare, but had the profoundest effect on the whole community when they occurred. For example, in 1899, when the *Emeline* of Mousehole was lost on the return journey from Lowestoft, donations flooded in from all over England, especially from Methodists. The loss of the lugger *Jane* within 200 yards of Penzance pier on 7 October 1880 inspired many Newlyn paintings. It was also one of the dating tools used by older folk when recalling past events.[249]

MARITIME AND OTHER OCCUPATIONS

Fishing Related Occupations

Boatbuilding Registration of vessels, including larger fishing boats, began in the late 18th century. Three-fifths of the boats belonging to Newlyn and Mousehole owners were then locally built; between 1800 and 1872, 66 vessels of 15 tons or more were built at Newlyn and five at Mousehole. All but six of the rest were built elsewhere in Cornwall, for instance, The *Hugh Bourne* from St Ives, named after one of the founders of Primitive Methodism.[250]

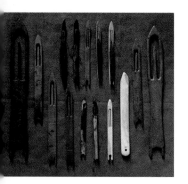

Figure 76 A selection of Newlyn beeting needles, some with owners' initials. The smaller needles are made of bone and the larger (up to six inches long) of wood.

By the early 20th century there had been changes in the pattern of boat building with the rise of Porthleven near the Lizard as an important centre. A third of the 315 fishing boats and trading vessels registered to owners from Newlyn and Mousehole between 1902 and 1914 were built in this port. This contrasts sharply with Newlyn's share, which was just under a quarter, and Mousehole's, which was less than a tenth. Newlyn had six boat-builders in 1896 with '20 hands [employed] in all', but 'trade had considerably decreased'. At Mousehole there was then only one boat builder employing one or two men.[251]

Net making In the early 19th century, when 14 Mousehole and Newlyn girls were sent to teach net making to reluctant Scilly Islanders, the craft was women's work, carried out in the winter months. Net making (breeding) and mending (beeting) continued generally to be so regarded, although some men at Mousehole made their own mackerel nets. Seine nets had the smallest mesh; then came pilchard, herring and mackerel drift nets in ascending order of mesh size. Netting needles were either made of bone (if small) or pliable wood. Children and old people loaded needles with twine, twenty being wanted at a time to keep a net breeder at work. By the late 19th century cheaper machine-made nets were available, but women went on mending nets for a shilling a day.[252]

Others By the 1840s there were four rope-walks at Newlyn and Tolcarne, but none at Mousehole. The three Newlyn rope-walks were all on the south side of the town: Tonkin's at Bowjey, William Chirgwin's south of Gwavas battery and Henry Warren's at Roskilly. The 1851 census shows that there were then 21 rope-makers living in Newlyn. In 1851 there were also sailmakers, although they were fewer with three to four at Newlyn and two at Mousehole. In 1896 Mousehole had a sailmaker's loft with two men working in it, while Newlyn had three lofts, employing six men each (40 feet by 20 feet was the minimum space needed to lay out a sail).[253]

Nets and sails were weather-proofed with cutch or tree bark, giving the sails their distinct red-brown colour. This work was carried out in barking houses, equipped with a furnace and chimney. In 1896 Newlyn had six or seven such establishments and Mousehole four; those at Mousehole were a little bigger than those at Newlyn, each employing two men rather than one. Greens at either end of Newlyn, meadows, and railings on the cliffs were used to dry the freshly barked sails and nets.[254]

Other Occupations

While the majority of those gainfully employed made their living from the sea, by no means everyone was linked to maritime occupations. In 1851, 17.5 per cent of the men in Paul parish farmed or gardened, and about five per cent were craftsmen and five per cent tradesmen. Only 1.5 per cent had professions or unearned incomes (annuities or land rents); and a mere one per cent were miners or quarrymen. Among women, 9.5 per cent were in domestic service, six per cent were in the craft sector, and three per cent each in trade and the professions.

In 1891 about ten per cent of men were engaged in farming and market gardening, a significant decline since 1851. Crafts were up to nine per cent with trades at five per cent and professionals and independent people now at three per cent, the same as miners and quarrymen. Female occupations were less commonly recorded than in the 1851 census, but seven per cent of women were in domestic service, six per cent were associated with crafts, and six per cent with trades. Mining or other maritime associations are represented by single examples, but almost 80 per cent of women were not credited with an occupation. This could reflect a social change noted elsewhere in Cornwall. After 1851 the role of women in the work place was questioned in reports and they were encouraged to become home makers instead.[255]

Crafts might include activity specifically generated by the fishing industry. In 1896, in addition to the many bootmakers at Newlyn, there was also one firm making seaboots at Mousehole. Basket-making was a speciality of Tolcarne in Newlyn, while oilskins were usually home-cured, though creosote was beginning to be used at Mousehole by the 1890s. Artists, the new elite, provided some additional employment for local people from the 1880s, as models or landladies (chapter 9).[256]

Penzance also drew on Newlyn and Mousehole for its work force with a few from Newlyn working at the Wherrytown serpentine works in 1861 to 1881 and 'nearly a score of Newlyn workfolk

Figure 77 'Memories' by Walter Langley evokes loss at sea. Dated 1885, it shows net mending being done indoors (the common practice). The net-maker gazes out to sea, while her daughter reads an illustrated magazine (the source of pictures for their cottage walls). Only the grandmother concentrates on the task in hand; loading netting needles with twine.

Figure 78 Market gardening at Newlyn as captured by Walter Langley in 'The Sunny South'. The gardener is William Curnow, an eminent botanist and member of the Penzance Natural History and Antiquarian Society.

and apprentices' worked for a Penzance outfitters in 1896. A trade directory of 1878 allows comparisons to be made between the Mount's Bay towns. There were then five shops each in Marazion and Mousehole, 16 in Newlyn and over 70 in Penzance, including 41 butcher's shops. W.H. Smith's later replaced Newlyn's second-hand bookshop. Newlyn also had a knitting factory employing at least four 'knitting machinists' in 1891.[257]

Mining and Quarrying Tin and copper mining were never very important here. Wheal Elizabeth (Betsy) on Chywoone Hill and Wheal Tolvadden at Gwavas were worked in 1851-2 and 1859-65, respectively. Trereife smelting works was at Stable Hobba in Paul parish, but better tin and copper lodes for mine 'adventurers' lay west and north of Paul parish.[258]

Quarrying became important at the end of the century. A demand for roadstone led to the opening of quarries at Penlee and elsewhere in Paul parish. The metarphosed slate (a hard dolerite with calcium intrusions) quarried on the coast is known locally as blue elvan. The original quarry in Great Cliff field at Penolva was leased to James Runnalls of Penzance. In December 1880 he agreed to pay a rent of £10 per year. Runnalls was 'to vigorously and effectually work' the quarry and the blue elvan stone was 'to be placed in proper heaps, properly measured and cubed'.[259]

When work began at Gwavas Quarry in 1890 the name Penlee Quarry was transferred to it. (As usual, Penzance Natural History and Antiquarian Society were interested in visiting this new enterprise as early as 1890-1.) Stone was taken by rail to the south pier ('stone pier') at Newlyn. Only four quarry workers are listed in the census of 1891 and all were Mousehole-born. By 1901, there were granite quarries at Sheffield in Paul parish and Lamorna, too. At least 80 quarry workers are listed in the census, with 16 being elvan workers, and 21 granite quarrymen. Of the 80 quarrymen and stonecutters, 31 came from other parishes and most were farm labourers' sons. A seaplane station was based on the beach below the quarry during the First World War, and thereafter some fishermen became quarrymen.[260]

Some men continued to work on the land. By the end of the century some of the crops produced by local farmers and market gardeners, such as early potatoes and broccoli (cauliflower) were grown for the London market and sent up by train. In 1914, besides 9,000 tons of fish, large quantities of broccoli, potatoes and flowers went to the capital from Penzance.

Chapter 8

Social Life in the 19th Century

How were Mousehole and Newlyn governed in 1800? As we saw in chapter 3 apart from parish registers, there are no parish records for Paul parish before 1834. The absence of churchwardens' accounts, vestry minutes, constables' or highway accounts, and Poor Law records contrasts with Penzance, Marazion and Madron (including the Tolcarne part of Newlyn) which are much better documented. Cornwall's early quarter session records – the county end of local government – are also missing.

What follows is an attempt to tease out the general strands relating to life in the 19th century. The underlying theme is the way in which Methodism became dominant in both Mousehole and Newlyn, and the impact that this had on the way of life in the two communities. The religious census of 1851 provides an indication of the success of Methodism and the context for an Anglican revival. Methodists rather than Anglicans took the lead in providing places of worship and schools in the two towns.

Figure 79 Newlyn from Tolcarne by John Blight, c.1860. Behind the *Tolcarne Inn* on the right is Trinity Wesleyan Chapel and the clock tower cupola belongs to the 1858 Wesleyan School at Fradgan. Beyond Newlyn Town is West Tolvaddon mine (now Penlee Quarry). A cartful of seaweed and a fishwife in traditional red jacket complete the picture.

GOVERNING MOUSEHOLE AND NEWLYN

It is not possible to say very much about the early 19th-century local government or the impact of Methodism in Mousehole and Newlyn. Paupers seeking settlement were questioned on work

Figure 80 The
administrative boundaries
of west Cornwall.
Newlyn and Mousehole
were governed by Paul
Urban District Council
between 1894 and 1934
when they became part
of the enlarged Penzance
Borough.

and family matters and their answers recorded, but none has
been found for this period for a Paul parishioner. Poor children
were apprenticed to wealthier parishioners to save money. Ann
White went to work for William Pascoe at Tolcarne mills in 1818,
while Priscilla Murrish was apprenticed to W.O. Gurney and John
Downing at Tolcarne brewery in 1833.[261]

Some crime by the early 19th century was dealt with at Bodmin.
Between 1821 and 1848, 32 men and 14 women from Paul parish
were imprisoned in the Bodmin Bridewell for minor offences.
Behaviour was also regulated by the Archdeaconry court for
Cornwall, which had the power to excommunicate (keep people
from the Christian rites of marriage, burial etc). Paul cases cover
the usual range of adultery, bastardy, fornication, incest, libel, and
disputed wills. In an incest case of 1801, in which an uncle married
his pregnant niece, the man was pursued as far as St Austell by Paul
churchwardens.[262]

Parish, Poor Law and Paul Urban District Council

The New Poor Law Act was passed in 1834 as a cost-saving
measure. It lasted until 1930. From 1834 the able-bodied poor were
expected to go to workhouses if they needed relief, rather than to
receive weekly handouts, which had included clothes, shoes, and
furniture. Madron workhouse served the whole of west Penwith;
and Paul parish, like other Penwith parishes, elected one or more
Poor Law guardians. Settlement examinations for this period
include that for Rebecca Jewell of Paul parish of 1842, whose
husband, a miner, had gone to seek work in America. In practice,
outdoor relief continued in Paul, as elsewhere, although it was
queried by the London-based Poor Law commissioners in 1858.
Public health issues were dealt with separately by local boards,
which became sanitary authorities in 1872.[263]

The only surviving pre-1890s parish record from Paul, apart
from parish registers, is a vestry minute book which was begun in
1872. Most of the recorded business was concerned with church
restoration. The vestry had four members from Mousehole but
only three from Newlyn, probably because Paul church was
much nearer to Mousehole. All of these members, except for one
from Newlyn, were from key fishing families (chapter 3). The
rural members came from the farms of Gwavas, Kemyel (two
representatives), and Trungle.[264]

Major change came in the late 19th century. County Councils
were established in 1889 and Urban and Rural District Councils
replaced the local sanitary boards in 1894. Paul UDC took over
the sanitary board's Church Town office, minute book and
membership. The first UDC committee meeting was held on

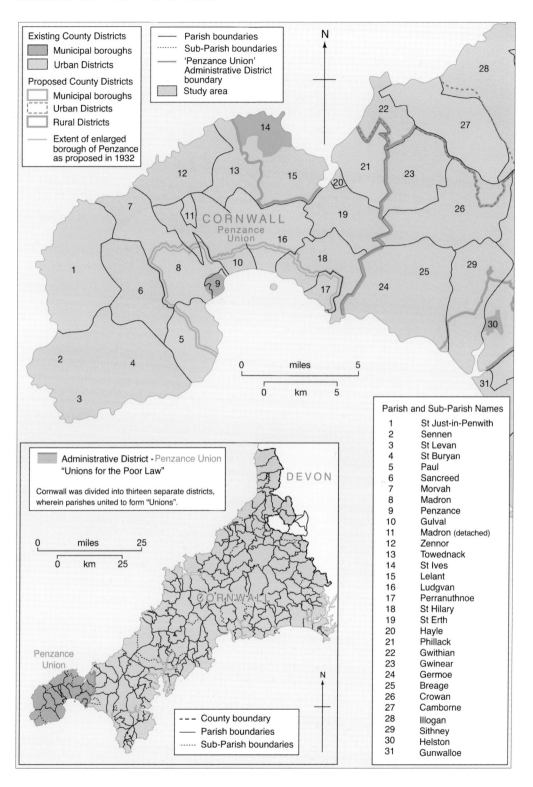

Existing County Districts
- Municipal boroughs
- Urban Districts

Proposed County Districts
- Municipal boroughs
- Urban Districts
- Rural Districts

Extent of enlarged borough of Penzance as proposed in 1932

— Parish boundaries
···· Sub-Parish boundaries
— 'Penzance Union' Administrative District boundary
Study area

N

CORNWALL
Penzance
Union

0 miles 5
0 km 5

Administrative District - Penzance Union
"Unions for the Poor Law"

Cornwall was divided into thirteen separate districts, wherein parishes united to form "Unions".

0 miles 25
0 km 25

DEVON

CORNWALL

Penzance
Union

N

- - - County boundary
— Parish boundaries
···· Sub-Parish boundaries

Parish and Sub-Parish Names

1	St Just-in-Penwith
2	Sennen
3	St Levan
4	St Buryan
5	Paul
6	Sancreed
7	Morvah
8	Madron
9	Penzance
10	Gulval
11	Madron (detached)
12	Zennor
13	Towednack
14	St Ives
15	Lelant
16	Ludgvan
17	Perranuthnoe
18	St Hilary
19	St Erth
20	Hayle
21	Phillack
22	Gwithian
23	Gwinear
24	Germoe
25	Breage
26	Crowan
27	Camborne
28	Illogan
29	Sithney
30	Helston
31	Gunwalloe

1 January 1895. Members included a cooper, an ice merchant and a boat owner from Newlyn. William Baily of Lynwood, who was also a county councillor, at least four farmers and the local vicar, were the other members. Parish officers were chosen by rotation from the middle ranks of the parish.[265]

METHODISTS AND ANGLICANS

The Arrival of Methodism

Between 1747 and 1786 John Wesley, the Anglican minister who founded the religious movement known as Methodism, preached in Newlyn 11 times. On the first occasion he was rescued by Philip Kelynack (nicknamed 'Old Bunger') from Penzance trouble-makers. Trouble persisted and it was only on Wesley's fourth visit to Newlyn, in 1751, that his audience 'stood quietly in the rain for the most part'. Wesley came again to preach in Newlyn in 1760 and, for a place that was neither a market town nor a mining centre, his visits recurred with unusual frequency thereafter.[266]

Mousehole on the other hand saw Wesley only three times between 1766 and 1785, but became more staunchly Methodist than Newlyn thereafter. Methodism had already recruited in Mousehole two years before Wesley's first visit in 1766. Early converts included Richard Trewavas the elder, who in 1770 gave up 'all sinful ways – smuggling in particular'. The town became 'one of the liveliest societies' and in 1784 had a preaching house with a Wesley 'preaching rock' nearby. In 1821 Mousehole chapel had 163 members, 13 more than Newlyn.[267]

Methodism's formal split with the Church of England after Wesley's death in 1791 saw an increase in the provision of places of worship. The period also saw divisions within Methodism and the foundation of less hierarchical groups such as the Primitive Methodists and Bible Christians. Not surprisingly most new chapels around the bay were Methodist. The earliest were Wesleyan with Anglican-style pews, but later other groups also gained new premises with more egalitarian seating arrangements. Mount's Bay towns generally had two different Methodist chapels each during the 19th century, while Penzance had three.

The older nonconformist churches, long separate from the Church of England – the Baptists, Quakers, and Congregationalists – were based primarily at Penzance, where there was also a Jewish synagogue. There was one Quaker in Paul parish in 1745 and the Congregationalists established a chapel at the Bowjey in the southern part of Newlyn Town in 1810. Built on the site of Thomas Tonkin's orchard, it was later known as Foxell's Chapel after its first minister. Paul had a Baptist Church in 1821.[268]

Newlyn Parish

The parish of Newlyn was created in February 1848, one of a number of new parishes created in Cornwall by Act of Parliament in response to population growth. Extending almost as far as Wherrytown in the north and Bowjey in the south, it had 3,200 souls at its foundation. This was rather greater than the population of Newlyn as the parish's 386 acres included part of Penzance (where three new parishes were created in the second half of the 19th century). The old ecclesiastical parishes like Paul and Madron became the new civil parishes, continuing as a result to exercise powers of local government. This was a well known pattern in 19th-century towns.[269]

The Picture in 1851

On Census Sunday, 30 March 1851, Anglicans in the Penzance registration district (the whole of west Penwith) accounted for only 27.7 per cent – just over a quarter of all those attending a place of worship and almost five per cent of the rest were old dissenters, and one per cent Roman Catholics. About two-thirds – 66.3 per cent – were Methodists. This pattern was typical of Cornwall as a whole, although in Camelford and industrial areas like St Austell and Redruth Methodists numbered more than 70 per cent. The Wesleyans claimed the most worshippers, as many as 60 per cent of worshippers in Mousehole (where an additional spur may have been the fact that the Anglican church was uphill from the village) and 40 per cent in Newlyn.[270]

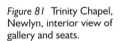

Figure 81 Trinity Chapel, Newlyn, interior view of gallery and seats.

Methodist dominance was in large part due to an active chapel-building programme in the first half of the 19th century. In Paul parish there were at least eight places of worship in 1851 but only two were Anglican – the parish church at Paul Churchtown (which had seating for less than a fifth of the population) and a temporary church in St Peter's Hill, Newlyn. Methodists, by contrast, could go to Wesleyan chapels in Mousehole, Newlyn or Kerris, a Bible Christian chapel at Mousehole, or a Primitive Methodist chapel at Newlyn. Their dominance, notable in both towns, was especially marked in Mousehole.

While no figures are available for the parish church, where the low numbers attending may have been due to the weather (the vicar inserted a clause to this effect in the religious census), at Newlyn's temporary church there were 110 morning attendees and 150 evening ones. By contrast, Wesleyan attendances totalled 230 in the morning and 540 in the evening at Mousehole, and 333 and 500 at Newlyn. A further 250-350 teetotal Wesleyans went to Mousehole's Mount Zion chapel in the morning and 300 in the evening, while Primitive Methodists at Newlyn numbered 360 in the afternoon and 350 in the evening. There was also an independent dissenting chapel (Foxell's) in Newlyn said to house 150 in the afternoon and 120 in the evening. These figures probably underestimate the extent of Methodist dominance in both towns, since 741 men and boys, including 100 Primitive Methodists from Newlyn, were at sea on Census Sunday.

Wesleyan Methodism and the Community

But enumerating the number of worshippers and chapels does not give a full picture of Methodism's impact upon the village communities. Noisy and exuberant Methodist revivals, at which penitents sobbed and sang and many were converted, formed a regular feature of religious life in south-west Cornwall. They began with the Great Revival of 1814 and recurred in Mousehole in 1818 and 1828, in Mousehole, Newlyn and Penzance in 1838-9, and at Mousehole and Newlyn in 1844, and at all three places again in 1849. They may have been encouraged at different times by fear of cholera, good or bad fish harvests, and bad weather leading to wrecks, but more probably they were the result of expectation among the community that these should be regular events with the aim of making converts; as many as one hundred people were converted at Newlyn on Easter Monday 1849.

The revivals in the tightly-knit, egalitarian communities of Mousehole and Newlyn seem to have begun among the people and involved all age groups, rather than being directed from above and aimed at the young as was the case at Penzance. Those

at Mousehole seem to have been relatively brief, curtailed by the
fishermen leaders being called away to sea, while Newlyn's more
varied industries supplied teachers who could sustain classes – an
important ingredient of revivals – over longer periods. There was
an enthusiasm for education among the Methodists in both places.
In Mousehole Wesleyans founded a day school in 1848, followed 11
years later by one in Newlyn. Mousehole patriarchs also ran a book
club and circulated volumes amongst its members. Despite this,
the Wesleyan hierarchy seemed to be remarkably tolerant of the
communities' traditional behaviour and superstitions, a tolerance
which may have encouraged more recruits.[271]

Church and Chapel in the Later 19th Century

In the second half of the 19th century Mousehole and Newlyn
both housed Salvation Army communities, who were encouraged
by General Booth's visit to Penzance in 1890. There were also
congregations of Plymouth Brethren. Temperance and teetotalism
were strong in both places: Band of Hope galas were held, and
a 'Religion and Temptation guarding you from Evil' banner
was displayed at the Primitive Methodist chapel at Newlyn. A
temperance exam was held at Newlyn Board School in April 1894.
Sabbath breaking (working on Sundays) was also frowned on by
these fishing communities and continued to be disapproved of well
into the 20th century.[272]

Churches and Chapels

Figure 82 Mount Zion
Chapel at Mousehole – a
simple, but architecturally
effective exterior of 1844
(and another view of
the plague stone). This
building was converted
to a house in the late
20th century.

Nonconformist Like the medieval chapels of St Edmund and
St Mary before them, Mousehole's Methodist chapels served
the two halves of the town. Chapel building began here in 1813
with the adaptation of an earlier Methodist preaching house.
The new chapel was called St Clement's Chapel after the former
medieval chapel on the island. St Clement's was rebuilt on a much
larger scale on this 'down-town' site in 1832-3 (pews of this date
survive) and enlarged again in 1905 with an organ and 21 stained
glass windows made in St Albans. The building is stuccoed and
dominates the harbour view.[273]

Mount Zion, Mousehole's second Methodist chapel, was built
'up town' in about 1844 in plainer style. It was probably built for
Wesleyan Teetotallers. In 1852 they joined the Wesleyan Methodist
Association which soon became the United Methodist Free
Churches. Sold at auction in 1860, and then bought back, the chapel
was still UMFC in 1908, but keeping going 'was a hard struggle'.[274]

At Newlyn a Wesleyan Methodist chapel is recorded by 1812,
replaced by Trinity Chapel on Chywoone Hill in 1832. Like Mount
Zion at Mousehole, this was built with a front of coursed killas

(locally quarried rough stone) and granite dressings; painted rubble forming the sides. The chapel had 310 seats including box pews and a gallery in 1851 and served the new middle classes in Street an Nowan. Chapel accounts begin in the 1860s and the gallery was improved and a new pulpit made in 1866, perhaps in response to the finishing of St Peter's Anglican church at Newlyn in this year. Similarly, in 1872, the 'beautification' of Trinity Chapel and re-gilding of its gallery coincided with the restoration of Paul church. A further chapel enlargement in 1893 included a rostrum to replace the pulpit. A Sunday School for 350 children was built next door and opened on 6 June 1913 with the ceremonial exchange of a silver key.[275]

The Ebenezer, or 'the fishermen's chapel' as it was usually called, Newlyn's other Methodist chapel, was built in 1834-5 on Boase Street, a central site in Newlyn Town previously occupied by a number of cottages. Now a house, it cost £900 and had seating for 400, soon increased to 600 as attendances rose to 500 on Sundays and 200 on weekdays. 'Dooring' the pews to prevent draughts took place in 1855 and west gallery minstrels were still playing there in 1856, by which time elsewhere harmoniums and organs had become the main musical instruments deployed to accompany singing. In 1908 fund-raising began for a larger chapel. Unlike Mousehole, Newlyn was at that time still well able to sustain two Methodist chapels.[276]

Anglican Church Paul church was topographically disadvantaged. 'Situated', according to its vicar in 1851, 'in a very exposed part of the parish on an eminence', it was 'a considerable distance from the two great masses of the population'. In many ways, its plain interior differed little from a Methodist chapel in the earlier 19th century: it had small-paned wooden windows, whitewashed walls, box pews and a gallery. The main differences were the wall monuments of wealthy parishioners which clustered towards the east end, and the bells used to summon worshippers, ring funeral knells and warn of foreign invasion (an episode in 1810 when the bells were rung without licence could relate to this last use).[277]

Plans to restore Paul parish church in 1872-3 had to be scaled down because of the difficulty of raising funds in a parish still dominated by Methodism. The subscription list noted that strangers gave more than Mousehole people. New pews got draught-proof doors, giving them an archaic feel, but the rest of John Dando Sedding's plans were rejected for being too expensive. Sedding (1838-91) was known for his rigorous restoration of Cornish churches, but because of this parsimony Paul church retains Georgian features such as its plaster ceilings.[278]

The temporary church of St Peter, a 'licensed room' on St
Peter's Hill, was in use from 1848, when the new parish of Newlyn
was created. Previously used by a 'congregation of Protestant
Dissenters', possibly Baptists, the room only had 150 seats, but
continued to serve as the Anglican church until 1865 because of a
lack of funds. By contrast, other newly created parishes at this time,
like Baldhu, built churches within a year or two of their creation,
while the Penzance parishes already had buildings when they
achieved parochial status.[279]

Finally, in 1864 a small plot at Tamlyn Row, near the top of
Chywoone Hill, was chosen as the site for the first permanent St
Peter's Church. From here the church would have dominated the
town, but the vicar of Paul objected that it would be too close to
his own church and so Brewery Meadow, an attractive site in the
Coombe beside the Newlyn river at Tolcarne, was used instead. John
Pope Vibert, the third vicar of Newlyn (1856-72), began the church
with James Perrow of Penzance, who had restored the neighbouring
church of Gulval, as architect. But Perrow died unexpectedly
and John Trounson, a Penzance architect, and Edmund Sedding
(1836-68), older brother of J.D. Sedding, took over.[280]

The new St Peter's, or 'the fishermen's church' as it was soon
known, opened on 20 February 1866. At this stage it consisted
of a nave, chancel and south aisle, seated 365 people, and had
cost some £1,600. There were teething troubles. The church
had a harmonium but there was no one to play it; one church

Figure 83 St Peter's
church Newlyn and
medieval bridge, *c.*1870s.

bell already had a cracked sound; and land in Tolcarne was 'so valuable for garden crops' that the vicar feared it would be impossible to build a vicarage there. Nevertheless, a vicarage, also designed by John Trounson was eventually built in 1875-6 for the Revd Wladislaw Lach-Szyrma, one of the most charismatic of Newlyn's vicars. Attracted to Newlyn because of his interest in the Cornish language, Lach-Szyrma chaired the new harbour committee, wrote science fiction and had 13 children. Planned to include six bedrooms, the vicarage was built of granite dressing stone brought from Sheffield Quarry in Paul parish and bricks from Bridgwater in Somerset.[281]

Early in 1886 St Peter's north aisle was added, housing the organ, and the Leah sisters of Cliff (Manor) House donated windows for the south transept, some with fishing themes, made by Fouracre of Plymouth. Reopened by the bishop of Truro at Whitsun 1886, the church by then had a strongly Anglo-Catholic tradition, reflected in features such as the reservation of the host (the bread consecrated at the communion service, known at St Peter's as mass). An oak screen was added in 1895 after Lach Szyrma's time with painted panels depicting the life of St Peter and a painting of the same date by London artist Gregory Jones hid damp spots on the east wall. Although a 70-foot spire had originally been planned, the church was eventually finished in 1906 with a modest bell-turret.[282]

Figure 84 Fishermen outside Fishermen's Rest at bottom of Church Street, Newlyn Town. As Anne Treneer noted: 'Newlyn fishermen, it is said, wear out their blue jerseys in front from leaning over the railings; and Mousehole men wear out their trousers at the back from leaning against the wall.'

St Andrew's Mission Church and the Fishermen's Rest

With the Anglican effort now focused at Tolcarne, missions were set up to cater for parishioners in Newlyn Town. The former Congregational church at the Bowjey was used at first, two services being held each Sunday. Paul Urban District Council passed plans for St Andrew's Mission Church on 1 December 1903 and it was built on the Green in 1904. The Fishermen's Rest at the bottom of Church Street was a more informal Anglican initiative which provided a reading room and meeting place for fishermen. Newlyn School artists including Frank Bramley (1857-1915) and John Mackenzie (1861-1918) assisted local clergy.[283]

SCHOOLING THE PEOPLE

Early Schools

Paul parish had well below average literacy levels in 1641 with only 18 per cent of men able to sign their names. Elsewhere in Mount's Bay literacy levels were usually rather higher: above a quarter at Madron and more than a third at Marazion and Penzance. Gradually, literacy improved, sometimes through private initiative; Lydia Tonkin of Newlyn, for example, was educated at home, at Kerris in Paul parish in the second half of the 17th century (Panel 4). By the mid-18th century 70 per cent of Paul fishermen could sign their names (only one per cent below the parish average). Private schools for the better off and charity and Sunday schools for the poor co-existed.[284]

The most important private school was run by Alexander Rowe (1727-1814) of Raginnis near Mousehole, 'one of the finest mathematical scholars in the West of England'. Some of his Mousehole pupils were later master mariners and Richard Pentreath a schoolmaster. When Rowe died in 1814 his goods included a deal bookcase and chest, several suits of clothes, 300 to 500 volumes of books, a telescope, two gold rings and £700 in cash. Another 18th-century schoolmaster is noted in the parish registers and there was an aged schoolmaster at Newlyn in 1829.[285]

Charity schools in Paul parish included a National school in 1824. Set up on the south side of the village green in Churchtown, it was painted by Elizabeth Forbes ('School's Out'). The bishop of Exeter gave schoolbooks, which were soon worn out, and scholars were expected to attend the parish church. It was replaced with a new school built in 1883 near Boslandew House and the new cemetery.[286]

Government grants were given from 1833 to the National Society (Anglicans) and British and Foreign Schools Society (non-Anglicans) to build more charity schools. At this date well

Figure 85 Fradgan School (today without cupola) and school house now replaced by Tolcarne School.

over 500 children were being educated in 11 schools, all but one private, in Paul parish. There were also well-established Methodist Sunday schools at Mousehole and Newlyn with more girls than boys as pupils. Built by Wesleyan Methodists, Mousehole School dates from the late 1840s and Fradgan school, Newlyn to 1858, the latter being the successor to the school-room loft noted in Nicholas Kelynack's will of 1854. Fradgan was built on Thomas Curnow's garden above the harbour slip, later named Champion's Slip after John Champion, headteacher.[287]

Adult Education

Adult education was also encouraged with a book club set up at Mousehole by local Methodists in 1818. Newlyn had a reading room in St Peter's Hill in the 1840s, which was refounded in 1865. At the latter date it had 100 members, and more than 460 books and newspapers to instruct 'the hardy sons of toil' at little cost. Navigation evening classes were held in most schools into the 20th century.[288]

Mass Education

The 1870 Education Act made schooling compulsory and led to the creation of new schools and enlargement of others. A report of 1869 noted that 'in Mousehole and Newlyn our Schools suffer thro' the lack of efficient teachers; the population consists principally of fishermen and their families – the men, old and young are much from home & cannot regularly aid in school work.' In this maritime environment, truants were described as a 'floating party who come and go as the fit takes them'.[289]

A National school was set up at Newlyn *c.*1870 and had close connections with St Peter's church from the start. In 1873 it had only 50 pupils, but in 1881 a second 'iron school' by the church was built for girls and infants. When Wladislaw Lach-Szyrma offered four treats a year instead of three (the common practice at other Newlyn schools) and lower fees, he was accused of poaching pupils from the new Board School.[290]

Newlyn Board School was yet another Methodist foundation. Built near the top of Chywoone Hill in 1879-80 with places for 385 children, it had a museum in the 1890s-1900s and was also known as Newlyn Hill School. The Board school succeeded at the expense of the Anglican National School, which had to close in 1881 despite its recent expansion. The old National school building then became the Newlyn Institute with a reading room, and later the Ship Institute was built on the site. The new school at Paul church town in 1883 was also a Board School.[291]

Infant schools were built in both towns in 1901-2 at Trewarveneth Street, Newlyn and opposite the old school at Mousehole. The latter had a large room and classroom with cloakroom and lavatories too high for the infants who could only reach them 'by kneeling on a form'. 'Two depressing seasons in fishing and farming' meant that the school was in debt when it opened. Despite this, Mousehole Junior School was built in 1911 behind the Infants School by the Redruth firm of Perkin and Caldwell. Most local schools came under council control in 1911-12 and this finally broke the Methodist monopoly of education here.[292]

Other Schools

Private schools, including dame schools, continued alongside the new institutions provided by the state. Dame schools were early primary schools, usually taught by women from their own homes; Newlyn's included Miss Allen's held in a thatched cottage at the lower end of Primrose Court in 1871-81, and another at Mrs Barrett's vegetable shop below Frank Bramley's studio in Trewarveneth Street. Needlework and art were also taught in Newlyn, at Mrs Rebecca Thomas's ladies' school in Antoine Terrace, for about 30 years in the late 19th century. A major development in 1899 was the opening of Newlyn Art School with studios in Bateman's Meadow off Trewarveneth Street (chapter 9).[293]

THE REVIVAL OF CORNISH

Fragments of Cornish survived into the 1930s at least in Paul parish, usually as old sayings, counting rhymes or weather signs. Families like the Kelynacks of Newlyn, or Pentreaths and Victors of Mousehole collected these oddments. The surviving fragments (some themselves survivals of the 17th century and later revivals) combined with a new interest in Dolly Pentreath. Prince Lucien Bonaparte, the nephew of Napoleon with an interest in Celtic languages, visited Paul in the late 1850s and paid for a monumental tombstone to her in 1860 with a Cornish inscription written by a Truronian. The centenary of Dolly's death was celebrated in 1877 and the stone was moved nearer to her grave. This produced a second revival of Cornish in and around Mousehole and Newlyn.[294]

Wladislaw Lach-Szyrma, who was also interested in the Cornish language, had taken the living at Newlyn in 1874. By 1875 he was introducing Henry Jenner, a 'figure-head for the emerging (Cornish revivalist) movement', to parishioners who knew the Cornish numbers and in 1876 both men met Lucien Bonaparte. Lach-Szyrma published *A Short History of Penzance* in 1878, which included a chapter on 'The Old Cornish language' and both he and Jenner compiled Cornish grammars. These activities clearly had an impact in the locality; when the *Cornishman* newspaper held a competition in 1879 for an essay on the Cornish language, the only entries came from Mousehole men, Bernard Victor and W.P. Pentreath. The tradition of interest in Cornish established at St Peter's appears to have continued, as a later curate, James Sims Carah, who left Newlyn in 1896 for Penponds near Camborne, was to become one of the first bards after the foundation of the Cornish Gorsedd.[295]

THE NEWLYN RIOTS OF 1896

By the end of the 19th century the range of local occupations and activities was increasingy, particularly with the opening up of quarrying, but the people of Newlyn and Mousehole still looked predominantly to the sea, either as fishermen themselves, or through work on land connected with the sea. In a scene reminiscent of the Boston tea party, Newlyn fishermen threw more than 100,000 mackerel into the sea from Lowestoft and Yarmouth boats on the morning of Monday, 18 May 1896. The official cause of the riots was the east coast practice of Sunday fishing contrary to local tradition. Although local Methodists strictly kept the Sabbath, it was the glutting of the markets on Mondays that local fishermen really objected to. Lowestoft drifters were bigger and capable of catching more fish because they set more net than local drifters,

Figure 86 Telegram sent by Hobson to the Home Secretary on the day after the Newlyn Riots began. There are no photographs of the riots because the fishermen confiscated all cameras.

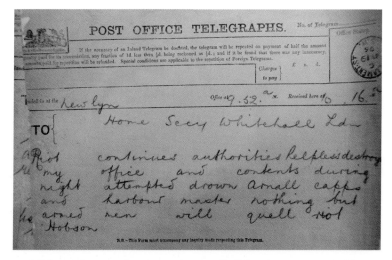

and fish stocks were low. As a Yarmouth fish salesman put it: 'the grievance is not the old one of Saturday and Sunday nights fishing, but it is the boats being here at all.'[296]

With the total breakdown of law and order that followed, Mr Hobson, an east coast fish dealer, sent an urgent telegram to the Home Secretary asking for a gunboat. The rioters retaliated that night by wheeling Hobson's new wooden office off the edge of the north quay into Newlyn harbour. While this was going on Paul band played and young men and old women danced.[297]

Next day, 19 May, a crowd of rioters on either side of the Larigan river – the Newlyn parish boundary – watched the arrival of 330 soldiers at Wherrytown as well as three gunboats. When the soldiers went into the old serpentine works for tea, the rioting began again – Newlyn, St Ives, Porthleven and Mousehole men against those of Lowestoft, Yarmouth and Penzance. A badly injured man was taken to Penzance infirmary, and martial law declared in Newlyn. The battalion of the Royal Berkshire Regiment 'resumed their interrupted meal' and stayed for a week. Schoolboys played truant, nine Newlyn fishermen were sent for trial and the six found guilty were bound over to keep the peace for a year.[298]

Somewhat surprisingly Newlyn fishermen received little support from their Methodist leaders. This was because leading Trinity Chapel Methodists – the Bazeleys and harbourmaster Strick – sided

Figure 87 Fish weathervane from the Lowestoft vessel General Gordon reputedly stolen by the rioters.

Figure 88 G.P. Bazeley of Trinity Methodist Chapel marches with the military at the time of the riots.

with the forces of law and order. By contrast, James Sims Carah, the Anglican curate at Newlyn, 'worked tirelessly behind the scenes' to get the fishermen released. At least two Anglican artists, Percy Craft (1852-1934) and John Mackenzie (1861-1918), supported the fishermen either with a 'stout cudgel' or letter of support to a local newspaper. Craft painted 'Tucking a School of Pilchards' in 1897 as a tribute to the rioters (chapter 9). The riots did not drive the east coast fishermen away and an uneasy period of co-existence and annual gunboat visits in fishing season continued into the 20th century, as we shall see in chapter 10.[299]

Chapter 9

Artists and Other Visitors

'The most painted spot in the British isles' is how one travel writer described Newlyn in 1911. By then its quaint corners could be seen on the walls of many art galleries in Britain and around the world and Newlyn had already played host to one of the liveliest British art colonies for nigh on 30 years. Newlyn was well known as a centre for naturalistic art, and shared characteristics with other art colonies set up in the late 1870s or early 1880s around the coast of Britain. Those colonies included Kircudbright and Cockburnspath in Scotland, Cullercoats in Northumberland, Staithes in Yorkshire, Walberswick in Suffolk, and (in the 1890s) St Ives and Lamorna in Cornwall.[300]

The new fashion for naturalistic painting executed from life, outdoors (*en plein air*), was made practical by the invention of tubes for oil paints in the earlier 19th century, and was promoted in the French and Belgian schools by Jules Bastien-Lepage (1848-84). It is worth noting that most of the leading painters of the school, for instance Stanhope Forbes, Frank Bramley, Thomas Gotch, and Norman Garstin, trained at Paris, Antwerp or both places. In an English context this was the time of the Pre-Raphaelites, of the Arts and Crafts movement, and the search for and idealisation of rural life. Not all of the artists who made their homes at Newlyn were painters; some were craftsmen in copper or enamel, most notably John Mackenzie and John Pearson, and at least one art student, Charles Lee, pursued a successful career as a writer.

Many of the painters of the Newlyn school were born in the midlands or the north of England. Very few were local. The only significant exceptions came from Penzance; Frank Bodilly (1860-1926), who was there at the start of the Newlyn art colony, but only stayed a couple of years, and Harold Harvey (1874-1941), who grew up in Penzance in the 1870s and '80s, just as the artistic colony was developing. But although mostly outsiders, in the 1880s many artists became (at least for a time) resident, establishing a different and greater interaction with the locality than earlier tourists or visitors.[301]

EARLY VISITORS TO MOUNT'S BAY

Mount's Bay attracted visitors from an early date. The earliest, like John Leland, were interested in piers, medieval chapels, and

the submerged forest. Later antiquarian visitors included William
Borlase, vicar of the nearby parish of Ludgvan in the 1750s, and
the brothers Daniel and Samuel Lysons in 1805 and later. These
early tourists also took an interest in new things like the 'ring
and thimble' stones (figure 4) and John Badcock's 1784 tomb in
Paul church. Badcock's eccentric cousin, John Price, who owned a
sugar-plantation and slaves in Jamaica had paid for all of these the
'thimble' being a sugar cone.[302]

With the temporary ending of continental travel during
the Napoleonic Wars, Mount's Bay became a favourite holiday
destination. The displaced 'Grand Tourists' called Penzance 'the
Montpelier of England'. By 1839 there were two museums in the
town and the promenade opened in 1844. Visitors to Mousehole
and Newlyn often stayed at Penzance, as no respectable lodging
houses then existed in the fishing towns.[303]

The Attractions of Mousehole

The word 'pretty' was first applied to Mousehole by Leland as early
as 1538. John Ayrton Paris, a physician, who published one of the
first guides to Mount's Bay in 1816, singled out the fishery here and
at Newlyn but also spoke of the Spanish Raid of 1595 and Dolly
Pentreath. Somewhat earlier, on 5 May 1803, the Plymley family

from Shropshire, who were staying in Penzance for some months, met the sexton who had dug Dolly Pentreath's grave and spoke with two other people who had known Dolly well. Artists were attracted by Mousehole's semi-circular harbour ringed with white-washed houses. In the early 19th century Mousehole's people were considered picturesque, too:

> both men and women exhibit the finest specimens of Cornish strength and beauty … The broad and muscular outline of the male, and the luxuriant contour of the female form, here evince that the climate, food, or employment of the people … are highly conducive to the maturation and perfection of the human figure.[304]

Amateur artists included Luttrell Wynne (1738-1814), later rector of St Erme, who sketched the northern half of Mousehole *c.*1777 as part of a coastal tour (Mousehole cave also features in this sketch book). Sketches of Mousehole from the Island and Mousehole harbour mouth by local artist Henry Pendarves Tremenheere (1774-1841) and visiting artist Thomas Allom (1804-72) were published in 1804 and 1830, respectively.[305]

Newlyn's More Dubious Charms

In 1803 Newlyn remained 'a very ugly small fishing town, close built and very populous', although it was then admitted that 'two or three houses at the farther end of the town are pleasant, built on a cliff and command a fine view of the bay'. Cliff Castle, Pembroke House, and probably Cliff Manor House, are likely to be the places

Figure 90 Newlyn Harbour at low tide, by E.W. Cooke, 1846, showing how 'Newlyn harbour dries out completely'.

meant. The 'pretty view' was also noted earlier in 1795. Newlyn, because of its more linear settlement pattern, was harder to capture in one picture than Mousehole. The most dramatic view (now obscured by trees) was from Tolcarne looking south across the harbour to Newlyn Town.[306]

The earliest artistic activity at Newlyn was local: H.P. Tremenheere produced a drawing of Jackford and Tolcarne, which was published as an engraving in 1804. He was the younger brother of Walter Tremenheere (1761-1855) of Penzance. Walter was also well known as an amateur artist and made several pen, ink and wash sketches of the Mount's Bay area at this time. Non-local artists who sketched at Newlyn rather later, from the 1820s to 1840s, included J.S. Prout (1805-76) and Royal Academician, E.W. Cooke (1811-80). Cooke's view of the old harbour at low tide was published as an engraving in 1849 (figure 90); in the foreground are fishwives with their characteristic cowels (fish carrying baskets), a popular subject with other artists like Mousehole-born Richard Pentreath (1806-69), for instance.[307]

The Impact of Railways

Railways made travel to Cornwall much easier, as elsewhere. Although the completion of the London to Penzance line in 1859 made Newlyn and Mousehole more accessible, not all visitors were impressed. In 1862, for example, Newlyn was characterised as being made up of 'grotesque homes huddled together, many of them at the edge of a narrow cliff', as having dangerous highways and bad drains, and as being inhabited by 'gaping and staring' natives of both sexes. Although Mousehole from a distance appeared 'a desirable little town for a summer residence', the same visitor found

Figure 91 Mousehole viewed from the south (Raginnis Hill), by George Wolfe, 1860. The medieval and early 19th century harbour lies in the centre and Gemick Street, with its living accommodation raised above fish cellars, runs south by the shore (bottom right). Paul church is wrongly placed too far down the hill.

'their streets and lanes were horrible'. Houses lacked proper fronts
and were not 'tastefully laid out'. Again there was much 'gaping and
staring' by the local inhabitants. The biggest disappointment was
that there was no guidebook or well-informed aged person to point
out places of historic interest.[308]

Guide books, notably that produced by John Murray as part
of a series for the pockets of the new railway travellers in 1859,
encouraged artists to go to Newlyn. According to Murray, it
was a 'colony of fishermen, with narrow paved lanes, glistening
with pilchard scales in the season – with external staircases and
picturesque interiors'. Even the 'mun' pits of decomposing fish,
destined for the fields, had a pretty edging of shells or pebbles.
Murray concluded that Newlyn 'will exceedingly delight artists who
entertain a proper sense of the value of dirt'.[309]

The artistic challenge was immediately taken up. Camberwell-
born Henry Martin arrived at Newlyn in 1860 and stayed for
more than 20 years. In the same year a Bristol-based painter,
George Wolfe (1834-90), painted Mousehole from Raginnis
Hill, its harbour full of fishing boats. Day-trippers came from
Penzance attracted by the beach auctions at Newlyn. As one such,
John Blight (1835-1911), noted in 1861: 'sketchers are often to be
seen transferring to their canvas portions of the busy scene …';
Blight also painted Keigwin House in Mousehole. Henry Pope
of Birmingham (1843-1908), Charles Napier Hemy of Falmouth
and Truro-born artists Richard Carter (1839-1911) and John
Uren (1845-1932) were among those who came to Newlyn in the
1860s-70s.[310]

THE EMERGENCE OF THE ARTIST COLONY

The overcrowding of continental art schools led to a search for
new locations closer to home. In the late 1870s and early 1880s
like-minded artists were setting up semi-permanent artistic
communities where they could learn from, and compete with, each
other. Fishing communities were especially attractive, as they were
well served by railway and transport links to London that gave
artists the opportunity to exhibit at the Royal Academy. Fisherfolk
also provided the essential local colour of 'peasants' at work.
Arguably Cullercoats in Northumberland was the first of these
British art colonies in the late 1870s, while Newlyn was ripe for
rediscovery. Still lacking up-to-date harbour facilities, Newlyn lay
only a mile from the south-western railway terminus. Walberswick
in Suffolk, Staithes in Yorkshire, Cockburnspath and Kirkcudbright
in Scotland were among these first British art colonies with
Lamorna and St Ives joining them in the 1890s.[311]

Figure 92 Newlyn
Harbour, by Caroline
Burland Yates (later
Gotch), 1879. One of
the first products of the
Newlyn Art Colony, but
predating its foundation
by some three or four
years. Nets are hung to
dry between the masts
of a fishing lugger and on
the rails.

The census of 1881 records only two resident artists at Newlyn:
Henry Martin, then aged 45, who was living at Cliff Castle, with
his Herefordshire-born wife Helen, and Charles Durdin, then 31,
who was living next door at Pembroke House with his widowed
Irish mother. Martin was in fact producing his best-known Newlyn
work, showing the old harbour and Newlyn Town, just before this
date, but neither he nor Durdin stayed on to be joined by the group
of artists who were just starting to arrive.

The marriage of artists Thomas Cooper Gotch (1854-1931)
and Caroline Yates (1854-1945) at St Peter's Newlyn in 1881,
with Francis Bodilly as a witness, may perhaps be regarded as an
important milestone in the setting up of the artistic community.
Gotch, the scion of a well-educated nonconformist family from the

Figure 93 A Fish Sale on
a Cornish Beach, 1885
by Stanhope A. Forbes
RA (1857-1947). The
painting (oil on canvas;
signed/dated 1885) shows
the primitive conditions
that attracted Forbes to
Newlyn. The painting is
a good example of the
square brush technique
and was well received
at the Royal Academy.
By the end of the year
the south pier had spoilt
this view. Collection:
Plymouth City Museum &
Art Gallery: photo©
©Bridgeman Art Library

midlands, had started training as an artist in Antwerp and Paris in the 1870s, and visited his future wife Caroline at Newlyn, where she was painting, in 1879. After his marriage, Gotch returned to Paris with his wife, but they continued to visit Newlyn and settled there in 1887. In the meantime, other artists were already resident, including Walter Langley (1852-1922) and Edward Harris (1855-1906), both from Birmingham, and Ralph Todd (1852-1932), a Londoner. Most crucially, in 1884 they were followed by Stanhope Forbes (1857-1947). Forbes, a Dubliner, who had trained in Paris, quickly became a leading figure in the emerging colony. The success of the paintings he exhibited at the Royal Academy at this time, in particular *A Fish Sale on a Cornish Beach*, did much to establish the reputation of the colony and to attract visitors, including the Canadian-born artist Elizabeth Armstrong (1859-1912), whom he married in Newlyn in 1889. Widely regarded as the leader of the colony, by this time Forbes had been joined by, among others, Gotch, Frank Bramley (1857-1915), and (briefly), Henry Scott Tuke (1859-1929).[312]

Figure 94 'Tucking a School of Pilchards', 1887, by Percy Robert Craft, shows fishermen as individuals (some were once named on the back). Tam o'shanters were brought back from Scotland and became the artists' favourite head gear.

In the 1880s, probably its best period, Newlyn became the liveliest of the new British artist colonies, its members regularly exhibiting at the Royal Academy. Young artists came by the train-load fresh from the ateliers of Antwerp, Paris and Brittany in the 1880s and 1890s. As well as colourful fish sales on the beach, artists were attracted by the mild climate, which encouraged painting out doors all year round. The incomers mainly comprised middle-class couples and bachelors; about a sixth were women. A generation younger than

Figure 95 Newlyn copper charger with fish designed by John Mackenzie and worked by Philip Hodder, 1899.

the French Impressionists, they were influenced by the new *plein-air* rustic realism promoted in Paris by Jules Bastien-Lepage (1848-84). Forbes' earlier works in particular owed much to Lepage and his circle. It was probably, however, from his former school-fellow at Dulwich College, Henry La Thangue (1858-1929), that he learned the square-brush technique, which was also employed by other continentally-trained Newlyn artists, such as Bramley, which often gave their paintings a somewhat unfinished look.[313]

While the leading incomers were thus painting in a rather advanced style, the people of Newlyn had very different tastes. They liked to paste up on their cottage walls 'coloured drawings from the illustrated papers … a classic head or frieze in chalk, a coloured sketch of fruit or flowers'. Unframed and with curling corners, they appear in several Newlyn School paintings (figure 77). More than anything else, they illustrate the gulf in artistic taste between the painters and painted.[314]

The Newlyn Industrial Class

The setting up of an industrial class on Arts and Crafts principles in 1890 was an attempt to put something back into Newlyn. John Mackenzie played a key role, together with other socially conscious artists like Thomas Gotch, Percy Craft, and Reginald Dick (1868-1941), and the project was supported by T.B. Bolitho, the local MP. Gotch had already helped to found the New English Art Club as an antidote to the stuffiness of the Royal Academy.[315]

The class was intended to provide a suitable occupation for fisher lads during periods of enforced idleness caused by bad weather or lack of fish. According to the artist Norman Garstin (1847-1926), writing in *The Studio* in 1896, initially the students worked in wood in a fish cellar in Newlyn, but then some artists became involved 'who seemed to feel the inadequacy of fretwork or woodcarving to keep Satan at bay, so copper and brass were introduced.' In 1892 John Pearson, who had earlier probably worked for William De Morgan in London, was bought in to teach the technique of repoussé (working the metal by hammering from the reverse side). Designs of galleons, fish, fruit, flowers and birds were produced at the Champion's slip premises in Street an Nowan. Plaques for the art gallery established at Newlyn in 1895 (figure 96) and the galleon weathercock for the Seamen's Mission of 1911 were designed and made here, as well as domestic products like candlesticks and pin trays. Copper stencils for marking barrels for the local fishery were also produced. The industrial class provided useful by-employment for a handful of fishermen. In 1913 it was renamed the Newlyn Copper Works and moved to New Road, Tolcarne.[316]

The Passmore Edwards Art Gallery

Forbes, Bramley, Langley and Gotch wished to build a permanent
art gallery at Newlyn, and to that end approached John Passmore
Edwards, a Cornish-born newspaper proprietor and patron of
the arts. The building commissioned by Passmore Edwards in
1895 was sited on the sea front at Tolcarne on land given by the
LeGrice family and was to display new work by Newlyn painters
before it was sent for exhibition in London. Initial plans to have a
reading room as well as a gallery were not realised, giving rise to
local suspicions that high-handed artists were more interested in
establishing a club for themselves than in providing for local needs.
The building, designed by James Hicks of Redruth (1846-96),
had an imposing gabled front of dressed granite laid in random
patterns with wooden bargeboards supported on granite corbels.
Hicks' original design had included a Grecian frieze, but this was
replaced by copper panels of the four elements, designed by John
Mackenzie and Thomas Gotch in an advanced art nouveau style
and made in Newlyn at the industrial school (figure 96).[317]

In 1895 the Newlyn Society of Artists was formed to promote
and manage the exhibitions with trustees responsible for the
building and maintenance. Forbes and Craft were prime movers
and put much effort into setting up the project. Henry Rheam
(1859-1920) and Reginald Dick served successively as the first
honorary secretaries of the executive committee, which drew its six
members from the trustees and Newlyn Society of Artists, while
Gotch and Langley were active members. The opening exhibition
included works by 47 artists of whom two-thirds were, or had

been, Newlyn-based. At least seven St Ives artists also exhibited, alongside Lord Leighton, the only English artist to be made a peer. A total of 51 exhibitions had been held by 1914, with those in 1899 being more cheerful in theme because 'the weird and sad' paintings were absent.[318]

The Newlyn School of Art

The founding of the Passmore Edwards Gallery inaugurated a change in the dynamics of the local artistic community. There was no longer a unity of vision, Gotch preferring Symbolism to Naturalism. Several of the founding generation moved away, including Bramley, who left for Grasmere in 1895, and Craft, who eventually moved to London. In 1899, in part to counter this exodus and attract younger artists to Newlyn, Stanhope Forbes, his wife Elizabeth, and George Sherwood Hunter set up the Newlyn School of Painting. At the same time they also encouraged the building of studios by making a roadway from Trewarveneth Street to a suitable site at Bateman's Meadow. The Meadow and Anchor Studios were built there. Further large studios were set up for pupils of the school at Belle Vue and Gwavas in the first decade of the 20th century.[319]

At its peak in 1904, the school may have had as many as 80 pupils of both sexes. Fees were three guineas a month or 22 guineas a year and nude models came from London. Some star pupils married each other and settled in Newlyn permanently, like the Forbes and Gotches in the first generation. Ernest Procter (1886-1935) came to study at the Forbes' school in 1907, where he met Dod Shaw (1892-1972), and after a spell in Paris they married in 1912, settling at North Corner in Newlyn Town. The etcher Geoffrey Garnier (1889-1971) came to the Forbes school in 1912 and in 1917 married his cousin and fellow pupil, Jill Blyth, who had come to Newlyn with her mother in 1913; afterwards the Garniers lived at Belle Vue. Children of first generation artists who studied at the school at this time included Arthur Todd (1891-1966), son of Ralph Todd, and Rosamund Fletcher, daughter of William Teulon Blandford Fletcher (1858-1936).[320]

Norman Garstin and Ernest Procter also ran an art school at Newlyn for a time and there were close links with the artists' colonies at St Ives and Lamorna. Harold and Laura Knight came briefly to Newlyn in 1907, before moving to Lamorna where they stayed until 1918, and Charles Simpson, who later ran the school of painting at St Ives, also stayed here, complaining about the bad state of roads in Paul parish in 1916.[321]

BECOMING NEWLYNERS

Figure 97 Jill Garnier (née Blyth), self portrait.

How far were Newlyn artists and craftsmen a part of Newlyn life? The question is a complex one because on the one hand Newlyn artists were well known for keeping themselves to themselves (home entertainments and cricket matches being key examples of this), while on the other they were quick to support local causes.

Newlyn artists used local models, rented houses or lodgings, and used local builders to build permanent homes there. Although initially wary of employing Newlyn servants, almost all did by 1901. Newlyn landladies were sometimes chaperones and a few became friends. For example, Caroline Yates (later Gotch) lodged with the Tonkins in Gwavas Terrace when she first came to Newlyn in 1879. Annie Tonkin was a witness at her wedding and looked after her when she was ill in 1883.[322]

Resident artists often appear in the records of the Paul Urban District Council. For example, in 1898 and 1904, Ralph Todd and then Reginald Dick were in trouble for not disposing of ash properly, the latter preferring to use a 'boy and a wheelbarrow' rather than the council sanitary cart. Walter Langley complained of refuse 'and other offensive matter thrown out on the beach near his studio wall' on 14 July 1899 and about poor drainage there in October 1907. George Sherwood Hunter was worried about drains and slop water overflowing into his Belle Vue garden and about sewage arrangements for the new Park an Sheeta estate. Drains in Shute Lane were of concern to Lionel Birch in 1908. Later artists applied for planning permission for new studios, extensions to houses, and garages.[323]

Marriage at Newlyn St Peter's, whether to a fellow artist or to a local inhabitant, could lead to settlement and participation. The former example set by the Gotches and the Forbes in the first generation was later followed by the Harveys, Proctors and Garniers. Marriage to a local inhabitant, though somewhat frowned on, was especially likely to lead to integration. Ralph Todd, who had moved to Newlyn, in 1883, married a local builder's daughter in 1888, probably at Penzance, after several failed courtships, while in 1898 Ernest Blackburne (1864-1947) married the vicar of Newlyn's daughter. On the whole, however, integration did not extend to sending children to local schools. A significant exception was Arthur Todd, only son of Ralph Todd and his Newlyn-born wife Vasilessa, who attended Tolcarne school and won several art prizes there in the early 1900s. He went on to study at the school of painting and became a professional artist.[324]

Edwardian Pageants and Folk Culture

Figure A: *1907 Pageant ship, Newlyn harbour.*

Edwardian pageants, also known as Parker's pageants (after their founder), began in Sherborne (Dorset) in 1905 and became very popular throughout the 20th century. Newlyn's pageant of 1907 copied Parker's original and was not only the first held in Cornwall, but one of the first to be put on anywhere. Pageants emphasised the past 'as community drama, arranged in short chronological episodes'. Newlyn's pageant was certainly copied at Lanner, a Cornish mining parish near Redruth; 'Perkin Warbeck' landing up there, too, in 1909.

By contrast many folk customs started as church festivities – saints' days and seasonal festivals being celebrated with processions and plays. The medieval church was at the centre of social life. When religious elements were forcibly removed at the Reformation, these customs lost their meaning. To antiquarians folk customs seemed pagan, prompting searches for prehistoric roots. Shaming rituals escaped from church control to become 'riding the stang' (an example is noted in 19th-century Newlyn) or Skimmington rides. Records of folk customs are usually found in antiquarian manuscripts and journals, personal memoirs, oral history recordings and newspapers. By the 19th century folk customs came under attack from the anti-drink lobby and had to adapt to survive.

Paul parish shared in West Penwith's rich folk culture, much of which was not unique to Cornwall and is now lost. Cornish elements here included plays (performed in a now lost plain an gwarry or playing place), hurling and wrestling. Carols are another Cornish tradition and new ones were being composed in the early 1800s. One carol composer, William Broad, a Penzance maltster and gentleman, retired to Newlyn and died there aged 81 in 1833. At least one of his compositions survives.

Of the seasonal festivals, May Day was particularly popular. Paul had a hobby horse in 1595, which the Spaniards found stored in Paul church (they treated it as a pagan idol and burnt it), and in the mid-17th century Newlyn Green still had its maypole and rousing chorus of 'Haile an Taw' (like Helston's 'Hal an Tow'). Well into the 20th century Paul parishioners were woken by blasts from tin May horns (or huers' trumpets), but children then danced round Paul's maypole. Midsummer is celebrated today by the Golowan festival at Penzance (formerly burning tar barrels were carried as still occurs at Ottery St Mary in Devon). Guise dancing followed Alantide (oversize apples being given out on 1 November) and women and girls dressed as men at Mousehole. At Newlyn in the mid-19th century there was a St George's mummers play and one about David and Goliath at Christmas.

Tom Bawcock's Eve (23 December), Mousehole's best known folk custom today, cannot certainly be traced back before 1927. It probably derives from fishermen's dinners, like that held at Madron in 1865.

Joanna Mattingly and Margaret Perry

Edwardian Pageants: P. Readman, 'The place of the past in English culture c.1890-1914', *Past & Present* (2005), 168-75, 185-7.

Responsible Artists

As we have seen, Newlyn artists were much involved in ensuring
the exhibition of their work locally, initially in the studios in
Bateman's meadow and then in the new gallery. Less willingly,
perhaps, they also held parish offices on occasion. Frank Bramley
and Reginald Dick, for instance, were overseers of the poor of Paul
parish in 1893-4 and 1915-16, respectively. Other Anglican artists
served the church; Lionel Birch being churchwarden of St Peter's
Newlyn and Frank Bourdillon and John Mackenzie assistants there.
Indeed, so close was the link between Newlyn's Anglican church
and the artists that St Peter's parish magazine had a regular section
entitled 'News from the Studios'.[325]

The prominent role of artists is also clear in the mid-1890s
when there were three disasters at Newlyn – a flood, fire and riot;
artists were involved with the first and last of these. In December
1894, Gotch headed the flood relief fund committee, while in 1896
John Mackenzie and Percy Craft helped local curate, James Carah,
during and after the Newlyn riots (chapter 8). When Carah left
to become vicar of Penponds near Camborne at the end of June,
grateful fishermen also presented Mackenzie and Craft with gifts
of a napkin ring each. Thomas Gotch was also involved with the
local Boy Scout movement, while the wife of Norman Garstin was
treasurer of the Newlyn nursing association.[326]

Providing Entertainment

Despite accusations of only entertaining themselves, Newlyn artists
also put on plays for the public and raised money for good causes.
Percy Craft, a trained actor, and Norman Garstin organised public
shows at St Peter's church hall in Newlyn and St John's at Penzance
in the 1880s-90s. Ernest Blackburne organised a 'nigger minstrel
show' in 1894 and Gotch gave talks on art to the Newlyn Nursing
Society.[327]

The Newlyn pageant, held on 9 August 1907, was 'the crowning
effort of the [Art] colony as a whole. The idea of John Stead Patrick
Fagan, the new vicar of St Peter's, it was in aid of the parish room
there. With a cast of a thousand and costumes and sets made
by Newlyn artists, it included ships, wagons, equestrians and
pedestrians, and the villagers felt in an indefinable way that the
artists "belonged"'(Panel 9). At Newlyn the main scene was the
Landing of Perkin Warbeck, a pretender to the throne during the
reign of Henry VII; this event at Whitsand Bay in Sennen led to a
Cornish rebellion in 1497. There were also scenes of Phoenicians
and Ancient Britons, King Arthur's knights, Don Diego de
Brochero and the Spaniards (the 1595 raid), and Fairfax and his

troopers (the Civil War). The fishing community contributed four marshals for the water and land processions and a giant Phoenician (William Stevenson), while most other named actors, including Gladys Hynes (1888-1958) who played Lady Katherine Gordon, were students at the Forbes art school. Forty-seven children from Newlyn Board School played truant in order to take part, while the artist Lionel Birch had the only speaking role. The event was not a financial success, raising only £42 for St Peter's church hall fund. Much later, at the time of the Newlyn Clearances, Phyllis Gotch nicely mixed fact and fantasy when she mentioned Perkin Warbeck once walking the streets of Newlyn.[328]

In July 1908 local Methodists responded to this Anglican event with 'Ye olde English Newlyn fayre'. Significantly, Newlyn artists were not involved apart from giving money. In aid of the new Primitive Methodist chapel, sets for this three-day indoor event were designed and made in Liverpool. The centre-piece was an Elizabethan street scene with stalls named 'Ye Signe of ye Diligent Housewife (Ladies)' or 'Ye Signe of ye Green Man (Gentlemen)'.

Figure 98 Martyrdom of St Morwena at St Hilary by Gladys Hynes.

Rain spoilt the second day and Newlyn's Primitive Methodists had to wait 20 years for 'the most important and moving (day) in their lives' – the opening of the new Centenary Chapel.[329]

Chapter 10

Newlyn and Mousehole since 1914

THE FIRST WORLD WAR

Shortly before midnight on 4 August 1914, Great Britain declared war on Germany. Apart from the low attendance at the Newlyn Carnival of that year prompted by concern over the unfolding international crisis, the response from Cornish coastal communities such as Newlyn and Mousehole to entering the war was one of uncharacteristic enthusiasm. The strong traditions of nonconformity and liberalism, often associated with pacifism, ensured that throughout Cornwall, the outbreak of war was met with muted indifference. The coastal communities were however different: many of the men of villages like Newlyn and Mousehole were Royal Navy and Royal Navy Volunteer reservists. Following the declaration of war thousands of seafarers across Cornwall were issued with their call up papers and told to report to the naval base at Devonport in Plymouth, departing from their local communities to much excitement and emotion. It has been suggested that as many as half of Great Britain's fishermen in 1914 were called up as reservists and the West Briton newspaper of 14 September 1914 reported that Cornwall's contribution to the Navy was, in proportion to its population exceeding that of any other county in the United Kingdom.[330]

The men of Cornwall were more reticent when it came to signing up for the army, although by the later years of the war, a number of Newlyn and Mousehole's inhabitants had joined the Duke of Cornwall's Light Infantry or the Devonshire Regiment and were fighting on the Western Front: men like Cecil Blewett of Mousehole and Nicholas Harvey of Newlyn died within a day of each other during the second battle of Albert, in late August 1918.[331]

Those who remained at home would have been forgiven for not noticing the change to wartime conditions. The threat of enemy bombs and attack from the sea caused alarm, but two flights of Short 184 sea planes (424 and 425 flights, later 235 squadron) operating from the Newlyn seaplane station and motor launches kept the harbours relatively safe from aerial attack and German submarines.[332]

The artist community of Penwith was divided between those who decided to fight, and those who were pacifists, but in the end the ethic of service to the community led most to join up alongside

Figure 99 The Newlyn War Memorial.

young fishermen and quarrymen. Those who fought included students from the art school, seven of whom are commemorated on the Newlyn war memorial. A few, including Norman Garstin, Harold Knight and Ernest Procter were pacifists, although Ernest, as a Quaker, served in the Friends' Ambulance Corps and became an official war artist in France in 1918-19.[333]

Some first generation artists were Volunteers (home guard) and helped in the defence of Newlyn quay, while Thomas Gotch, who had trained in Antwerp, was also treasurer of a committee to help Belgian refugee artists. In 1916 Mrs Blyth, soon to be the mother-in-law of Geoffrey Garnier, set up the Newlyn War Hospital Supply Depot, which specialised in iodine field dressings for the Belgian Army with instructions written in French. Her daughter Jill became registrar for the Women's Labour Bureau in Newlyn, despite the fact that local farmers mostly opposed the idea of women workers. As part of the war effort, in 1916 she was also a 'walking-talking doll' in her mother's fund-raising Waxworks show.[334]

Stanhope Forbes, whose only son was killed in the war, became artistically and emotionally involved in the Newlyn war memorial, placed in a prominent position overlooking the harbour. Designed by Edward Prioleau Warren (a friend of the artist Thomas Gotch's brother) who had already built the Ship Institute, the memorial had a carved granite cross by local sculptor Arnold Snell, and its bronze plaques were designed and made by London-based L. S. Merrifield. One of the names on the war memorial is that of Richard Quick, a 37-year-old fisherman from Mousehole who was stationed aboard HMS *Warrior*. *Warrior* joined the Grand Fleet in 1914 and was part of the 1st Cruiser Squadron at the Battle of Jutland, the greatest naval engagement of the war. On the first day of the battle, 31 May 1916, *Warrior* was badly damaged and Chief Stoker Quick was wounded. He was transferred back to Devonport before succumbing to his wounds. He died on 11 June 1916.[335]

LIFE IN INTER-WAR NEWLYN AND MOUSEHOLE

Following the First World War, life in Newlyn and Mousehole returned quickly to some sort of normality. The names of Penwith's lost sons were immortalised on the war memorial, unveiled on 23 July 1920 and the census of 1921 recorded the population of Paul Urban District, which included the village of Mousehole and the civil parish of Newlyn, as 5,398. Of that figure, 3,031 (a decline of 169 from 1848) lived in Newlyn and 1,398 lived in Mousehole with the remainder in the rural areas of the ancient parish of Paul.[336]

Fishing and Other Occupations

The social and economic life of Newlyn and Mousehole was
still dominated by the traditional fishing industry, which unlike
Cornwall's other major industries, china clay and tin mining, had
not seen major unemployment caused by the wartime closure of
major export markets. While pilchards and mackerel remained
plentiful off the Cornish coast, the fishing industry stuck to its
traditional methods. The growing demand for white fish, generated
by fish and chip shops established in both Newlyn and Mousehole
by 1926, was partly satisfied by Devonian trawlers from Brixham,
which had been using Newlyn as their 'western rendez-vous' from
1900, and continued to do so after the First World War. Trawling
involved a bag-shaped net being dragged along the sea-floor, a
well-established method of catching demersal (sea-bed) fish, the
kind sold in the new shops.[337]

In Newlyn, the pilchard and mackerel fisheries were still
important. Indeed, 1930 was a record year for pilchards, a catch
worth over £29,500 being landed and processed. At that time 17
pilchard exporters worked there, including the Italian firms of
Cippolina and Parodi, the Stevensons, and Bath and Hunkin, the
last pair having a fish store at the Gernick in Mousehole, too. As
earlier, the port towns of Genoa, Naples and Leghorn (Livorno) on
Italy's western coast were the main markets to which the fish were
sent. By 1939 only 32 boats fished for pilchards, but the Second
World War encouraged demand, since tinned fish could be used
as food for the troops. The production of tinned fish did not take
place in Newlyn and the only canning factory in Cornwall was at
Mevagissey.[338]

Some fishing families diversified. The Stevensons ran a bakery
in Trewarveneth Street, and in the Second World War a number of
local women made camouflage nets: 'They were awfully messy. You
were constantly brushing your kitchen and we did them [the nets]
in behind the door'. But 'for many youngsters who left school then
at 14, the choice of work lay between fishing and quarrying'.[339]

Penlee Quarry When production resumed after the First World
War, Penlee Quarry employed 200 men, and boats were loaded
with stone up to three times a day, depending on tides, by teams
of 20 men. The stone went to Germany, France and Belgium, and
to Cornwall County Council for roads or, in the form of concrete
blocks, for housing. A new tramline and bridge were put up in
1929 and there was an inclined conveyor which carried quarried
stone over the road from 1931 until the late 1980s.[340]

Figure 100 This Cryséde design (Trembath) celebrates the local violet industry.

Life in the quarry 'was a grim one, being very dusty', and only in 1956 was the quarry face 'benched' (cut in steps) to improve safety. Many quarry workers later developed emphysema and the dust also upset house-proud Newlyners, who had to clean their homes up to three times a day. Blasting caused damage to houses, too, though Newlyn people could set their watches by these 'quarry guns'. As a sort of compensation, Tolcarne school children had Penlee Quarry to thank for their annual Christmas tree.[341]

Crafts The Newlyn Copper Works struggled during the First World War, but from 1920 copper working was revived as a commercial business by Tom Batten and John Payne Cotton, two former members of the Newlyn industrial class. John Mackenzie who produced many designs for copper art-works, died in 1918, but by 1920 Obed Nicholls, a disabled protégé, worked from his home in Duke Street, Newlyn, while at Mousehole, Herbert Dyer, an engineer, also had a workshop in Curter Lane off Virgin Place. Batten's company, Newlyn Art Metal Industry, was still working in the 1930s but production ceased during the Second World War.[342]

Another commercial enterprise stimulated by the presence of the artistic community was the textile printing factory known as Cryséde, started in Newlyn by Alec and Kay Walker (the latter one of Forbes's art students) in 1919. The first factory was at Sambo's Row in St Peter's Hill and a shop then opened in New Road, Tolcarne, with 3,000 mail-order clients. A second dyeing factory was set up at Florence Terrace, Tolcarne, in November 1923. Although a drying room was added to the original factory in 1925, there was less than one 'sanitary convenience' for every 25 females working there on 3 May 1926. Cryséde relocated to St Ives, but kept its Newlyn premises until 1932.[343]

Market Gardening Market gardening was well set up in these coastal areas by the 20th century. From January to May 1933, 887 tons of 'mainland' flowers were sent to market by train from Penzance, two-thirds the amount supplied by the Scilly Isles. At Mousehole there were 'small steep meadows … for the cultivation of violets, daffodils and other winter and spring flowers'. Flower boxes came in flat pack form from Scandinavia, while the dealers were based in London, Birmingham and elsewhere. Early potatoes were also grown on the cliffs in tiny fields and in 1917 the urban district council considered employing German prisoners-of-war to help plant them. You can still see some of these fields on the cliffs between Mousehole and Lamorna. There was also a demand for allotments; in 1919 the pressure was such that John Francis, an ex-serviceman, used his war record to jump the queue.[344]

The Beginnings of Tourism

The opening of Brunel's Royal Albert Bridge across the Tamar River on 2 May 1868 and the leasing of the West Cornwall Railway by the Great Western Railway from 1866 meant that it was possible to travel directly to Penzance from London, making Mount's Bay a more attractive tourist destination. The development of southern Cornwall as a tourist destination during the late 19th century grew from a desire within the English middle-class for healthy holidays, away from large resorts and characterised by a certain landscape aesthetic. This elite tourism by the 20th century had spread to the masses (thanks in no small part to promotional tours by GWR Road Motors advertising destinations on their routes) who were drawn by the remoteness, solitude and mild climate offered by the coastal settlements of Mount's Bay.[345]

Despite the failure of a scheme to construct a light railway linking Newlyn and Penzance, a bus service was in operation between Penzance station and Newlyn from 1903 and by 1936 the Western National Service provided regular buses between Penzance and Newlyn and Mousehole increasing their viability as tourist destinations.[346]

Limited accommodation for tourists to stay overnight in Mousehole was available from the early 20th century. By 1914 Polmear House, at the top of the Parade, was offering visitors 'board residence, facing Mount's Bay, good fishing and bathing and motor accommodation'. Visitors complained about guides touting aggressively for business in 1921 and by the 1930s there were three tea rooms, three boarding houses and a cycle agent. Polmear was transformed into the *Old Coastguard Hotel* and soon afterwards

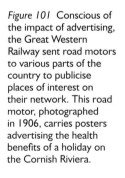

Figure 101 Conscious of the impact of advertising, the Great Western Railway sent road motors to various parts of the country to publicise places of interest on their network. This road motor, photographed in 1906, carries posters advertising the health benefits of a holiday on the Cornish Riviera.

Figure 102 In this Great
Western Railways
advertisement of 1925,
English holiday makers
are encouraged to 'See
your own country first',
with two women in
the national costumes
of Cornwall and Italy
depicted to draw
similarities between the
two destinations.

in 1937 the newly opened *Lobster Pot Hotel* played host to Dylan
Thomas and his fiancée Caitlin Macnamara. Despite its greater size
there was less provision for tourists in Newlyn than in Mousehole.
At the beginning of the 1930s Mrs Mabel Chirgwin was running
a boarding house in Newlyn West and Home-a-Long on Paul Hill
was being run as a boarding house by Mrs E. Curnow, while the
Dolphin was inter-war Newlyn's only hotel. [347]

The Artist Colony

Important artists continued to be based at Newlyn after the
First World War and into the 1930s, some, such as the Proctors
and the Garniers, trained at the Newlyn school. Others came on
a more temporary basis. Vorticists, like Cedric Morris and his
friend Arthur Lett Haines, members of the short-lived British art
movement which tried to capture movement in images, were there
in 1918-20. Mousehole had its artists, too. Phyllis (Pog) Yglesias
(1892–1978) settled there in 1923, while home-grown talent
included William George (1851-1945), a Mousehole fisherman
turned artist, his more famous grandson Jack Pender (1918-98),
and T.H. Victor (1894-1980). [348]

At St Peter's church, the vicar of Newlyn from 1936 to 1955 was
Allan Wyon (1882-1962), an 'eminent sculptor and engraver' who
exhibited at the Royal Academy and in Paris and designed postage
stamps. In the late 1930s he created the present church interior,
removing the screen and installing a west gallery. He also included
some of his own sculptures and an altarpiece and font cover by

Figure 103 Mousehole Harbour by William George, mid-20th-century.

Figure 104 St Peter's Newlyn, altarpiece by Martin Travers.

Martin Travers (1886-1948). Travers was not local but was one of the most distinguished church furnishers of his day.[349]

The art school closed in 1938, but resident artists continued to make their presence felt in the local community. In 1937 their favourite locations were threatened by a slum clearance scheme begun in 1935 by the Penzance Borough Council, and they took a leading role in opposing the changes. Of the original Newlyn artists at least three, Stanhope Forbes, Caroline Gotch and Harold Harvey, still lived in Newlyn. In addition, some pupils of the art school including the Garniers and Dod Proctor had also made their homes there. A 'Save Newlyn' campaign was mounted, with a committee set up and chaired by Geoffrey Garnier (figure 106), like his wife a pupil of Forbes. Forbes himself became the president, and Phyllis, Marquise de Verdières (figure 105), daughter of Thomas and Caroline Gotch, the secretary. She proved to be an enthusiastic and successful publicist, and when Garnier had the idea of sending a fishing boat, the *Rosebud*, to London to draw attention to the cause (see below), she made sure that at least 80 newspapers country-wide and in America carried the story. Newlyn was declared to be of national importance, and Belfast, Birmingham, Bournemouth, Gloucestershire, Kilmarnock, Lincoln, Liverpool, Manchester,

Figure 105 Phyllis, Marquise de Verdières at the time of the Newlyn Slum Clearances. Her title, acquired in a short-lived second marriage, proved useful in the campaign.

Swansea, and Sunderland were among the British places that took an interest in its fate. H.M. Bateman, a 'famous artist', who had spent the winter of 1936-7 in Newlyn, wrote an article defending the town, illustrating it with his own cartoons.[350]

The artists were joined in their protest by other local inhabitants and a committee was set up including a number of local fishermen and the artistic vicar of Newlyn, Allan Wyon. Here then, in a matter close to their hearts, the resident artists showed that, when they chose, they could become fully involved and even take a leading role in the affairs of their adopted community. This set them apart from other visitors and artists who merely passed through.

CHANGE IN NEWLYN

Paul Urban District Council had begun to tackle unsatisfactory slum housing at Newlyn during the First World War, participating in a movement for clearance which had started in the Victorian period with the Artisans' and Labourers' Dwellings and Improvement Acts passed in 1868 and 1875 and the Housing of the Workers Act passed in 1885. Houses with no back doors, deemed to be slums, were generally in badly planned areas of narrow streets and courts, and often had dwellings in their back-gardens or yards.

Although most of the 'slums' in Newlyn were clean and well looked after by the standards of the time they had no sanitary facilities or water supply. The worst were in the area of the Bowjey and Navy Inn Court. Other patches of poor housing were to be found elsewhere in Newlyn Town and in the Fradgan area of Street an Nowan. Mousehole had to some extent avoided the problem by major rebuilding in the Victorian period, but plenty of houses there, as at Newlyn, did not have a back door.

Properties condemned in March 1915 in Newlyn Town included 11 houses in Factory Row, which lay behind and to the west of Navy Inn Court and butted onto Bowjey meadow, and three in Fore Street near the Old Quay (probably including the Bosons old mansion). Two houses were also condemned at Farmer's Meadow and two more at Dolphin Court, off Jack Lane, in Street an Nowan. Slums were rare and not always a sign of destitution. When Martin Kemp, whose wife had earlier been committed to Bodmin asylum, was removed to Madron workhouse in 1916, his dirty house at Bowjey contained £997 10s. in cash and over £100 worth of jewellery.[351]

The review of the state of the housing stock continued after the First World War. In August 1920, a woman inspector found up to 30 'unfit houses' and 'two unhealthy areas' in Paul. Picturesque

Figure 106 Geoffrey Garnier, painted by his wife Jill.

Figure 107 Navy Inn, early 20th-century. The porch was supported by brick pillars dating to 1799 (with a passing resemblance to Keigwin).

thatched cottages at Church Lane, Newlyn Town, including the reputed birthplace of William Lovett, the Chartist, were demolished in November 1921. Newlyn Town surveyors in 1931-2 found a row of seven old houses at Bowjey Terrace with skirting boards eaten away by rats and no closets at all, and 'very old' houses at Navy Inn Court with stone ground floors and weather-boarded upper floors lacking light and air.[352]

New Buildings and Services

New houses and terraces were going up during and after the First World War, some developers taking advantage of housing subsidies. Cairn William Terrace, on the southern side of St Peter's Hill in Newlyn Town, was built in 1915, while in November 1920 sites for 32 houses were approved (16 at Newlyn and eight each for Mousehole and the rural district). With three bedrooms, a living room, parlour and 'other offices', these houses had twice as many rooms as most old cottages. Bungalows were built at Mousehole from 1921 (including one for the Yglesias family on Raginnis Hill) and others at Newlyn by 1925. In the early 1930s work was started on Kenstella Road, a private enterprise named after the children of the builder. The development was designed to close the hillside gap between Newlyn Town and Street an Nowan, but by the outbreak of war only the eastern side had been completed, with its uniform pairs of semi-detached houses. [353]

In this period Newlyn got its first cinema – the Gaiety in the Coombe at Tolcarne *c*.1920 – and in 1928 Centenary Chapel at the top of Newlyn Town was finished, a century after Primitive Methodism started. The chapel was on the site of the Church Lane cottages. Tolcarne School replaced Fradgan School in 1923, and had playing fields from the start. This was also a time when war memorials were put up, perhaps the oddest being the McGrigor lamp stand at the top of Newlyn Town slip. Made of granite and commemorating a First World War nurse who died of overwork, the lamp never functioned.[354]

Electricity reached Mousehole via Newlyn in 1929, but many properties were not connected to the mains supply until after the Second World War. A bigger issue, perhaps, was sanitation. Like many fishing communities, Newlyn and Mousehole were seen as unhealthy places by outsiders, although in fact sanitary conditions were no worse than in many other places. Chickens were kept in a Fradgan kitchen at Newlyn in 1916, while Mousehole had pigs and a farm at Pengarth on the Parade into the 1950s. In both Newlyn and Mousehole stables were mixed up with houses, and streams and gutters polluted with fish offal and raw sewage. Building rubble, near Keigwin in Mousehole, harboured a rat colony in 1915-16.

Figure 108 Cairn William Terrace, Newlyn was included in a slum clearance scheme in 1936.

Figure 109 Centenary Chapel, Newlyn. Built after 20 years of fund-raising, the original plan was for a building twice this size. Its opening day was for many Newlyn people 'the most important and moving in their lives'.

Figure 110 House of late 17th-century date with sideways-sliding sashes on the corner of High Mountains and Boase Street. The blue enamel street sign dates from 1932 and is one of 67 ordered then as one of the last acts of the Paul Urban District Council.

Diphtheria, typhoid and other infectious diseases remained a problem and a diphtheria epidemic was recorded at Newlyn as late as 1941. The nearest isolation hospital was at Penzance.[355]

The First World War was blamed for holding up water and sewerage schemes, including a new sewer planned for Tolcarne. The ore mined from the Wheal Betsy adit at Newlyn was found to be impure and Belle Vue reservoir insufficient. New reservoirs were made at Trewarveneth by March 1920 and the Coombe (a Madron-Paul initiative) in 1932. At Mousehole the hilly landscape made it difficult for one water source to supply the whole town. A source at Penolva was abandoned by 1920 and Foxes Lane and Trevithal were investigated instead. Public latrines were needed in 1925 for summer visitors and standpipes came to Mousehole in 1929. Trevithal reservoir dates from 1932, but even then water rationing was necessary in summer.[356]

Newlyn's poor water supply was a major problem for artists, and Harold Harvey of Maen Cottage, Elm Terrace, was the most frequent complainer. Another artist, Henry Rheam of Belle Vue House (later Orchard Cottage), refused to pay water rates in 1915 because supplies were restricted to two hours a day. Artists, however, may have made the situation worse. The Cryséde factory at Tolcarne used a large amount of water in 1923, while in July 1929 Geoffrey Garnier needed 10 gallons a week 'to wash the acid used [for his aquatint engravings] from the plates'.[357]

Figure 111 Map
showing the redrawn
administrative boundaries
following the enlargement
of Penzance Borough in
1934.

Naming Newlyn's Streets One of the last acts of the Paul Urban
District Council (UDC) was to put up street nameplates in Newlyn
(though not in Mousehole) as a belated response to regular Post
Office appeals. On 5 September 1932 the council ordered 67 blue
enamel nameplates from Wildman and Maguyer Ltd. with brass
screws at a cost of £8 10s. Some still survive in the Fradgan, Belle
Vue and Newlyn Town.[358]

Penzance Municipal Borough and the Inter-war Clearances

In spring 1934 the borough of Penzance was enlarged to include
part of the parish of Gulval, Heamoor in Madron, the parish of
Newlyn and most of the parish of Paul including Mousehole.
Madron and Paul urban district councils were abolished, the last
meeting of the latter being held on 26 March 1934. The population
of the enlarged Penzance Borough was nearly 20,000 people in 1939.
The councillors of the new authority were imbued with a vision of a
modern future, in a style inspired by Vienna and Paris. An Art Deco
lido was built between Newlyn and Penzance on an acre of land at
Battery Rocks in 1935. Emptied and refilled with the tide, Jubilee
Pool lies opposite the similarly Art Deco, 'liner' style, *Yacht Inn*.[359]

Slums were defined in a 1932 report as the 'specific creatures of
19th century industrialism', representing a 'primitive tendency to
herd together as closely as possible'. Penzance's clearance project
at Newlyn, expedited by the 1930 and 1933 Housing Acts which
reclassified 'Unfit' to cover bad housing, began with a compulsory
purchase order for Navy Inn Court at Newlyn Town in January
1935, at a time when many other towns and cities across the
country were taking similar action. Before this, a new estate of 242
houses had already been planned for the hillside fields above and
to the south of Newlyn Town. The land between Trewarveneth and
Gwavas Lane was compulsorily purchased from the LeGrice family
of Trereife on 31 October 1935, and then augmented by an extra
field (Love's Land) to the south-west (on which Treveneth Crescent
was to be built). Plans for the Gwavas estate, as the new area was to
be known, were drawn up in 1936 and in 1937 the first inhabitants,
mostly from Navy Inn Court and Factory Row, moved in. The
housing was arranged around a curving central spine, Chywoone
Avenue, from which Chywoone Crescent led off to the north and
Trewarneth Crescent to the south. Houses were mainly semi-
detached or foursomes, with three to four bedrooms, bathrooms,
hot and cold water and gardens.[360]

Seven or eight compulsory purchase orders followed in 1936
for Lower Green Street, Fore Street, St Peter's Hill, and Vaccination
(now Dolphin) Court, again all in Newlyn Town. An area of at

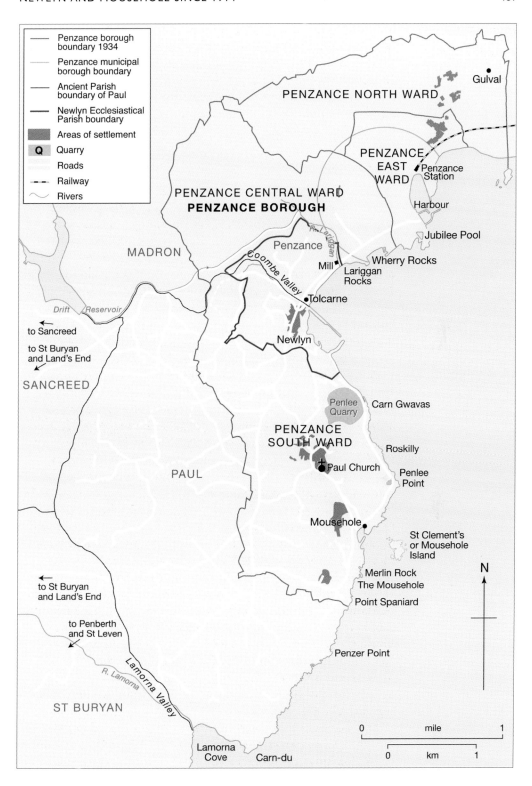

Penzance borough boundary 1934
Penzance municipal borough boundary
Ancient Parish boundary of Paul
Newlyn Ecclesiastical Parish boundary
Areas of settlement
Q Quarry
Roads
Railway
Rivers

PENZANCE NORTH WARD
Gulval

PENZANCE EAST WARD
Penzance Station

MADRON

PENZANCE CENTRAL WARD
PENZANCE BOROUGH

Harbour
Jubilee Pool

Penzance
R. Lariggan
Coombe Valley
Mill
Wherry Rocks
Lariggan Rocks
Tolcarne

Drift Reservoir

to Sancreed

to St Buryan and Land's End

SANCREED

Newlyn

Penlee Quarry
Carn Gwavas

PENZANCE SOUTH WARD

Roskilly

PAUL

Paul Church
Penlee Point

Mousehole

St Clement's or Mousehole Island

to St Buryan and Land's End

Merlin Rock
The Mousehole

N

to Penberth and St Leven

Point Spaniard

Penzer Point

R. Lamorna
Lamorna Valley

ST BURYAN

0   mile   1

0   km   1

Lamorna Cove   Carn-du

Figure 112 The Gwavas Estate. A well-planned modern estate of the 1930s with a strong sense of community today.

least 6¾ acres, including several houses, was thus acquired for redevelopment.[361]

The Newlyn scheme was notable for a lack of consultation, in strong contrast to that at St Ives. In 1935 the Society for the Protection of Ancient Buildings published a report on the use of Old Cottages at St Ives, on the need to do rehousing work there. This was drawn up with the consent of St Ives Borough and local artists desirous to see 'a better England built from the past'. At Newlyn, worried locals were uncertain about the purpose of the compulsory purchase orders – whether they related to slum clearance, road widening, or to new town planning. Protesters commissioned their own report from Stanley Adshead, a retired professor of town planning, only for it to be ignored by Penzance Council. The Council for the Preservation of Rural England was not consulted, although in the end it approved Penzance's plans for reconstructing Newlyn.

Opposition and the Voyage of the *Rosebud*

Despite the lack of consultation and higher rents, many of Newlyn's inhabitants were keen to move to the new Gwavas Estate. While there was general agreement to the removal of the worst slums, like Navy Inn Court, many clearly felt that the council's scheme went too far. After a five-day public enquiry, the protest committee met the Newlyn and Mousehole representatives of Penzance Council on 23 August 1937. Nearly 1,100 people, including owner-occupiers, fishermen and artists, signed a petition against the clearances which was to be sent to the Houses of Parliament at London by

Figure 113 The *Rosebud* at Westminster 1937. An early colour photograph taken by Charles Hoyland.

fishing boat. Some younger people were, however, persuaded that the protest committee was acting against their best interests, and 400 of them signed a counter-petition.[362]

The council seems to have adopted a divide-and-rule strategy, seeking to press ahead with the clearances in Newlyn while promising Mousehole that there would be no changes there. The secretary of the protest committee, Geoffrey Garnier, who like most second-generation Newlyn artists lived in an old house, was well aware of this. He warned members of his committee from Mousehole that, although they would be told that they faced no 'alterations', the truth was that 'to save Newlyn is to save Mousehole'.[363]

Despite divided local opinion, the protest committee nevertheless pressed ahead with the scheme to send a fishing boat to London. The voyage of the *Rosebud* fishing boat took four days, beginning on Monday 19 October 1937 at Newlyn's south pier. When she came up the Thames her captain Cyril Richards noted: 'sirens were blown on big and little ships, and everybody was waving to us'. Billy Roberts, the oldest of the Newlyn crew, left no one in any doubt as to why they were there: 'The Cornish boys are here to fight for their homes – the homes that their fathers and mothers lived in.'[364]

The voyage was romantic, iconic and worthy of re-enactment 70 years on, but how effective was it in stopping the Newlyn clearances? In 1938 new compulsory purchase orders were ready and included the home of the *Rosebud* captain in Lower Green Street. Almost 350 houses were now condemned, mostly in Newlyn Town, although some were in Street an Nowan, too. Over a quarter of Newlyn's population (some 1,027 people) were evicted and many moved to the new Gwavas Estate as houses there became available. Although Navy Inn Court had been demolished by 1939, and plans for replacement blocks of flats, Bowjey Court and

Navy Inn Court, approved, many of the other properties that were purchased stood empty and derelict. By 1940, only 58 of the 350 condemned houses had been demolished but the Newlyn of 'little whitewashed houses, tar on the bottom, geraniums in the window', had largely vanished.[365]

THE SECOND WORLD WAR

Cornwall, like the rest of Britain in the Second World War, saw much of its population either conscripted into the army, called up to the Royal Navy or doing war work on the Home Front, all the time surviving on wartime rations. Men like Sidney Vivian Hitchens, a Newlyn blacksmith who, having served as a stoker during the First World War, re-enlisted in 1940 aged 47. The county also welcomed a good many evacuees: children, new mothers and expectant mothers, who were sent from the towns to areas where it was thought they would be safer. There were also naval bases in Cornwall and other troops were stationed there, too, including soldiers from the West Yorkshire regiment.[366]

Figure 114 The Jubilee Pool, Penzance, was constructed in 1935 in an extravagant Art Deco style and was designed to empty and refill with the tide. Built on the site of a former battery, it was again put to military use during the Second World War, serving as a defensive battery manned by the Home Guard.

In Newlyn itself there was gunfire overhead from enemy planes seeking strategic targets such as Falmouth and Plymouth, and some bombing; a particularly long campaign took place in June 1941 shortly before a lull prompted by Hitler's invasion of Russia. The Jubilee Pool at Penzance was fitted with two four inch Naval Guns and two .303 Bren machine guns to form 394 Coast Battery, predominantly manned from 1943 by the Home Guard, responsible for preventing the ingress of hostile shipping to within a radius of 5,000 yards. Newlyn harbour could also take bigger ships and

because of this minesweepers and torpedo boats worked out in the bay in addition to the Royal Air Force high speed launches which were responsible for rescuing downed RAF airmen.[367]

Belgian refugees – mainly fishing families – lived in some of the condemned houses at Newlyn during the Second World War, put there by Mr Austin, town clerk of Penzance (an instigator of the clearances). The 'better houses' in Farmer's Meadow at Street an Nowan 'were rapidly cleaned and aired' and neighbours lent mattresses, blankets, pillows, cushions and beds in May 1940. A further 24 Belgian fishing boats came to Newlyn in 1943 when Brixham in Devon was needed for D-Day preparations. Overall an estimated 500 to 700 Belgian refugees lived in Newlyn during the war together with a smaller number of evacuees from London and other urban centres.[368]

POST-WAR DEVELOPMENTS AND THE FINAL CLEARANCES

There was more new building after 1945. To the north-west of Newlyn Town, the eastern side of Kenstella Road was finished in the 1950s and the Alverton estate north of Tolcarne was built between 1949 and 1953. The completion of this estate merged the town as a whole with Penzance, a physical change already anticipated by the joining together of the two settlements' rugby clubs to become the 'Pirates' in September 1945. Plans for Navy Inn Court and Bowjey Court flats had been approved in 1939, encompassing one of the main clearance sites around and behind the old *Navy Inn*. Building work from 1949 was not completed until about 1953; workers from the Alverton estate being seconded to this project. Some attempt was made to integrate this early post-war public housing with the older housing stock, using distinctive local detail including granite and render frontages, slate hanging, and external steps providing access to levels higher up the hill. This was the only part of Penzance's grandiose scheme ever realised. On the whole, the authority was more effective at pulling things down than rebuilding; a local builder who worked on Navy Inn Court and Bowjey flats, and the Alverton estate, thought that Penzance 'pulled down the best part of Newlyn … when they came over slum clearing'.[369]

Although some threatened houses were reprieved during the Second World War, including that of the artist Dod Procter at North Corner, demolition continued to change the character of Newlyn Town. In 1943 Dolphin Court in Street an Nowan was demolished, followed by much of North Corner in 1945. By 1948 it was the turn of Farmers Meadow at the top of the Fradgan, where the Belgian refugees had been housed. Many long derelict properties in Newlyn Town, including St Peter's Place and Square,

Figure 115 Navy Inn Court, Newlyn – a bold new venture with architectural merit. This nods at the local vernacular tradition of slate hanging.

and the surrounding area, went in 1951. In the following year a visitor, although pleased to see that 'Newlyn still has many narrow alleys just behind its waterfront, where dark little cottages crowd together', also found that 'a group where I had sketched two years ago was now a car-park'. This may well be a reference to St Peter's Square, a focal point and still in fact a car-park. The final, large-scale clearance was a block of houses in the Fradgan in 1955.[370]

By 1968 there had been a change in government policy, marked by the publication of a White Paper 'Old Houses into New Homes', and in Newlyn the last clearance was at Lower Green Street in 1978 following the replacement of Penzance Borough by Penwith District in 1974. But by the 1980s a former artists' model could

Figure 116 The car park that has taken the place of the St Peter's Hill slum area.

Figure 117 Harbour Road of 1908, fish market and ice works at Fradgan.

describe the town as 'all torn to pieces … like a dress – all moth-eaten'. About 130 – or a third – of the houses originally condemned had survived at Newlyn. Mousehole had escaped altogether.[371]

POST-WAR FISHING

The fishing industry had been badly disrupted during the war with a ban on night fishing but the end of the war brought new opportunities for those prepared to grasp them. Between 1945 and 1954 nine short-lived pilchard canning factories were set up in Newlyn and later the Pilchard Works exported pressed salt-cured fish (with a taste like anchovy) to Italy, but closed in 2006 as eating habits changed and demand fell. The mackerel fishery almost ended with the Second World War but then boomed in the late 1970s and early 1980s. As in 1896, the bonanza period attracted unwelcome outside competition in the form of factory ships from Eastern Europe as well as east coast, Irish and Scottish boats.[372]

A variety of fishing methods were used to catch mackerel – line fishing, purse (Danish) seining and, eventually, trawling. The introduction of trawling at Newlyn after the Second World War represented an important change. Like Brixham in Devon, Newlyn had housed Belgian trawlermen during the war and local men learned from them. The Stevenson family built up a trawler fleet by buying up decommissioned Motor Fishing Vessels. These 75-foot vessels were built for 'the Admiralty during the war with a view to conversion and use in the fishing industry when hostilities ceased'. When William Stevenson died in 1974, he owned 17 boats, far outstripping his original ambition, which had been to 'own five boats, one landing on each weekday'. Trevelyan Richards, coxswain of the Penlee lifeboat in 1981, was skipper of the *Excellent*, a Stevenson trawler, and in 2001 the Stevensons had an ageing fleet of 36 vessels.[373]

Through the efforts of the Stevensons and others Newlyn had risen to become a 'second division port' by the 1970s. Thereafter, failures elsewhere in distant water trawling and the cod fisheries pushed Newlyn (and Brixham) into the first. This was no doubt a direct result of the Icelandic Cod Wars which severely hampered the efforts of the North Sea trawler fleet (at the time the largest in Europe), during a series of altercations between 1958 and 1976. In September 1945, President Harry S. Truman issued a proclamation concerning US offshore rights, asserting the right of any state to establish conservation zones off its shores to protect its fishery resources. This led to Iceland extending the limits of its fishery zone on 1 September 1958 from four nautical miles to 12 nautical miles and again to 50 nautical miles on 1 September 1972 and imposing an annual quota capping the amount of fish that the British fleet could remove within this area. Throughout the periods of conflict, Great Britain declared that her trawlers would continue to fish these waters as the British Government did not recognise the extended fishery zone and that trawlers would be protected by British warships. British trawlers were regularly fired upon and had their nets cut by the Icelandic Coast Guard. In 1975 Iceland extended its exclusion zone to 200 miles and after further hostilities in 1976 the British Government agreed to its fishermen staying outside Iceland's exclusion zone, ending the 'Cod Wars'. Iceland's successful enforcement of the quota had an extremely detrimental effect on the British North Sea trawler fleet, much to the benefit of Newlyn and Brixham, unaffected by these events.[374]

In 1980 Newlyn was the seventh wealthiest British port (outside Scotland) in terms of the values of fish catches. The Mary Williams Pier was built in 1980, deep-water berths were made and landing facilities improved; Penlee lifeboat moved to the inner harbour. In 1987 Newlyn reached second position and despite the stricter regulation of the total allowable catch by the European Union's Common Fisheries Policy, between 1997-2007 Newlyn was the top port (a position recently taken by Brixham in Devon), only Peterhead, Aberdeen and Fraserburgh in Scotland having more valuable catches. It owed this position to the fact that it specialised in shellfish and mackerel rather than white fish. In 2006, 80 per cent of Cornwall's 1,500 or so fisherman and 172 of Cornwall's 672 registered fishing vessels were located at Newlyn. Today more scallops are being landed than ever before and the value of mackerel is increasing with the discovery of the health benefits of omega three oils.[375]

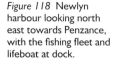

Figure 118 Newlyn harbour looking north east towards Penzance, with the fishing fleet and lifeboat at dock.

Mousehole, with its more constricted site and the off-shore island, could not compete with Newlyn in fishing. After 1945 its fishermen mostly worked out of Newlyn and in 1981, four of the Mousehole lifeboat crew at Penlee earned their livings at Newlyn.

The decline of fishing at Mousehole encouraged a diverse range of occupations. In 1949, of the 19 trustees of the settlement's Methodist church of St Clement, only three were, or had been, fishermen. An equal number were market gardeners, while others included builders, carpenters, motor drivers and schoolteachers, and a butcher, clerk, grocer, hairdresser, and lifeboat mechanic. One traditional local industry which closed down entirely was quarrying. Penlee ceased operation in the late 1980s because blue elvan was judged too slippery a surface for roads. On the other hand crafts developed in both settlements, especially Newlyn. In the 1960s and 1970s they provided the location for at least six studio potteries, including Leaper, Celtic and Troika.[376]

THE GROWTH OF TOURISM

Unlike Newlyn, Mousehole invested in tourism, which developed there rapidly after the Second World War taking the place of the fishing industry as Mousehole's principal economy. Visitors soon returned, including former evacuees. Pleasure boats had begun to frequent Mousehole by the 1950s, although the harbour was not deep enough for yachts. Visitors stayed in guesthouses or rooms over the pub. 'People in the village who had a spare room would often let it, the guests seeming to be quite content with outside lavatories and no baths'. A few couples, to make extra money, slept in the attic or net loft and let out their own bedrooms. There were as yet no houses to let, but tourist souvenirs were already available; serpentine (a marble-like red stone from the Lizard) souvenirs were sold from St Clement's chapel car park.[377]

The rise in the popularity and affordability of the motor car in the 1950s and '60s led to an increase in the numbers of seasonal visitors to Cornwall, making tourism the staple industry of the county's coastal communities during the second half of the 20th century. The same conditions which made Cornish harbours suitable for seine fishing, a sheltered bay without strong current or tides also made them suitable for bathing, and by the mid-20th century Mousehole had copied many other holiday resorts around the Cornish coast by importing sand to establish a beach. A bird hospital in Mousehole, founded by the Yglesias sisters in 1928, became an unexpected tourist attraction and earned national recognition when the oil tanker *Torrey Canyon* went aground and spilt its cargo in 1967. But by this date there were still only a few houses to let.[378]

A guide to Penzance and district published in 1976 illustrates the growth of tourism in Penwith. Newlyn is listed as having six hotels and Mousehole three, while the area around North Corner, formerly home to the Newlyn artists, had become a centre of self-

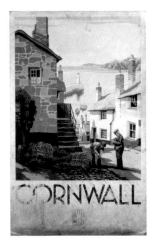

Figure 119 By the 1930s, Cornwall's fishing heritage had become a marketable element of its tourist appeal. This Great Western Railways poster by John Bee depicts two fishermen in front of a staircase, characteristic of houses with a pilchard cellar. The composition emphasises the steep topography leading from the harbour and is reminiscent of Newlyn and Mousehole.

Figure 120 The dramatic harbour light display and celebrations, held annually at Mousehole on 23 December are one of the major reasons for high visitor numbers during the Christmas season.

catering accommodation, with 35 North Corner, 'Studio Cottage' and 'In a Long' all advertised to let. The guide also highlights how Cornwall's old ports and fishing centres had developed into tourist attractions in their own right. Both Newlyn and Mousehole were described as, 'picturesque', and the guide placed special emphasis on the latter, 'with its stone cottages clustered around the harbour wall and scattered up the steep hillside'.[379]

The growth of tourism in Newlyn and Mousehole really took off during the 1980s with the development of the holiday letting business and second-home ownership. Today over 93 holiday cottages in Mousehole and 35 in Newlyn are advertised on the internet. Three quarters of the visitors are accommodated in Mousehole with the Christmas season especially popular, due to the harbour light display and the celebrations on Tom Bawcock's Eve (23 December), a midwinter festival commemorating the efforts of the probably mythical Tom Bawcock to lift famine from the village. The story cannot be traced earlier than the beginning of the 20th century, but is charmingly retold in *The Mousehole Cat*, in which Mowzer the cat, and Tom, the old fisherman, brave the Great Storm to try to save their village.

Second homes are even more numerous than holiday cottages: 166 in Mousehole and 99 in Newlyn. Self catering holiday units let for more than 20 weeks a year add a further 20 and nine, respectively. Of the total housing stock, 31 per cent at Mousehole and five per cent at Newlyn are second homes.[380]

Despite the changes and the rise of tourism, both Newlyn and Mousehole remain an important part of Cornwall's artistic heritage. Although few descendants of the original Newlyn artists still live in either town today, there is a vibrant artistic community and a strong sense of continuity. Pupils of the Forbes' School of Art, like Dod Procter (only the third woman to become a Royal Academician), continued to paint at Newlyn until the early 1970s. The sculptor Dennis Mitchell and painter John Wells both had studios in Trewarveneth Street in the 1980s and Jeremy Le Grice, who knew Dod Procter and other second generation artists, still paints in the Garniers' old studio at Belle Vue. More artists can be found here and at other historic studios in Newlyn. Newlyn and

Figure 121 Annie Metcalfe, one of the artists in residence in a Garnier studio.

Mousehole are still among the most painted and photographed places in the British Isles.

THE PERILS OF THE SEA

Figure 122 Memorial statue by Tom Leaper unveiled by HRH The Princess Royal in 2007.

The loss of the Penlee lifeboat, the *Solomon Browne*, on 19 December 1981 with its crew of eight brought Mousehole unwanted international fame. The *Solomon Browne* had gone to the aid of the *Union Star*, a container ship in hurricane conditions, and had rescued four people before both vessels were lost with all hands. Three of the lifeboat crew were cousins, another was the landlord of the *Ship Inn*, and all were at the centre of Mousehole life. Coxswain William Trevelyan Richards was posthumously awarded the Royal National Lifeboat Institute's gold medal and the rest of the crew bronze medals. The tragedy is still commemorated at Mousehole today by the annual dimming of the Christmas lights on 19 December at 9.22 pm (when radio contact was lost with the lifeboat).[381]

A major donation of £350,000 made possible the construction of a new lifeboat and the move to a new station in Newlyn harbour. The old station has been fully maintained as a memorial, surrounded by an attractive garden. A further memorial to the men who were lost has been placed in Paul church; a large granite block, surmounted by a glass octagon enclosing a glass chalice and patten, it evokes a lighthouse. In 2007 a complementary memorial to fishermen lost at sea was installed at Tolcarne next to the Passmore Edwards Art Gallery. Unveiled by HRH The Princess Royal, it takes the form of a fisherman gazing out to sea.

Into the 21st Century

Figure 123 Penlee
Quarry ceased operation
in the late 1980s. Will
its redevelopment as a
marina be beneficial for
the Mount's Bay villages?

In 2001 there were 25,062 people living within the six wards which make up Penzance. In turn they represented nearly 40 per cent of the 63, 058 people who live in the District of Penwith. Of particular interest are the figures for Penzance South which included Newlyn, Mousehole and Paul. Altogether, 4,919 people lived in the ward, 93 per cent of whom were born in England. Of the 1,920 actively employed people aged 16-74, 72 per cent worked less than six miles from their home, confirming a continuation of a tradition of local employment. The nature of their employment was also interesting: only 98 people, five per cent of the employed population, were working in the fishing industry, while 394 (20.5 per cent) were working in the hotel and catering, and real estate and renting sectors.[382]

These figures illustrate the shift from fishing to tourism as Mousehole's and to a lesser extent Newlyn's principal source of income. At Mousehole this shift, evident as early as 1945, has progressed so far that today there is no fishing or even pretence of fishing, the industry's long history being invoked only by the dominant harbour and the characteristic external staircases over the numerous pilchard pressing cellars. Newlyn, in contrast, remains very much an active fishing port, the largest in Cornwall, while its physical character, much altered by the 20th-century clearances and proximity to Penzance, ensures that the contrast with Mousehole is retained.

These differences however, are becoming blurred again in the 21st century. Although the rural area has a much reduced population (232 in 2001), it has become less rural, a place to retire to (some 20 per cent of the ward are retirees) or commute from. Second-home ownership and holiday lets have led to a fall in the population at Mousehole from 830 in 2001 to 759 today, with only a quarter of residents from old Mousehole families (in 1981 half the lifeboat crew were Mousehole-born). Newlyn's population has also declined from 4,165 people in 2001 to 3,687, but it might have been less had not the older cottages that survived the clearances come to be considered as highly desirable residences. The fishing industry, for so long at the heart of Newlyn life, is also under serious threat following an investigation by the Marine Fisheries Agency and DEFRA into an alleged quota fraud by a number of Newlyn fishermen in 2002.

Since Richard earl of Cornwall's dramatic landing in 1242, Mousehole, and later Newlyn, too, have been popular with visitors, whether foreign traders or tourists and, as the 21st century nears the end of its first decade, that shows no sign of changing. Cornwall, unlike many other parts of the UK, has not seen the dramatic decline in the popularity of the British seaside holiday caused by the growth of package holidays to Mediterranean destinations which guarantee good weather. The county's success is also perhaps due to its offering self-catering rather than serviced accommodation, which has become increasingly unpopular with British tourists since the 20th century. Newlyn is promoted today for its scenery and heritage and as a convenient base from which to explore major Cornish attractions such as the Eden Project, the Tate Gallery at St Ives, and the Scilly Isles. The improvements to the A30 south of Bodmin completed in July 2007 also ensure that the west of Cornwall remains a popular tourist destination.

Penwith is one of the 50 most deprived local authorities in the country, the west of Cornwall continues to defy the falling property values prevalent in the country at the time of writing. Penzance, with its direct rail link to London, continues to represent a safe investment, while the marina which has been proposed for the disused Penlee Quarry site, appropriately half way between Mousehole and Newlyn, should lead to significant investment in Newlyn. This poses an interesting question regarding Newlyn's future. Moushole, spared the worst of the 20th-century clearances, has been preserved and is physically the same village which existed at the beginning of the 20th century, although it is socially very different. Newlyn has seen a century of upheaval and change in its physical character, although its fishing industry has survived. With the redevelopment of the Penlee quarry site and the potential for additional investment from outside the region, there is some debate as to whether what remains of old Newlyn should, like Mousehole, be preserved in aspic. Ultimately, it will be market forces which decide the fate of this area beyond 2009.[383]

Endnotes

The following abbreviations are used throughout the endnotes.

Arch. Rep. A-B	Berry, E. and Cahill, N., A. 'Keigwins, Mousehole' and B. 'Mousehole – historic settlement survey (VCH EPE reports, 2007)
Assize I-II	C. Henderson transcripts of Assize Rolls
BL	British Library
Bodleian	Bodleian Library
CA	Cornish Archaeology
Cal. Chart.	*Calendar of Charter Rolls*
Cal. Close	*Calendar of Close Rolls*
Cal. Fine	*Calendar of Fine Rolls*
Cal. Inq. Misc.	*Calendar of Inquisitions Miscellaneous*
Cal. Inq. p.m.	*Calendar of Inquisitions post mortem*
Cal. Pat	*Calendar of Patent Rolls*
Cal. SP Dom.	*Calendar of State Papers Domestic*
Carew	Chynoweth, J. et al., *The Survey of Cornwall By Richard Carew* (*DCRS*, 2004).
Cat. Ancient Deeds	*Catalogue of Ancient Deeds*
CAU	Cornwall Archaeological Unit now part of the Historic Environment Service of Cornwall Council
CAVA	Cornwall Audio Visual Archive
CFHS	Cornwall Family History Society
Coll. Cornub.	Boase, G.C., Collectanea Cornubiensis (1890)
CP	*Cornish Post*
CS	Cornish Studies
CT	*Cornish Telegraph*
Cullum	Cullum, D., 'Society and Economy in West Cornwall *c.*1558-1750' (Exeter PhD, 1993)
CRHC	The Council for the Research on Housing Construction
CRO	Cornwall Record Office
CSL	Cornish Studies Library
CSMR	Cornwall Sites and Monuments Register
DCNQ	*Devon and Cornwall Notes and Queries*
DCRS	*Devon and Cornwall Records Society*
Dir.	Directory
Douch *Muster*	Douch, H.L., ed., *The Cornwall Muster Roll for 1569* (1984).
DRO	Devon Record Office
ESF	Starkey, D.J., et al. England's Sea Fishing
GP	General purposes committee of Paul UDC
Havener's a/cs	Kowaleski, M., *The Havener's Accounts of the Earldom and Duchy of Cornwall, 1287-1356* (DCRS, 2001)
Henderson Cal	C. Henderson transcripts of original documents 1910s-33
ICS	Institute of Cornish Studies, University of Exeter
JRIC	Journal of the Royal Institution of Cornwall
Ledbury MS.	Materials for a history of the Keigwin family compiled by F.J. Ledbury and now owned by E. James.

Leland Itin. I	Toulmin Smith, L. ed., The Itinerary of John Leland, I (1964).
L&P Hen. VIII	Letters and Papers of Henry VIII
Mag.	Magazine
Morrab	Morrab Library
Newlyn Life	Chesher, V. ed., *Newlyn Life 1870-1914 – The Village That Inspired The Artists* (2003)
Newlyn Report	Russell, S., Newlyn- Historic Characterisation report (2003).
ODNB	*Oxford Dictionary of National Biography*
OC	*Old Cornwall*
OS	Ordnance Survey
Padel *Bosons*	Padel, O.J., *The Cornish Writings of the Boson Family* (1975).
Padel *Place-names*	Padel, O.J., *A Popular Dictionary of Cornish Place-names* 1988)
Pat. R.	Calendar of Patent Rolls
PLHG	Penwith Local History Group or History Group
PNHAS	Penzance Natural History and Antiquarian Society
Pool *Penzance*	Pool, P.A.S., *The History of the Town and Borough of Penzance* (1974)
PRO	Public Record Office (see now The National Archives)
RCG	*Royal Cornwall Gazette*
RCPS	*Royal Cornwall Polytechnic Society journal*
Reg. Brantyngham	Hingeston-Randolph, Revd F.C., *The Register of Bishop Brantyngham 1370-94* (London & Exeter, 1901)
Reg. Grandisson	Hingeston-Randolph, Revd F.C., *The Register of Bishop Grandisson 1327-70*, I (London & Exeter, 1894)
Reg. Lacy	Dunstan, G.R., *The Register of Edmund Lacy, Bishop of Exeter 1420-55*, I-V (Exeter: DCRS, 1963-72)
Reg. Stafford	Hingeston-Randolph, Revd F.C., *The Register of Bishop Stafford 1395-1419* (London & Exeter, 1886)
Reg. Stapeldon	Hingeston-Randolph, Revd F.C., *The Register of Bishop Stapeldon 1308-26* (London & Exeter, 1892)
RIC	Royal Institution of Cornwall (The Courtney Library)
RS	Record Series
Spriggs *Cornish*	Spriggs, M., 'Where Cornish was Spoken and When: A Provisional Synthesis', *CS*, 11 (2003), 228-269
Stoate *Hearth Tax*	Stoate, T.L. ed., *Cornwall Hearth and Poll Taxes 1660*-1664 (1981)
Stoate *Protestation*	Stoate, T.L., Glencross, R.M. and Douch, H.L., ed., *The Cornwall Protestation Returns 1641* (1974).
Stoate *Subsidies*	Stoate, T.L. ed., *Cornwall Subsidies in the Reign of Henry VIII 1524 and 1543 and the Benevolence of 1545* (1985).
Stoate *Survey*	Stoate, T.L. ed., *The Cornwall Military Survey 1522 with the Loan Books and a Tinners Muster Roll c.1535* (1987).
T/A	Tithe Apportionment (in CRO).
Tax. Eccl.	*Taxatio Ecclesiastica ... circa AD 1291* (Record Commisssioners)
TNA	The National Archives
UDC	Urban District Council
Univ.	University
Val. Eccl.	*Valor Ecclesiasticus*
VCH	Victoria County History
VCH *Cornwall*	Victoria County History of Cornwall volume 1
VCH Penwith	Victoria County History of the Hundred of Penwith
WB	*West Briton*
WMN	*Western Morning News*

INTRODUCTION, pp. 1-4

1 James J. Keigwin, the last of the Keigwins actually died in 1883 but for three generations the family had not resided in Mousehole. See *JRIC*, viii (1883), 106.
2 Newlyn report, 3ff.

CHAPTER 1 Origins and Early Settlements, pp. 5-24

3 ***Pertusum muris:*** Luard, H.R. (ed.), *Annales Monastici* (RS, 1864-9), I, 128.
4 **Richard earl of Cornwall:** *ODNB*; **St Edmund:** M. Powicke, *The Thirteenth Century 1216-1307* (1962), 56-7.
5 C. Bristow, *Cornwall's Geology and Scenery* (1996), 65-6, 130-1.
6 **Submerged forest and coastline:** *Leland Itin.* I, 189; N. Johnson and P. Rose, *Cornwall Archaeological Heritage* (1990), 1.
7 **Pounder:** CSMR, Raginnis, artefact scatter, 163744 [OS: SW 467256]; **axe:** Penolva, findspot, 169321 [OS: SW 467269]; **urns:** Tresvennack, Findspot, 28707.1 [OS: SW 441278]; Trevelloe, findspot, 28781.1 [OS: SW 447261]; **lunula:** A.M. Jones, J. Marley and J. Mattingly, 'Five Gold Rings? –Early Bronze Age gold lunulae from Cornwall', *JRIC* (2009), forthcoming; **'imitation' Greek coins:** D.F. Allen, 'The Paul (Penzance) Hoard of Imitation Massilia Drachms', *Numismatic Chronicle*, 7th ser., no. 1 (1961), 91-106.
8 **Hill fort and rounds:** V. Russell, 'Parish of Paul', *CA* 2 (1963), 65; **courtyard house:** CSMR, Castallack, hut circle, 28917.1 [OS: SW 448254].
9 **Bracelet:** CSMR, Corn929E07, Portable Antiquities [OS: SW438256]; **coin hoards:** Kerris, Findspot, 28841.2 [OS: SW 440260], Tredavoe, Coin Hoard, 18783 [OS: SW 450280]; **Trevelloe pottery etc:** Trevelloe, Findspot, 28704 [OS: SW 446254].
10 N. Orme, *The Saints of Cornwall* (2000), 211-13; G.H. Doble, *Saint Paul of Leon* (1941).
11 CSMR, Kerris, Inscribed Stone, 60504 [OS: SW 443271].
12 **Devon:** H. Fox, *The Evolution of the Fishing Village* (2001), chapters 5-6.
13 C. Henderson, 'Topography of the Parish of Paul', *RCPS* n.s. 9 (1941), 58, 62, 65.
14 **Domesday:** C. and F. Thorn (ed.), *Domesday Book: Cornwall* (1979), 5,1,11; P.A.S. Pool, 'The Penheleg Manuscript', *JRIC* n.s. 3 (1959), 218.
15 VCH Penwith, 49.
16 **Alverton:** VCH Penwith, 49; *Book of Fees*, I, 394; **Kemyel:** Henderson, 'Topography of the Parish of Paul', 59;**Fee Marshall:** *Pat R*, n.s. 15, 169 (Padel,'Cornish place-names index').
17 **Porthenys:** *Cal. Chart.* 1257-1300, 75; **Raginnis:** *Selden* 68, 411 (Padel,'Cornish place-names index'); *Cal. Inq. Misc.* 1387-93, 5.
18 **Manor of Newlyn:** CRO, AR1/1005/2; **Manor of Trewarveneth:** VCH Penwith, 50; **Alverton sub-manors:** P.A.S. Pool, 'The Penheleg Manuscript', *JRIC* n.s. 3 (1959), 218.
19 **Roger of St Constantine:** T. Peter, *The History of Glasney Collegiate Church* (1903), 106, 108; **income:** *Tax. Eccl.* 148; **Porthenys:** *Cal. Chart.*1257-1300, 75.
20 **Paul fair:** *Cal. Chart.*1257-1300, 62; **Fairs:** 'Gazetteer of Markets and Fairs to 1516: Cornwall', Centre for Metropolitan History, 23 February 2005. http:www.history.ac.uk/cmh/gaz/cornwall.html (accessed 16 January 2006); **Paul Aurelian:** Doble, *Saint Paul of Leon*; Orme, *Cornish Saints*, 212-13; **Newlyn fair:** *Pigot's Dir. Cornwall* (1844), 29.
21 **Porthenys fair:** *Cal. Chart.*1257-1300, 75. **Mousehole fairs:** *Cal. Chart.*1257-1300, 489; 1327-41, 270.
22 **Two settlements:** CRO, R1152; Henderson, 'Topography of the Parish of Paul', 63
23 This and the following paragraphs depend upon Arch. Rep. B.
24 Arch. Rep. B., 14-15.
25 **Infilling:** RIC, Assize I, 66; **shops:** RIC, Assize II, 121; **seld:** *Cornwall Feet of Fines* I, 330-1; **1327:** TNA, E179/87/33/6.
26 For the rest of this section see Arch. Rep. B.; D. E. Benney, *Cornish Water Mills* (1972), 9.
27 **Northern mills:** TNA, E134/11&12 Charles I/Hil 19, m.9; Bodleian, Rawl. C 789 (RIC microfilm); **southern mills:** RIC, HK/7/3; BB/4/10; TNA, C108/67 (21 July 1488); RIC, BB/4/10.

28 **Income:** *Tax. Eccl.*; **appropriation:** *Cal. Close* 1296-1302, 26.

29 M.I. Somerscales, 'Lazar Houses in Cornwall', *JRIC* n.s. 5 (1965), 91-2.

30 **Chaplain:** *Reg. Stapeldon*, 454; RIC, Assize II, 121; **Edmund Bosvenning:** TNA, C108/67 (1366); **St Edmund's:** N.M. Pender, *A Short History of Mousehole* (1970), 10 (lost deed); *Reg. Lacy*, I, 12, 115, 385; II, 197, 247; C.S. Gilbert, *History of Cornwall*, 2 (1820), 730.

31 **St Mary's:** *Reg. Brantyngham*, 500, 637; Pender, *Mousehole*, 10; in **ruins:** *Reg. Stafford*, 260; **John Patry:** *Reg. Lacy,* I, 12, 115; **St Clement's:** *Leland Itin.* I, 189, 319.

32 **Nancothnan 1469 will:** TNA, PROB 11/5, f.233v (N. Orme, *Cornish Wills* (DCRS, 2007), 205); **Polyphant:** VCH Penwith, 34, 80.

33 **Royal writs:** *Cal. Close* 1296-1302, 101ff.

34 **Burgesses:** *Cal. Inq. p.m.* VII, 24; **taxpayers:** TNA, E 179/87/7, m.12..

35 **Alverton court:** TNA, SC 2/156/15; **hundred court:** VCH Penwith, 3; TNA, SC2/161/174, f. 13; **maritime court:** *Havener's a/cs*, 41-3, 137, 153; **tithings:** P.A.S. Pool, 'The tithings of Cornwall', *JRIC* n.s. 8 (1981), 302-6.

36 **Black Death:** *Havener's a/cs*, 200-3; **1377:** TNA, E179/33; C.C. Fenwick, *The Poll Taxes of 1377, 1379 and 1381* (1998), 80-9.

37 **1522:** TNA, E179/87/122, ff. 30v-33; **1524-5:** /127, ff. 6v-7; /136, ff. 7; **1545:** /188, ff. 4v-5; **1549-50:** /197, f.6v; Douch *Muster*, 114-15 seems to show a declining population in 1569; **household size:** T. Gray, *Harvest Failure in Cornwall and Devon* (1992), xx-xxv; **'Porthenys alias Mowseholle':** TNA, C108/67 (1557).

38 **Newlyn:** Padel, *Place-names*, 128; VCH Penwith, 51; Newlyn Report, 11-14; **mansion:** CRO, R1154-5.

39 **Jackford:** RIC, Assize I, 14; **other place names:** P.A.S. Pool, *The Place-Names of West Penwith* (1985), 51, 69; **bridge:** CRO, AR2/102, f.3.

40 **Chapel:** *Leland Itin.* I, 319; CRO, J212; BL, Add. 9420, f. 430; **taxpayers:** TNA, E179/87/7, ff.11-12; **Newlyn:** *Leland Itin.* I, 189, 319; W. Lach-Szyrma, *A Short History of Penzance and Land's End* (1878), 83.

41 **Maritime courts:** *Havener's a/cs*, 137, 153; **shipwreck:** *Gentleman's Mag.* n.s. XIII (Jan.-June 1840), 79; **shops:** RIC, Assize II, 112; TNA, C1/363/10; **mills:** TNA, E134/11&12Chas1/Hil 19, f. 6.

CHAPTER 2 Mount's Bay and its Ports to 1600, pp. 25-38

42 **Porthplement:** *Havener's a/cs*, 21 (note 77).

43 **Mousehole's pre-eminence:** *Cal. Close*1296-1302, 101; VCH Penwith, 50.

44 *Cal. Pat.* 1391-6, 247.

45 **Site:** Pender, *Mousehole*, 10 (lost deed); Arch. Rep. B, 28; **royal enquiry:** TNA, C143/416/4; **quayage:** *Cal. Pat.* 1391-6, 247.

46 **Pier and pilgrims:** P.A.S. Pool, 'The Penzance Harbour Charter of 1512', *JRIC* n.s. 6 (1971), 230-1; **royal letter:** *Cal. Pat.* 1413-16, 10; **fair:** *Cal. Chart.* 1341-1417, 430.

47 **Mount quay:** *Cal. Pat.* 1422-9, 447; **Newlyn quay repairs:** *Reg. Lacy* II, 45; CRO, P19/5/1, f.39v; **16th-century maps:** BL, Cotton MS. Augustus I, i.34, 35-9; **Mousehole quay repairs:** *Reg. Lacy* I, 306; CRO, PD 322/1, f.42 (B. Hull transcript p. 58).

48 **Marazion and Penzance:** Padel *Place-names*, 115, 136; VCH Penwith, 53-4, 77; Pool *Penzance*; **markets:** *Cal. Chart.* 1341-1417, 430; *Leland Itin.* I, 319; **foreign inns:** TNA, E179/87/80; **ships:** *Cal. Pat.* 1446-52, 448-9.

49 **1520s :** TNA, E179/87/127 and /136 (taxpayers multiplied by six or more); **1540s:** /188; L.S. Snell ed., *The Chantry Certificates for Cornwall* (1953), 42 (see also Stoate *Survey* and *Subsidies*); **Paul only:** TNA, E179/87/197ff; **1595:** R. Dickinson, 'The Spanish Raid on Mount's Bay in 1595', *JRIC* n.s. 10 (1988), 181-2; **Marazion charter:** *Cal. SP Dom.* 1591-4, 553.

50 **English exports:** G. Hutchinson, *Medieval Ships and Shipping* (1994), 88-103.

51 **Noght and Taverner:** *Cal. Pat.* 1330-4, 144; *Havener's a/cs*, 160; **Tyes:** VCH Penwith, 41.

52 **Victuallers:** RIC, Henderson Cal. 40, pp. 33-4, 36; **Portuguese ship:** *Cal. Pat.* 1441-6, 289-90; **puffins:** *L&P Hen. VIII*, VI, 271; **baker as surname:** TNA, SC2/161/74, f. 12; **oven:** Bodleian, Rawl. C 789, 47 (RIC microfilm).

53 **Bastard's wine etc:** TNA, JUST 1/117A, ff.67-8; **wine and honey:** *Havener's a/cs*, 241; **Bordeaux:** *Calendar of Chancery Warrants*, I, 507; **Bristol and London:** TNA, PROB 11/5, f.233v (N. Orme, *Cornish Wills* (2007), 205, 235); *Cal. Close* 1429-35, 305.

54 **Nicholas Taverner:** RIC, Assize, II, 112, 121; TNA C1/363/10; *Cornwall Feet of Fines* I, 330-1; **wine cellars:** *Havener's a/cs*, 164, 186; TNA, SC6/818/11, f.5.

55 **War disruption:** *Havener's a/cs*, 30 fn; **1470s:** TNA, SC6/822/2, f. 14; **1541-2:** E122/116/16; **1592-4:** E190/1018/13.

56 **Salt:** *Havener's a/cs*, 220, 277 TNA, E122/116/16; **corn:** *Havener's a/cs*, 276-7; E190/1011/22; 1019/6; /25; f. 25v; **oranges:** E122/116/16, f. 25v; **'frysse':** CRO, AR 2/898.

57 **Cloth:** *Cal. Pat.*1361-4, 496; **hides:** *Havener's a/cs*, 160; TNA, E122/116/16; E190/1011/10; **Saint Michael:** *Cal. Close* 1349-54, 25-6.

58 **Lamorna:** *Cal. Close* 1399-1402, 569; **tin:** *Cal. Pat.*1485-94, 461; TNA, E122/115/8-/206/10 (J. Scantlebury list); E190/1010/5-/1012/15; **1540s:** E122/116/16.

59 **Port rents:** *Havener's a/cs*, 21-2; **fish:** TNA, E122/116/16.

60 M. Kowaleski, 'The Western Fisheries' in *ESF*, 28.

61 **Fishing methods:** Fox, *Fishing Village*, 59-61; Hutchinson, *Medieval Ships*, 130-3; **whale:** *Havener's a/cs*, 245.

62 **14th century:** *Havener's a/cs*, 181, 241; **Mount's Bay hake:** *Cal. Pat.* 1422-9, 447; **fishing fleet and other fish:** TNA, E122/116/16; E190/1012/13; /1018/13.

63 *Havener's a/cs*, 258.

64 **Dried hake:** *Cal. Pat.* 1364-7, 11; **train oil:** TNA, E190/1019/33.

65 **Mousehole boats:** *Cal. Inq. p.m.* VII, 24; **St Ives:** *Havener's a/cs*, 203; **Irish fleet:** TNA, E122/116/16; Fox, *Fishing Village*, 168; **mixed crews:** RIC, Henderson Cal. 11, 266.

66 **Newhall:** TNA, C1/1041/16-17; TNA, E122/206/3, 8 (J. Scantlebury list); RIC, Henderson Cal. 3, 115; **William Cockes will:** TNA, PROB 11/21, f.32v; Orme, *Cornish Wills*, 170, 221-2; **wealth:** E179/87/122, f. 32; /127, f. 6v; /136, f. 7v; /188, f. 4v.

67 **Fish merchants:** *Cal. Pat.* 1364-7, 32; TNA, E122/115/8ff (J. Scantlebury list); **Spanish apprentice:** *Cat. Ancient Deeds*, IV, 10022 (p.495).

68 **Gascon:** RIC, Henderson Cal. 40, 33-4, 36; **inns:** TNA, E179/87/80; **foreigners:** /122, f.33; *L&P Hen. VIII*, XX (1), 568; **black man:** CRO, P172/1/1 (28 Feb. 1596).

69 **Poitou:** TNA, E179/87/7; **others:** *Havener's a/cs*, 180-1, 232; **salt traders:** TNA, SC 6/817/6, f. 10v.

70 Fox, *Fishing Village*, 177-8.

71 **Loges:** *Cal. Inq. p.m.* VII, 24; CRO, AR 2/139; RIC, TRM/4, 8; *Cat. Ancient Deeds*, IV, no 9104 (p.392); **Penzance:** Bodleian, Rawl. C 789 (RIC microfilm).

72 *Cal. Pat.* 1317-21, 293; 1330-4, 497; 1340-3, 587.

73 **Wreck:** TNA, JUST 1/119, ff. 4-v, 5v, 9v; *Cal. Pat.* 1307-13, 255-6; **1371:** *Cal. Pat.* 1370-4, 173.

74 **1284:** RIC, Henderson Cal. 40, pp. 33-4; **1310 (x2):** *Cal. Pat.* 1307-13, 257; *Cal. Close* 1307-13, 194; **1326:** *Cal. Pat.* 1324-7, 329; 1327-30, 49; **1368:** *Cal. Inq. Misc.* IV, 66; **1387:** *Cal. Close* 1385-9, 359; *Cal. Inq. Misc.* IV, 218; VCH Penwith, 66; **1392:** 66; **1398:** *Cal. Inq. Misc.* VI, 101-2.

75 **Hailes abbey:** *Cal. Pat.* 1327-30, 8ff; **St Buryan:** *Reg. Grandison* I, 358-9; **illegal imprisonment:** TNA, JUST 1/124, f. 12; **Newlyn case:** C1/5/158.

76 **Spanish account:** R. Dickinson, 'The Spanish Raid on Mount's Bay in 1595', *JRIC* n.s. 10 (1988), 178-83; **Cornish account:** Carew, 156-9. Unless otherwise specified the Cornish account has been used.

77 *Cal. SP Dom.*;1595-7, 77.

78 TNA, E190/1019/33 Dickinson, 'Spanish Raid', 182.

79 **Letter:** *Cal. SP Dom.* 1595-7, 77; **cannon request:** 1591-4, 511; **Keigwin burial:** CRO, P 172/1/1; **mass:** Dickinson, 'Spanish Raid', 183.

80 **Burials and baptism:** CRO, P 172/1/1; **unsatisfactory tax returns:** *Cal. SP Dom.* 1595-7, 246.

CHAPTER 3 Living off the Sea, 1600-1800, pp. 39-50

81 **Bounty:** T. Pawlyn 'The Cornish Pilchard Fishery in the Eighteenth Century', *JRIC*, n.s.II.2 (1998), 67-8; **1699 case:** TNA, C 7/194/32.

82 Cullum, 277.

83 **Background:** T. Gray, 'Inshore fisheries of the South West, *c.*1530-1630' and T. Pawlyn, 'The South West pilchard, trawl and mackerel fisheries, 1770-1850' in *ESF*, 82-7; Pawlyn, 'Cornish pilchard fishery', 67-90; **pots and willows:** CRO, CN 1628; ML 475.

84 **Huers' huts:** M.E. Perry, 'Penolva' in V. Chesher and J. Palmer ed., *Three Hundred Years on West Penwith Farms* (1994), 121; **Mount:** CRO, ML 472.

85 TNA, CUST 68/12.

86 **1649:** TNA, E134/31&32Chas2/Hil22; **1762:** CRO, ML 749; **1750s:** Pawlyn, 'Cornish pilchard fishery', 75.

87 **Maritime survey:** T. Gray, *Early Stuart Mariners and Shipping* (1990), xviii, 78-9; **1679:** TNA, E134/31&32Chas2/Hil12.

88 CRO, P172/1/6 – parish literacy was 71%. **Pentreath tribes:** RIC, Jago MS., p.1254; **Rouffignac:** TNA, PRO, PROB 11/1209, f. 309; **Grusilier:** Cullum, 98.

89 **Thomas Bosun's fleet:** Cullum, 74 (as Edward not Thomas Boson); CRO, AP/B/851/2. **John Richards:** CRO, AP/H776/2; /R365/2.

90 CRO, CN 1642.

91 CRO, AR1/1002.

92 **Tregurtha:** CRO, AP/T/2706; **seine names:** ML 448.

93 **Fair-maids:** R. Morton Nance, *A Glossary of Cornish Sea Words* (1963), 76-7; **Fryer:** CRO, AP/F/127/1; **train oil and Penzance:** Cullum, 74, 277.

94 **Inventories:** CRO, AP/N315/2; /C2679; **poor fishermen:** CN 1645.

95 **Hake bulks:** CRO, AP/H61/1; F127/1; H776/2; **salt re-use:** FS/3/1105/7; **other inventories:** AP/C3344/2; /S 1847/2.

96 **Noye:** CRO, AP/N315/2; **cellarwomen:** ML 450.

97 **Thefts:** CRO, ML 464-5; **Penberth women:** ML 481; **quote:** CN 1672/1.

98 **Exports:** VCH *Cornwall*, 583; CRO, ML 448; **Chancery case:** TNA, C 7/194/32.

99 **Dolly:** RIC, Jago MS., 1250; **Martha Blewett:** CRO, P172/1/3.

100 **Goats:** CRO, AP/R1246; 1753a/2; **winter marriages:** Cullum, 284-5.

101 **methodology:** all women's inventories and highest and lowest value inventories were excluded in each case to reach an average; **Cornish average:** M. Overton et al., *Production & Consumption in English Households 1600-1750* (2004), 141; **Sampson:** CRO, AP/S1551; **subletting:** Cullum, 284-5.

102 CRO, AP/H4871.

103 **quote:** CRO, ML 467 (2); **1652:** VCH, *Cornwall*, 502; **18th-century impressment:** TNA CUST 68/5.

104 **background:** T. Gray, 'Turks, Moors and the Cornish Fishermen: Piracy in the Early Seventeenth Century', *JRIC* n.s. 10 (1990), 457-75; A. Duffin, *Faction & Faith: Politics and Religion of the Cornish Gentry before the Civil War* (1996), 134-43; **1640:** *Cal. SP Dom.* 1640, 328, 438, 449; **other pirates:** 1629-31, 296; VCH, *Cornwall*, 496; **defences:** *Cal. SP Dom.* 1625-6, 91, 207, 242.

105 **first case:** TNA, E190/1055/11; **Falmouth packet:** CUST 68/11 (10 Aug. 1780).

106 **quote:** TNA, CUST 68/5 (23 Nov. 1761); **customs books:** TNA, CUST 68/1-18; **1749:** /2 (1-26 Feb. 1749); *Polly:* /2-3 (17 May-17 Nov. 1750); **Smuggling voyage:** TNA, CUST 68/8 (23 Feb. 1773).

107 **dissenter:** TNA, CUST 68/14 (17 Jan. 1789); **Rowling:** /6 (28 Dec. 1767-21 Jan. 1768); **May Day:** /1 (28 Feb. 1740).

108 **assault:** TNA, CUST 68/11-12 (8 Feb. 1781-26 Aug 1782); **Odgers murder:** /7 (14 Nov. 1768); *Wolf* **marriages:** CRO, P172/1/6; **John Pentreath:** TNA, CUST 68/7 (12 Jan. 1771).

109 **Mousehole case:** TNA, CUST 68/14 (24 Feb. 1789); **Rickard:** /13 (Dec. 1788).

110 **Trewavas family:** TNA, CUST 68/13 (29 June 1786); **murder:** CRO, P172/1/3.

111 **wrongful arrest:** TNA, CUST 68/13 (9 Feb.-18 July 1788 – John Carnepezzack was arrested instead of his son, both were probably millers; **Carey:** /14 (11 Mar. 1789).

CHAPTER 4 The Expansion of Newlyn, 1600-1800, pp. 51-74

112 Pool *Penzance*, 30; **collections:** J. Foster Williams ed., *The Early Churchwardens' Accounts of Hampshire* (1913), 198; St Boltoph Aldgate. London- information form

Kate Thompson [Ms 9234/5], Guildhall Library; **mortality crisis:** Cullum, 30-1.

113 **1613:** CRO, ARD/TER/349; **constable:** RIC, Henderson Cal. 4, p.26; **vestry room:**
M. Cook ed., *The Diocese of Exeter in 1821*, 1 Cornwall (1958), 64; **way wardens:**
CRO, QS/1/5-6.

114 Madron parish records include CRO, P133/5/1-10; /12/1-13; 16 (B)/1-2.

115 **Hutchens almshouse:** CRO, P172/25/43; 46; **Verran's bed:** /12/2, f.92.

116 VCH Cornwall, 52

117 **Cornwall's population:** J. Whetter, *Cornwall in the 17th* Century (1974, rep. 2002),
10; **west Penwith:** Cullum, 32, 90, 95-6.

118 **hearth tax:** Stoate *Hearth Tax*, 88-9 and information from T. Arkell; **Paul
population:** Cullum, 245, 305; **town populations:** J. Barry, 'Towns' in Kain, R. and
Ravenhill, W., *Historical Atlas of South-West England* (1999), 417. Barry's figures for
*c*1660 need to be adjusted upwards using 1641 Protestation returns and Cullum's
growth rates.

119 **1641:** Stoate *Protestation*, 52; **mayor:** Pool *Penzance*, 279.

120 **exporters:** TNA, E190/1041/3-1051/2 (Keigwins: 4 masters, 8 merchants; Bosons: 2
masters, 1 merchant); **Alverton:** 'VCH Penwith', 41.

121 **Lawyer Boson:** TNA, C 10/514/96; **John:** TNA, E190/1019/33; **St Just:** RIC,
HHJ/2/57-70;

122 **quote:** BL, Add. MS., 28,554, f.10; **Gwavas:** *ODNB*.

123 *Carew*, 156v.

124 **wills:** TNA, PROB 11/105, f.127; /119, f.74v; /115, f.25; **old bells:** TNA, E190/1019,
25, 33; **former inscription:** J. Polsue, *A Complete Parochial History of the Country of
Cornwall* IV(1872), 24.

125 **inns:** CRO, X20/35; TNA, E 314/3Jas2/Mich32.

126 CRO, CY5012, f. 2.

127 **situation:** Newlyn Report, 12; **new houses:** TNA, PROB 11/126, f.329;
Trewarveneth: Stoate *Hearth Tax*, 88.

128 **Bretons:** Morrab Library, MAN/36/114/5; **Street an Awan:** RIC, Henderson Cal. 4,
158; TNA, PROB 11/105, f.127; **Tonkin will:** /126, f.329; **17th century quays:** CRO,
CN 1672/24.

129 **households:** TNA, E 134/Chas1/Mich41, mm.10, 14.

130 TNA, E 134/11&12Chas1/Hil19, mm.8-9, 15.

131 **Penkevil:** TNA, E 134/14Chas1/Mich41, m.4; **value:** /11&12Chas 1/Hil19, mm.6,
9-10; **rebuilding:** /4Geo2/Mich7, mm. 5, 7; **types of mill:** m. 4.

132 **proverb:** CRO, ML 573; **dispute:** M. Perry, *Newlyn* (1999), 30; Pool *Penzance*, 35-6,
66-8, 240-6; **ill dealing:** TNA, E 134/14Chas1/Mich41, mm.11-14.

133 **1664:** Stoate *Hearth Tax*, 88-9; Cullum, 277-8, 305; **ruins:** WH 4434; R. Potts, *A
Calendar of Cornish Glebe Terriers 1673-1735* (DCRS, 1974), 121; **chapels:** RIC,
Henderson Cal. 10, 133.

134 Arch. Rep. A.

135 **1610:** CRO, P126/4/1 (St Stephen by Saltash churchwardens' account book
reference found by Colin Edwards); **dendrochronological dating:** Alison Arnold
and Robert Howard, 'The Old Standard (Nos 1 and 2), Little Keigwin (No 5),
and Keigwin (No 7), Keigwin Place, Mousehole, Cornwall – Tree-Ring Analysis
of Timbers – Scientific Dating Report (Research Department Report Series No
10-2008 for English Heritage), 1-55; **Keigwin will:** Ledbury MS. (The original
will was not found but may be TNA, PCC Book of Pile, f.123); **ruins:** RIC, HD
11/239-40.

136 **fortlet:** M. Coate, *Cornwall in the Great Civil War* (1933), 363; **Pendennis:** Ledbury
MS.; **Gear:** M. Stoyle, *West Britons* (2002), 113-33.

137 **Penryn triumph:** J. Keast, *The Travels of Peter Mundy 1597-1667* (1984); 8; '**ethnic
undertow':** Stoyle, *West Britons*, 114.

138 **remodelling:** Arch. Rep. A, 24; **1670-89:** RIC, HD 11/143, CRO, WH 4475; **1668-
1708:** RIC, HD 11/142B; CRO, WH 3814, 3815.

139 **population:** Cullum and VCH 'Social and Economic History', 039; **cemetery:** DRO,
Faculty Causes, Paul 1; **1805:** BL, Add 9420, f.429.

140 **quote:** C.T. Gooch, 'A Journey to Cornwall in 1754', *OC* vi (1961-4), 58 (Gooch had

an interest in the fisheries here and later moved to Sunderland); **surgeon:** CRO, P172/1/6, 61; **peruke maker:** AP/H/6835; **other occupations:** H.L. Douch, 'Cornish potters and pewterers', *JRIC* n.s. 6 (1969), 57-60, 76 and 'Cornish goldsmiths', *JRIC* n.s. 6 (1970), 132-3; **black servant:** CRO, X573/246/1; AP/H/4377.

141   Morrab, MAN/36.

142   **pier plan:** CRO, BRA 1216/2; FS3/1105/6/1-8; **Penzance opposition:** Pool *Penzance*, 98; **wharf:** CRO, CN 1664/10.

143   **caption quote and deaths:** X573/114; CRO, P172/ 1/3; CN 1672/24; ML 873/1; **seine cellars:** CRO, CN1663/6; **Brick cellar:** CN 1662; **other cellars:** CN 943; Downing will: AP/D/1692.

144   **Boson's new house:** CRO, X573/179; **Balconey:** ML 871.

145   **infilling:** CRO X573/148; **street names:** X573/21/1; deed (D. Smart collection).

146   **Trewarveneth Orchard and Redes Meadow:** CRO, X573/138; BRA, 833/241-2.

147   Newlyn Report, 14-15; **Myrtle cottage:** information from Iris Green; **Belle Vue and Boase Castle:** I. Green, *Artists at Home* (1995), 10.

148   **Fradgan:** FS3/3/495; **Chywoone:** Newlyn Report, 15.

149   **Arundell rental:** CRO, X573/150; **shops:** X573/21/1; /6; **inns:** RIC, Douch MS; **tavern:** CRO, X573/110/1.

150   **Tolcarne:** CRO, P133/12/2-3; **boat-building:** X238/2; **lime kiln:** AR1/1010.

151   CRO, ML 736; 446.

152   **Chapel St.:** List descriptions; **Whitehall:** CRO, AD 482/17.

153   **wharf:** TNA, c114/138; **Gwavas offer:** Morrab, MAN/36; **quay:** CRO, ML 750, 756, **792;** CN 1662; **quote:** ML 756.

154   **Keigwin Arms:** H.L. Douch, *Old Cornish* Inns, 158; **shop:** CRO, AP/F/713; **salt ponds:** CN 1663/6.

155   J. Blight, *A Week at Land's End* (1861), 41-2.

156   **Mousehole girdle:** BL, Eg. 2657, ff.5v-6, no 7; Add 9445, f.198v; **other girdles:** CRO, AP/B/23/1-2; /P/332/1-2; **mayors:** Ledbury MS.

CHAPTER 5 Speaking Cornish in Mount's Bay, pp. 75-84

157   BL, Add. MS 28,554, f.158.

158   *Carew*, f.55.

159   D.H. Frost, '*Sacrament an Alter*: A Tudor Cornish Patristic Catena', *CS* 11 (2003), 291-307.

160   **Chivertons:** P. Hull, 'Thomas Chiverton's Book of Obits', *DCNQ* 33-4 (1975-8), 97ff; **'Cornish Bible':** M. Spriggs, 'Additional thoughts on the medieval "Cornish Bible"', *CS* 14 (2006), 44-55; **Camborne play:** Bodleian, Ashmole 1814, f.267.

161   J. Norden, *Speculi Britanniae* 1728 (orig. 1584), 21.

162   **Symonds:** C.E. Long ed., *Diary of the Marches of the Royal Army … by R. Symonds* (1859), 74; **Slanning's regiment:** T. Peter, 'Sir N. Slanning's Regiment in Great Civil War', *JRIC* 19 (1914), 491-6; **deserters:** Stoyle, *West Britons*, 141-2.

163   **1650s iconoclasm:** J. Mattingly, 'Stories in the glass – reconstructing the St Neot pre-Reformation glazing scheme', *JRIC* n.s. II, 3 (2000), 9-10; **Sennen case:** CRO, SF 285/68v.

164   **Ray:** E. Lankester ed., *Memorials of Ray: Itineraries* (1846), 189-90; **Boson:** Padel *Bosons*, 24; Spriggs *Cornish*, 253-4.

165   **monoglots:** Spriggs *Cornish*, 251-2; **Breton parallels:** information from B. Deacon.

166   **Ray quote:** Lankester, *Memorials*, 189 fn.; **Angwyn:** Spriggs *Cornish*, 251-3; CRO, F2/39, f 31v [52]; Davies Gilbert, *The Parochial History of Cornwall* (1838) IV, 218; C. Henderson, 'Nicholas Boson and Richard Angwyn', *OC* 2, pt 3 (1931-6), 29-32; Angwyn married Grace Fleming, great-granddaughter of Jenkin Keigwin (d.1595) in 1642; **bonfire:** CRO, AD/1863, p. 77; **Pendarves:** Bodleian, Ashmole 1814, f.267.

167   **Oliver:** Bodleian, Ashmole 1814, f.267; R. & O.B. Peter, *The Histories of Launceston and Dunheved* (1885), 320, 330; **Sherwood:** M. Spriggs, 'The Reverend Joseph Sherwood: A Cornish Language Will-o'-the-Wisp?' *CS* 6 (1998), 46-61.

168   CRO, F2/39, f.4v.

169   H. Woodhouse ed., *The Cornish Passion Poem* (2002), vi.

170   Stoyle, *West Britons*, chapter 7; M. Spriggs, 'William Scawen (1600-89) – a Neglected

Cornish Patriot and Father of the Cornish Language Revival', *CS* 13 (2005), 98-126; *ODNB*.

171 **tract:** *ODNB*; Bodleian, Ashmole 1814, f.20; CRO, F2/39, f.1; **helpers:** f.32r [53]; **letter writing in Cornish:** f.31r [51].

172 *ODNB*; CRO, F2/39, f.31v [52].

173 **Keigwins:** *ODNB*; **'higher house':** Bodleian, Ashmole 1814, f.101r; **'lower house':** BL, Add. MS 28,554, f.13.

174 **Sancreed:** Spriggs *Cornish*, 253; **proverbs etc:** Bodleian, Eng b.2042, f.144; **Charles letter:** BL, Add. MS 28,554, ff.139-140v; **Cornish dictionary:** Bodleian, Ashmole 1814, f.101r.

175 *Ordinalia:* Bodleian, Ashmole 1814, ff.20-1; **Isabella Keigwin:** Ledbury MS.; **omission:** BL, Add. MS., 28,554, f.14.

176 **Trelawny:** Spriggs, 'Scawen - Patriot', 110, 122, fn. 61; **Godolphin letter:** P. Berresford Ellis, *The Cornish Language and its Literature* (1974), plate 7.

177 *ODNB*; Padel *Bosons*, 24.

178 **Boson's autobiography:** Padel *Bosons*, 26, 28; **lands:** RIC, HHJ/2/66-7; **Gwavas:** information from M. Perry.

179 **Duchess:** Padel *Bosons*, 8-14; M. Spriggs, 'Who was the Duchess of Cornwall in Nicholas Boson's (*c*.1660-1670) "The Duchesse of Cornwall's Progresse to see the Land's End…"?', *CS* 14 (2006), 56-69; **hurling:** *Carew*, ff. 73v-75v.

180 *Nebbaz Gerriau:* Padel Bosons, 24-37; **'John of Chyanhor':** 14, 23; Bodleian, Ashmole 1814, f.267; **libraries:** Bodleian, Ashmole 1814, f.267; CRO, AR/B/2594/2.

181 **Thomas Boson:** *ODNB*; TNA, E190/1045/19; /1061/14, f.2; **hurling ball motto:** Padel *Bosons*, 38.

182 **John Boson:** *ODNB*; Padel *Bosons*, 15; **Kenegie:** TNA, C7/194/32, m.2; **new house:** CRO, X573/4/1, 179; **financial problems:** TNA, C11/30/12.

183 **pilchard curing:** Padel *Bosons*, 43-4; **epitaphs:** 48, 59.

184 *Bleau Pawle:* BL, Add. MS 28,554, ff. 3-4v (more correctly *Pleau Paul* or the parish of Paul); **quote:** Bodleian, Ashmole 1814, f.267; **helpers:** BL, Add. MS 28,554, f.13; 94v-5; 130-2; 135; **ship masters:** TNA, E190/1061/14; **Bodinar lease and will:** CRO, X573/25/1-2, TNA, PROB 11/622, ff. 45v-46; **mottos:** BL, Add. MS 28,554, f.148, 158; **John Boson's will:** CRO, AP/B/3320; **Chirgwin:** TNA, C5/231/16.

185 **fish tithe dispute:** T. Pawlyn, 'The Cornish Pilchard Fishery in the Eighteenth Century', *JRIC* (1998) n.s. II, 3, 78-9; **Boson witness:** Padel *Bosons*, 60; **quay:** Morrab, MAN/36.

186 **Tonkin:** BL, Add. MS 28,554, ff. 14-23; **Borlase:** f. 158; **Pryce:** W. Pryce, *Archaeologia Cornu-Britannica*.

187 **community language:** Spriggs *Cornish*, 252; **William Bodinar:** M Perry, *Mousehole* (1998), 46 ; **Keigwin:** CRO, AP/K/828; **Barringtons:** *ODNB*.

188 **Daines visit:** F.W.P. Jago, *The Ancient Language and the Dialect of Cornwall* (1882), 8-11; **Dolly:** *ODNB*; TNA, C114/138.

CHAPTER 6 Growth and Development 1800-1914, pp. 85-102

189 J. Thomas, *History of Mount's Bay* (1831), 73; **Brook Street boundary:** *CT*, Nov.-Dec. 1860.

190 **Up-long etc:** Phillips, K.C. ed., *The Cornish Journal of Charles Lee*, 10 (but note Lee's visit was 1893-4 not 1892-3).

191 **censuses:** W. Page ed., 'Social and Economic History', unpublished VCH volume, 040 and individual censuses; **background:** P. Carter and K. Thompson, *Sources for Local Historians* (2005), 34-6.

192 **emigration:** P. Payton, *Making of Modern Cornwall*, 99-118 and *The Cornish Overseas* (1999); **Farmer Giles:** CRO, DRB/WR/8, 324; **Kelynack emigration:** *Coll. Cornub.*, 1427; CRO, MSR/Penzance/2; **missionaries:** *CP*, 2 Jan. 1937 and further information from B. Deacon.

193 Newlyn Report, 22-43.

194 Newlyn Report, 16.

195 RIC, Douch pubs index; *Pigot's Dir. Cornwall* (1830), 25-6; **later inns:** *Kelly's Dir.*

Cornwall (1914), 250-2; **bakehouses etc:** CRO, DC/Pen/284, p.360;

196   **house types:** C. Lorigan, 'Newlyn and the Fishing Industry' unpublished report on
local housing 2006, 3-6; **overcrowding:** Razzell and Wainwright, *Victorian Working
Class*, 21.

197   **Penzance harbour:** Pool *Penzance*, 139-40; **Newlyn's plans:** Perry, *Newlyn*, 42.

198   **south pier:** Perry, *Newlyn*, 3; J. Holmes, *Penzance and Newlyn in Old Photographs*
(1992), 84; **accidental death:** *Coll. Cornub.*, 1077; **visit:** PNHAS (1888-9), 32; **light
railway:** CRO, DC/Pen/284, p.151.

199   **north pier:** R. Hogg, 'The building of the harbour and its environs' in *Newlyn Life*,
16-17; Perry, *Newlyn*, 3; **storm:** *Parish Mag.*, Feb. 1895 (M. Perry collection now at
CRO).

200   **harbour road:** CRO, DC Pen/285, pp.34, 240-1; Perry, *Newlyn*, 3; **Strand:** CRO, DC
Pen/285, p.425; *Star Inn:* p.430; **North Corner slip:** pp.136, 320; **Cippolina:** *Newlyn
Life*, 33-4; **Ship Institute:** Perry, *Newlyn*, 45-6; Penwith Local History Group, *West
Cornwall in the Twentieth Century* (2007), 3, 90; **weathervane:** H. Berriman, *Arts
and Crafts in Newlyn 1890-1930* (1986), 29.

201   **Dunn:** CRO, DC Pen/284, pp.247, 275; **Bazeleys:** /284, p.389, /285, pp.234, 271;
Bath: /285, pp.57, 69, 119; **ice works:** J.C. Jenkin, *Newlyn*, (2002); opp.119.

202   **thatch:** J.J. Beckerlegge, 'The thatched cottages of Newlyn within living memory', *OC*
4 (1944), 113-15; **Church and Boase Streets:** Lorigan, 'Newlyn', 6; **Eden Place:** OS
Map 1:25000, sheet LXXIV (1906 edn); **Navy Inn Street:** CRO, DC/Pen/284, p.408.

203   **Church Street:** CRO, DC Pen/285, p.180; **Olive Villa:** *Kelly's Dir Cornwall* (1889),
1095; **Penzer:** (1893), 1221; **Roseland:** W. Stevenson, *Growing up with boats* (2001),
14.

204   **glass studios:** C. Fox and F. Greenacre, *Artists of the Newlyn School* (1979), 26;
Bramley's studio: T. Cross, *The Shining Sands* (1994), 37.

205   **Westholme** *Kelly's Dir. Cornwall* (1883), 967; **Mount Vernon:** (1889), 1094;
Malthouse: P. Lomax, *The Golden Dream* (2004), 84.

206   **La Pietra:** CRO, X573/268, 275; **Higher Faugan:** B. Batten, *Newlyn of Yesterday*
(1983), 40; CRO, DC/Pen/285, pp.21, 40; **Wheal Betsy:** Lomax, *The Golden Dream*,
7, 135; **plans:** CRO, DC/Pen/286, p.247; **Morvah:** CRO, DC/Pen/288, p.91.

207   **Park Terrace:** DC/Pen/286, pp.206ff; **other terraces:** *Kelly's Dir. Cornwall* (1914),
250-2.

208   **Chypons:** *Kelly's Dir. Cornwall* (1926), 257; **Vivian House:** letters of 2 Mar. 1866, 5
and 20 Nov. 1870 (M. Perry collection); **Antoine House:** CRO, DRB/WR/19, p.213
(69).

209   Jenkin, *Newlyn*, 101 and information from T. Pawlyn.

210   **platforms:** Newlyn Report, 35; **Lane Reddin Terrace:** CRO, DC Pen/286, p.294;
Orchard Terrace: P172/25/45-61; **Kenilworth:** *Kelly's Dir. Cornwall* (1910), 244;
Bucca's pass: PLHG, *West Cornwall in the Twentieth Century* (2007), 87.

211   Newlyn Report, 31-2; R. Langley, *Walter Langley* (1997), 82, 103; **1871:** census.

212   **1817 storm:** Hitchens and Drew, *History of Cornwall*, 532; **Curnow:** PNHAS (1884-
5), 96.

213   CRO, DC/Pen/280.

214   **1874:** date stone; **railway:** letter of 26 July1875 (M. Perry collection); **Tolcarne
mills:** *Harrod's Dir. Cornwall* (1878), 883; **stone crushing:** *Kelly's Dir. Cornwall*
(1883), 967; (1897), 224.

215   **new road:** M. Waters, 'The new road from Penzance to Newlyn 1880-1886' in
Newlyn Life, 5-12; **old bridge:** CRO, DC/Pen/285, 93-4.

216   M. Hardie, ed., *100 years in Newlyn* (1995), 23-31; below, chapter 9.

217   **cholera:** J. Rowe and C.T. Andrews, 'Cholera in Cornwall' *JRIC* n.s. 7 (1974), 153-
64; **British death toll:** *Cornishman*, 10 Mar. 2005, p.45; **victim (Richard Mann):**
CRO, AP/M/3663; ARD 166/186/6.

218   **inns:** P.E. Razzell and R.W. Wainwright, *The Victorian Working Class* (1973), 21;
Ship Inn: *Kelly's Dir. Cornwall* (1897), 236; **bakehouses:** CRO, DC/Pen/284, 360.

219   **Salt ponds:** CRO, AD 482/10/1; **villas:** (1873), 830; **Lynwood:** CRO, AD/482/18, 32-
3; **Porthenys museum:** P. Harvey, 'William Baily' in *Mousehole Miscellanea* (1995),
9-11, 18.

220 **Salt quay:** TNA, CUST 68/32; **1838:** M. Perry, *Mousehole* (1998), 31.

221 **harbour:** Perry, *Mousehole*, 31-2; **quote:** *RCG*, 16 Sept. 1870; **slate cargo:** CRO, P172/8/1, 59.

222 **Duck Street and North Corner:** CRO, DC/Pen/284, p.51, /285, p.312; **standpipes:** /284, p.316; /285, p.103.

223 **Vibert:** *Coll. Cornub.*, 468; **disease:** CRO, DC/WPRDC/165; **fat cattle:** CRO, DC Pen/287, p.289; **tall beans and nets:** /287, p.178, /288, p.44.

224 **ruination of Newlyn:** transcript of Cordelia Dobson interview by Stephen Hall; **glass houses:** J. Cook et al., *Singing from the Walls – The Life and Art of Elizabeth Forbes* (2000), 115.

CHAPTER 7 Earning a Living, pp. 103-116

225 **batteries:** J. Palmer ed., *In and around Penzance in Napoleonic Times* (2000), 17-18, 94; **volunteers and Navy Inn:** *PNHAS* (1880-1), 76; (1888-9), 32; **press gang:** *The Life and Struggles of William Lovett in Pursuit of Bread, Knowledge and Freedom* (London: G. Bell & Sons, 1876, rep. 1920), 3. I am grateful to Margaret Perry for this reference.

226 **Napoleon:** Palmer, *In and around Penzance*, 92-3; *PNHAS* (1886-7), 232; **boats:** CRO, MSR/Penzance 1; **Spanish raid:** *RCG* 16 May 1807; BL, Add. 9420, ff.429-30; **poem:** extract from 'On the Burning of Mousehole by the Spaniards' by Richard Trewavas in R. Treffry, *Memoirs of Richard Trewavas, jun. of Mousehole* (1815), 165.

227 **Preventive service:** C. Noall, *Smuggling in Cornwall* (1971), 13, 83, 96; **Mousehole station:** TNA, CUST 68/19 (4 Feb. 1808); **boathouse:** /24 (21 Oct. 1817-18 July 1818), /27 (June 1821); **Newlyn:** /28 (19 Oct. 1821).

228 **Mousehole centre:** TNA, CUST 68/19 (31 Dec. 1804); **Prussia Cove:** Noall, *Smuggling*, 37-48; **spy:** A.K. Hamilton Jenkin, *News from Cornwall* (1951), 82-3; **bribery:** TNA, CUST 68/21 (19 Feb. 1813); *Two Johns*: /21 (18 Oct. 1814); **navy pensioner:** TNA, CUST 68/25 (Feb. 1819).

229 **1826:** TNA, CUST 68/31; **Guernsey:** /31 (14 Apr. 1829); /32 (6 June 1832); **last case:** /32 (2 May 1833).

230 **character of smuggling:** J. Rowe, *Cornwall in the Age of the Industrial Revolution* (1993), 288; **reformed smuggler:** /23 (7 Apr. 1817); **running away:** TNA, CUST 68/22 (1 Jan. 1816); /23 (10 June 1817); **coastguards:** /32 (1 June 1835); **keggers:** information from Tony Pawlyn.

231 **French prisoner:** P.A.S. Pool, 'The Journal of John Pollard of Newlyn, 1794-5', *JRIC*, n.s. II, 1 (1992), 200; **piracy:** P. Payton, *Cornwall* (1996), 182.

232 CRO, QS/1/7-8 (information from A2A index).

233 CRO, MSR/Penzance 1-3.

234 **organisation:** T. Pawlyn, 'The South West Pilchard, Trawl and Mackerel Fisheries 1770-1850' in *ESF*, 85; **Newlyn curers:** CRO, QS/1/5-6/3; /7-8/1-8 (information from A2A).

235 **St Ives:** Rowe, *Cornwall*, 299; **seines:** CRO, AP/D/(William Downing 1807).

236 **1849:** P.E. Razzell and R.W. Wainwright, *The Victorian Working Class* (1973), 17-19; **decline:** J. Rule, 'The South-Western Deep-sea Fisheries and their Markets in the Nineteenth Century', *Southern History* 22 (2000), 170.

237 **background:** Pawlyn, 'South West Fisheries', 85-6; Rule, 'Deep-sea fisheries', 68-9; *Nancy*: CRO, MSR/Penzance/1 (reg. 1822); TNA, CUST 68/32 (6 June 1832); **Irish fisheries:** *Coll. Cornub.*, 442; **Plymouth:** Rule, 'Deep-sea Fisheries', 170.

238 **toast:** J. Corin, *Fishermen's Conflict* (1988), 50; **jetties for pressing:** information from T. Pawlyn.

239 Rule, 'Deep-sea Fisheries', 164-82; Pawlyn, 'South West Fisheries', 86.

240 **fisherwomen's queen:** 'A Fisherwomen's Festival', *OC* (1937-42), 354; *RCG*, 17 Jan. 1862, p.6.

241 **women organiser:** C. Lee, *The Widow Woman* (1899), 20; **final quote:** *Cornishman*, 17 Jan. 1862.

242 CRO, RS/14; D. Smart, *The Cornish Fishing Industry* (1992), 10.

243 **peak:** Rule, 'Deep-sea Fisheries', 166; **crew lists:** MSR/1275-1518; *Pride of the Sea*: MSR/1451/1.

244 **boats:** Pawlyn, 'South West Fisheries', 86, 198, 200; CRO, RS/14; **harbour for strangers:** information from T. Pawlyn; **traditions:** CRO, RS/14; **mackerel counting:** *PNHAS* (1888-9), 184-5.

245 **yawlers:** M. Perry ed., *Looking at Penzance* (2006), 18-23; **rail freight:** Corin, *Fishermen's Conflict*, 86; CRO, RS 14; **early canning:** Pawlyn, 'South West Fisheries', 85.

246 **screw presses:** Pawlyn, 'South West Fisheries', in ESF, 85-6; **new methods:** *PNHAS* (1888-9), 30.

247 **curing houses:** CRO, RS 14; **Italian steamers and firms:** R. Hogg, 'fishing and Allied Trades' in *Newlyn Life*, 33-4 and information from T. Pawlyn;

248 **marginal quote and taboos:** Phillips, *Charles Lee*, 18; **Buccaboo:** *PNHAS* (1884-5), 36.

249 **dream:** Phillips, *Charles Lee*, 2; **Emeline:** MR PZ/152; **Jane:** J. Penwith, *Leaves from a Cornish Notebook* (*c.*1949), 36-9.

250 **registration:** CRO, MSR/Penzance 1-3; *Hugh Bourne:* /3.

251 **Porthleven:** CRO, MSR/Penzance/9-10; **local boat-building:** RS/14.

252 **Scilly nets:** M. Wright, *Cornish Guernseys and Knitfrocks* (1979), 12; **male net makers:** CRO, RS/14; **net making:** Phillips, *Charles Lee*, 3-4 and information from T. Pawlyn.

253 **rope-walks:** CRO, T/A; **1896:** CRO, RS/14.

254 CRO, RS/14.

255 C. Lorigan, *Delabole* (2007), 43.

256 **1896:** CRO, RS/14; **basket making:** information from Margaret Perry; *Kelly's Dir. Cornwall* (1914), 276.

257 **Penzance outfitters:** *Cornishman*, 28 May 1896; **1878:** *Harrod's Dir. Cornwall.*

258 **Wheal Betsy:** information from P. Lomax; **West Tolvadden:** R. Burt *et al.*, *Cornish Mines – Metalliferous and Associated Minerals 1845-1913* (1987).

259 CRO, P172/25/72/1-2.

260 **proposed quarry visit:** *PNHAS* (1890-1), 222; **seaplanes:** see P. London, *U-Boat Hunters* (1999), 46.

CHAPTER 8 Life in Mousehole and Newlyn in the 19th Century, pp. 117-132

261 **apprentices:** CRO, P133/16(B)/1; **brewery:** Penlee 2001.44, 62 (illustrations).

262 **Bridewell:** 'Bodmin Bridewell and its inmates 1821-1848' index by S.J. Pocock for CFHS; **incest:** CRO, ARD 151/113.

263 **Madron workhouse:** A. Bennett, *Cornwall Through the Mid Nineteenth Century* (1987), 6; **Rebecca Jewell:** CRO, P42/13/4/2; **outdoor relief:** *RCG*, 29 Oct. 1858.

264 CRO, P/172/8/1.

265 CRO, DC/Pen/283.

266 J. Pearce, *The Wesleys in Cornwall* (1964), 103, 106, 113, 116, 122, 128, 135-6, 169; **'Old Bunger':** *Collectanea Cornubiensis*, 441.

267 **Wesley at Mousehole:** Pearce, *Wesleys*, 146, 164-5; **revival:** Perry, Mousehole, 40; **Trewavas:** T. Shaw, *History of Cornish Methodism* (1967), 29; **preaching house:** CRO, AP/Y/109; **1821:** CRO, MR/PZ/51.

268 **Penzance:** *Universal Dir.* 1793-7, 282; **Quaker:** RIC, Henderson Cal. 10, 133; **Congregational chapel:** RIC, CLG/2000/08/3; **Baptists:** M. Cook, *The Diocese of Exeter in 1821: Cornwall* (DCRS, 1958), 64.

269 **1848 parish:** M. Perry collection; **other new parishes:** C. Henderson, *Cornish Church Guide* (1928), 152, 157-8.

270 **religious census:** CRO, FS/2/95 (J.C. Probert (ed.) *1851 religious census – West Cornwall and the Isles of Scilly*); **percentages:** B. Coleman, 'The Nineteenth Century: Nonconformity' in N. Orme ed., *Unity and Variety* (1991), 141; D.W. Bebbington, 'Culture and Piety in the Far West; Revival in Penzance, Newlyn, and Mousehole in 1849' in *Revival and Resurgence in Christian History*, K.Cooper and J.Gregory eds. (Eccl. Hist. Soc. 2008), 230.

271 Bebbington, 'Culture and Piety in the Far West, 225-50.

272 **Booth visit:** S. Bird, *Bygone Penzance and Newlyn* (1987), 99; **Plymouth brethren:** Pender, *Mousehole*, 32; **banner:** *Cornishman*, 18 June 1908; **temperance exam:**

CRO, SR/PAU/2/5.

273 **chapel building:** Perry, *Mousehole*, 41-2; CRO, DC/Pen/284, p.323; **1832:** CRO, ARD/149/103.

274 **Mount Zion:** *TheWesleyan Methodist Association Magazine* (1852), 487; *The United Methodist Free Churches Magazine* (1861), 124; further information from John Probert; Perry, *Mousehole*, 41; T. Shaw, *A History of Cornish Methodism* (1967), 8, 85; **teetotal chapel:** CRO, FS/2/95; **struggle:** MR/PZ/8.

275 **first Newlyn chapel:** CRO, AD 59/75; **Trinity:** MR/PZ/403; **seats:** FS/2/95; **'beautification':** MR/PZ/168; **rostrum:** /403; **Sunday school:** /170, /403.

276 **Ebenezer:** J.C.C. Probert, *Primitive Methodism in Cornwall* (1960s), 61-5; **building materials:** CRO, MR/PZ/390; **seating and music:** /393-4; B. Batten, *Newlyn Towners* (1978); **fund-raising:** WB, 20 July 1908.

277 **description:** CRO, FS/2/95; **wooden windows:** VCH Penwith, 51; **bells:** CRO, ARD 160/332/1-3; for a similar case see J. Chandler, *A Wiltshire Village - Codford* (2007), 144.

278 CRO, P172/8/1.

279 CRO, FS/2/95.

280 **1864:** letters of 7 & 14 Mar. (M Perry collection).

281 **opening:** *CT*, 28 Jan. 1866; **'garden crops':** letter of 2 Mar. 1865 (M. Perry collection); **Lach-Szyrma:** M. Perry, 'Eminent Westcountryman, Honorary Cornishman', *JRIC* n.s. II, 3 (2000), 154-67; **vicarage:** *Harrod's Dir. Cornwall* (1878), 882 and M. Perry collection.

282 **north aisle:** *Cornishman*, 10 Jun 1886; **Leah windows:** WMN, 9 July 1886; **High Church items:** *Parish Mags* 1895-1901; **painting:** *Cornishman*, 7 Jan. 1888; **spire:** M. Perry collection.

283 **mission work:** P.A. Waller, 'The Anglican Church in Newlyn' in *Newlyn Life*, 98-100;.**services:** *Parish Mag.* Jan. 1894; J. S. Carah, 'Meanderings of a Country Parson', *Tre Pol and Pen* (1928), 112; **plans:** CRO, DC/Pen/285, p.32; **1904:** *Kelly's Dir. Cornwall* (1906), 237; **Fishermens Rest:** *Newlyn Life*, 100.

284 Stoate, *Protestations Returns*, 52-3; 48-50, 54-5.

285 **Rowe:** J. and N. Parsons, 'Village Schoolmaster Extraordinary: Alexander Rowe', *CFHS* no 82 (1996), 28; **books etc:** CRO, ARD 165/39; **other schoolmasters:** P172/1/6, 61; ARD 166/82/1-3.

286 **Paul school:** Pender, *Mousehole*, 59, *Kelly's Dir. Cornwall* (1883), 974; **bishop's books:** CRO, FS/3/ 934.

287 **survey:** *Abstract of Education Returns* (1833) (copy at CRO); **Mousehole school:** Pender, *Mousehole*, 58; **Fradgan plans (1857):** CRO, SRP/56/1-5 and T/A; **loft schoolroom:** CRO, AP/K/1313/1.

288 **book club:** Pender, *Mousehole*, 30; **reading room:** M.Perry collection; *RCG*, 25 Oct. 1866; **navigation classes:** CRO, SRG/PAU. 1.

289 **report:** CRO, MR PZ/53; **truants:** SR/PAU/2/1.

290 **National school:** *Kelly's Dir. Cornwall* (1873), 824; **iron school:** W. Lach Szyrma, *Newlyn and its Pier* (1884), 23; **poaching:** Jenkin, *Newlyn*, 65; CRO, SR/PAU/2/1.

291 **Board School:** *Kelly's Dir. Cornwall* (1889), 1094; CRO, SR/PAU/2/2 (1897); Jenkin, *Newlyn*, 69; **museum:** SR/PAU/2/5, SRG/PAU. 1 (the school now houses a fishing museum); **Newlyn Institute:** Lach-Szyrma, *Newlyn and its Pier*, 25; **Paul Board School:** *Kelly's Dir. Cornwall* (1883), 974.

292 **Trewarveneth Infants:** CRO, SRV/PAU./2/7; Jenkin, *Newlyn*, 69; **Mousehole Infants:** CRO, MR/PZ/153; **Juniors:** SRG/PAU. 1; **council takeover:** /PAU. 2.

293 **dame schools:** S. Humphrys, *Some Recollections of Old Newlyn* (1980s), 10; **Miss Allen's:** J.J. Beckerlegge, The Thatched Cottages of Newlyn within Living Memory, *OC* (1943-51), 114-15; **others:** T. Cross, *The Shining Sands* (1994), 37, 59; **Antoine etc:** Humphrys, *Recollections*, 10, 12; *Kelly's Dir. Cornwall* (1873), 824; (1910), 245.

294 **survivals:** R.M. Nance, 'Traditional Cornish at Paul', *OC* 2, pt 12 (1931-6), 39-40, and 'A new-found traditional sentence of Cornish', *JRIC* 22 (1927), 284.

295 **Lach-Szyrma:** M. Perry, 'Eminent Westcountryman, Honorary Cornishman', *JRIC*, n.s. II, 3 (2000), 161-2; **Jenner:** D.R. Williams ed., *Henry and Katherine Jenner* (2004); **competition:** P. Berresford Ellis, *The Cornish Language* (1974), 145.

296 **religious question:** *Cornishman,* 11 June 1896; **Yarmouth view:** 28 May 1896.

297 **Newlyn riots:** Corin, *Fishermen's Conflict,* 9, 67; **telegrams:** TNA, HO 144/662/
     X58892, 1(closed archive until 2001); **Hobson's office:** *Cornishman,* 21 May 1896.

298 **second day:** *Cornishman,* 21 May 1896; **gunboats and trial:** Corin, *Conflict,* 9,
     79-80 but note that Alfred Green not Alfred Harvey was tried; **truancy:** CRO,
     SR/PAU/2/5;

299 **lack of Methodist support:** *Cornishman,* 28 May (letter), 4 June; **letter:** 26 June
     1896; **leading Methodists:** CRO, MR/PZ/168; Corin, *Conflict,* 66, 68-9; **Carah:** 80;
     letter of support and armed artist: *Cornishman,* 11 June 1896; 28 June 1896.

CHAPTER 9 Artists and Other Visitors, pp. 133-146

300 **Quote:** S Heath, *The Cornish Riviera* (1911), 36; L. Newton (ed.), *Painting at the
     edge – British Coastal Art Colonies 1880-1930* (2005).

301 G. Bednar, *Every Corner was a Picture* (1999), 12, 20.

302 **Leland:** *Leland Itin.,* I, 189, 319-21; **Borlase:** BL, Egerton 2657, ff. 5v-6, 40; **Lysons:**
     BL, Add. 9420, f. 429; **ring and thimble:** I.S. Spreadbury, *Impressions of the Old
     Duchy,* Book 1 (1971), 15; **tomb:** Shrops RO, 567/5/5/1/20-26 (Plymley journals);
     Price: E. Sparrow, *The Prices of Penzance 1734-1834* (1985), 3, 5.

303 Pool *Penzance,*120-2, 131, 157.

304 **pretty Mousehole:** *Leland Itin.,* I 319; **early guidebook:** J. Paris, *A Guide to
     the Mount's Bay and the Land's End…* (1816), 71; **Plymley family:** Shrops RO,
     567/5/5/1/20-26; Revd R. Warner, *A Tour through Cornwall in the Autumn of 1808*
     (1809), 174.

305 **Wynne:** CRO, PD 440; M. Brayshay ed., *Topographical Writers in South-West
     England* (1996), 172; **Tremenheere:** RIC accession lists; **Allom:** C. Wood, *The
     Dictionary of Victorian Painters* (2nd edition 1991), 22.

306 **Leland:** *Leland Itin.,* I, 319; **1803:** Shrops RO, 567/5/5/1/20-26; **1795:** Spreadbury,
     Impressions, 16.

307 **Tremenheeres:** *Penzance during Napoleonic Times,* 78-84; **Prout:** *Victorian Painters,*
     381; **Cooke:** 102; **Pentreath:** Penlee House Gallery and Museum exhibition
     catalogue 2006.

308 *RCG,* 21 Nov. 1862.

309 Murray's *Handbook to Cornwall* (1859), 189.

310 **Newlyn paintings:** T. Cross, *The Shining Sands* (1994), 11, 27; **Pope and Wolfe:**
     Victorian Painters, 526; **Blight:** J.T. Blight, *A Week at the Land's End,* 34; S. Bates &
     K. Spurgin, *The Dust of Heroes* (2006); **other artists:** Bednar, *Every Corner was a
     Picture* (2005).

311 **Art colonies:** Newton, *Painting at the edge,* 12, **Cullercoats:** 119.

312 **Gotches:** P. Lomax, *The Golden Dream* (2004), 11; **Forbes:** C. Fox, *Stanhope Forbes
     and the Newlyn School* (1993); *New DNB;* **other artists:** Bednar, *Every Corner was a
     Picture.*

313 **Bastien-Lepage:** Newton, *Painting at the Edge,* p.15; **square brush technique:** 11,
     15; **La Thangue:** A. Jenkins, *Painters and Peasants* (2000), 44-5:

314 *PNHAS* (1886-7), 232-3.

315 **industrial class:** H. Berriman, *Arts and Crafts in Newlyn 1890-1930* (1986), 13-18;
     New England Art Club: Lomax, *The Golden Dream,* 62ff..

316 **Garstin quote:** Berriman, *Arts and Crafts,* 13; **background:** 13-16.

317 **Foundation:** Newton, *Painting at the Edge,* 40; M. Hardie (ed.), *100 Years in Newlyn
     – Diary of a Gallery* (1995), 1-2; **design:** 6; Listing description; **Plaques:** 25-7.

318 **Newlyn Society of Artists:** *100 Years in Newlyn,* 2; **organisation:** 11-13;
     exhibitions: 31-3, 36; **Rheam:** Bednar, *Every Corner was a Picture,* 25; **Leighton:**
     Victorian Painters, 281.

319 **Newlyn School of Painting:** Newton, *Painting at the Edge,* 40-1; **roadway:** CRO, DC
     Pen/284, p.141; **other studios:** /284, p.405; /286, p.337.

320 **background:** J. Cook *et al., Singing from the Walls* (2000), 66, 120-5; **students and
     artists' children:** I. Green, *Posing the Model* (2002).

321 **other art school:** K. McConckey *et al., Harold Harvey* (2001), 97, 120; R. Pryke,
     Norman Garstin – Irishman & Newlyn Artist (2005); **Lamorna:** A. Wormleighton,

A Painter Laureate- Lamorna Birch and his circle (1995), 64ff.; **Simpson:** CRO, DC/Pen/295, p.3.

322 Lomax, *The Golden Dream*, 51, 54.

323 **ash disposal:** CRO, DC Pen/284, p.67; /285, p.118; **Langley:** /284, pp.127-8; /286, p.25; **Hunter:** /285, p.349; /287, p.292; **Birch:** /286, pp.69-70.

324 **Todd marriage:** *Ancestry.com*; C. Fox and F. Greenacre, *Artists of the Newlyn School* (1979), 121-2 (incorrectly states that Todd was unmarried in 1890); **Newlyn Board School:** CRO, SR/PAU/2/5-6.

325 **Overseers:** CRO, DC/Pen/283, p.266; /288, 197, 329; **Anglican artists:** Berriman, *Arts and Crafts in Newlyn*, 24; *Newlyn Life*, 97.

326 **flood:** CRO, DC/Pen/283, p.240; **fire (Mr Carter's shop May1895):** SR/PAU/2/5; **napkin rings:** *Cornishman*, 2 July 1896; **scouts:** Lomax, *The Golden Dream*, 7; **nursing association:** *Parish Mags* 1890s (In June 1895 East Coast fishermen gave £11 10s. to this cause).

327 **entertainments:** P. Lomax, 'The Newlyn Artists' Dramatic Society 1886-1890' in J. Palmer ed., *Treasures of the Morrab* (2005), 103-112; **Blackburne's show:** Fox & Greenacre, *Artists*, 35; **Gotch talks:** Parish Mag., Mar. 1899.

328 **Quote:** S. Humphrys *Some Recollections* (1980s), 13; **Newlyn Pageant:** *WB*, 12 Aug. 1907; *Cornishman*, 10 and 15 Aug. 1907; **Rebellion, 1497:** Ian Arthurson, *The Perkin Warbeck Conspiracy 1491-1499* (Alan Sutton publishing, Stroud, Gloucestershire, 1994); **Gladys Hynes:** Newton, *Painting at the Edge*, 159; B. Walke, *Twenty Years at St Hilary* (1935), 54-6;**truants:** CRO, SR/PAU/2/2; **Phyllis quote:** Morrab, Garnier archive.

329 **olde English fayre:** *WB*, 20 July 1908; *Cornishman*, 23 July 1908; B Batten, *Newlyn Towners, Fishermen and Methodists* (1978); **stalls:** *Cornishman*, 23 July 1908.

CHAPTER 10 Newlyn and Mousehole since 1914, pp. 147-170

330 **Response to War:** S. Dalley, 'The Response in Cornwall to the outbreak of Word War I', in *Cornish Studies*, 11, 85-109

331 **Soldier's Records:** http://military-genealogy.com, Records 295234 and 242116, accessed 13/05/2009

332 **Motor launches:** TNA, ADM 53/52586-9; **fear of bombs:** CRO, DC/Pen/288, p.189; **Sea Plane Station:** TNA, AIR/1/2423/305/18/34; **Flight Numbers:** From history of No. 235 Squadron, http://www.raf.mod.uk/bob1940/213to236.html accessed 25/05/2009

333 **Conscientious objectors:** R. Pryke, *Norman Garstin*, 154; **Procter:** E. Knowles, *Dod Procter RA 1892-1972* (1990 exhibition catalogue), 31-2; A. James, *Dod Procter* (2007).

334 **Belgian artists:** Lomax, *The Golden Dream*, 149; **hospital depot:** Jill Blyth scrapbook (Garnier archive); **Labour Bureau:** CRO, SRC/DC/8b/19.

335 **Richard Quick:** TNA, ADM/188/461

336 **Population Figures:** *Kelly's Dir. Cornwall* (1930), 262

337 **Trawl fishery:** T. Pawlyn, 'The South West Fisheries' and 'Fisheries of the West Country', in *ESF*, 86, 198-200; **fish and chip shops:** C Reid, 'From trawler to table: the fish trades since the late nineteenth century', in *ESF*, 157; *Kelly's Dir. Cornwall* (1910), 245; (1926), 275.

338 **Statistics:** *WB*, 28 Sept. 1939; **exporters:** W. Stevenson, *Growing Up with* Boats (2001), 138; **Gernick:** CRO, DC/Pen/296, p.156.

339 **Bakery:** Stevenson, *Growing Up with Boats*, 16-18; **camouflage nets:** CARET1-3, 29 (Penwith tape); **quarry quote:** B. Batten, *Newlyn of Yesterday* (1983), 17-18.

340 CRO, DC/293-4.

341 **Penlee quarry:** CURAT1; PAYWT1 (Penwith tapes): **damage:** CRO, DC/Pen/296, p.384; **quarry benching:** Batten, *Newlyn of Yesterday*, 20 and information from Mandy Morris; **Christmas tree:** CRO, SRG/PAU./5.

342 **Later history:** Berriman, *Arts & Crafts in Newlyn*, 19-20; **Dyer:** CRO, DC Pen/292, p. 6; /294, p. 98.

343 **Cryséde:** H. Berriman, *Cryséde* (1993), 11; *Kelly's Dir. Cornwall* (1926), 257; **factories:** CRO, DC Pen/291, pp.97, 278, 331, 347-8, 359; /294, pp.30-1; **sanitary**

conveniences: /292.

344   **Flower industry:** A. Brown, *Cornwall at Work* (1934), 28-37; **quote:** L. Tregenza, *Harbour Village* (1977), 13; **German POWs:** CRO, DC/Pen/288, p.419; **allotment:** /296, p.169.

345   **Tourism:** J. Lowerson, 'Celtic Tourism – Some Recent Magnets', in *Cornish Studies*, 2, 128-138; **GWR Road Motors:** P. Kelley, *Road Vehicles of the Great Western Railway* (1973), 101.

346   **Light Railway:** TNA, MT 6/948/5; **GWR Bus Service:** P. Kelley, *Road Vehicles of the Great Western Railway* (1973), appendix; **Western National Service:** TNA; RAIL 971/205.

347   **Mousehole guides:** CRO, DC/Pen/290, pp. 247, 258. 261; **Polmear and cycle agent:** *Kelly's Dir. Cornwall* (1914), 268 (1935), 263; **tea rooms etc:** *The Cornwall Dir.* (1931), 242-3; **Old Coastguards:** CRO, DC/Pen/294, pp.40(GP), 65; **Lobster Pot:** D. Williams, *Around Newlyn, Mousehole and Paul* (1988), 98-9; *Kelly's Dir. Cornwall* (1939), 265; **Newlyn Boarding Houses:** *Kelly's Dir. Cornwall* (1930), 245

348   **Lett-Haines:** /290, p.50; /296, p.178; Cedric suffered a dog bite on 4 November 1918 when he was living at Myrtle Cottage: /289, pp.213, 228; **Yglesias:** C. Wallace, *Women Artists in Cornwall 1880-1940* (1996), 36; **George and Pender:** S. P. Johns, *Jack Pender and his grandfather William J. George* (2007); F. Ruhrmund, *Jack Pender – A Tribute* (2008); **Victor:** J. Wood, *Hidden Talents: A Dictionary of Neglected Artists Working 1880-1950* (1994), 159.

349   **Wyon:** H. Berriman, *Arts & Crafts in Newlyn 1890-1930* (1986), 67-8; Margaret Perry research notes; **Travers:** Pevsner, *Cornwall*, 126; http://www.saintdunstan.org.uk/section3 (accessed 10 December 2008).

350   **Background:** M. Sagar-Fenton, *The Rosebud and the Newlyn Clearances* (2003), 12-13; S. Heath, *The Cornish Riviera* (1911), 36; **newspaper coverage and Bateman:** Morrab, Garnier archive.

351   **Condemned properties:** CRO, DC/Pen/288, p.184; **miser:** /295, pp.269-70; DRB WR77 (will).

352   **Inspector (Miss Aldridge):** CRO, DC/Pen/296, p.192; **Church Lane:** /290, p.274 and illustrated as 'The Evening Hour' in M.M. Mitford, *Sketches of English Life and Character with pictures by Stanhope Forbes* (1909), between pages 216-17; **Bowjey and Navy Court:** /294, pp.8-9, 64.

353   **Cairn William Terrace:** CRO, DC/Pen/295, p.176; /288, p.220; **new houses:** /290, p.120; **bungalows:** /296, pp.224, 435; **Kenstella:** information from M. Perry and Mrs Lockett; TNA, HLG 111/1007.

354   **Gaiety:** Jenkin, *Newlyn*, 147; *Cornwall Dir.* (1931), 319; **Centenary:** Probert, *Primitive Methodism*, 63-4; B. Batten, *Newlyn Towners* (1978); **Tolcarne School:** SRG/PAU.3; **McGrigor memorial:** DC/Pen/289, p.443; /296, pp.173ff; and information from Jane Rosen, Imperial War Museum.

355   **Electricity:** CRO, DC/Pen/293, p. 115; **chickens:** CRO, DC/Pen/295, pp.263-4; **rats:** /288, p.242; /295, p.283; **last epidemic:** SR/PAU./2/11, 36.

356   **Reservoirs:** CRO, DC/Pen/290, pp.3, 16; /294, p.33; **public latrines:** /296, p.426; **standpipes:** /293, p.43; **Trevithal reservoir:** /294, p.53.

357   **Harvey complaints:** CRO, DC/Pen/287, p.416; /289, p.272; **Rheam:** /295, p.225; **Crysède:** /296, pp.350-1; **Garnier's supply:** CRO, DC/Pen/293, p.102.

358   **Street name-plates:** CRO, DC/Pen/294, pp.47 (GP), 76.

359   Pool *Penzance*, 169; **Jubilee Pool etc:** 'Lidos', http://www.seasidehistory.co.uk/lidos.html (accessed 12 December 2006); **Vienna:** illustrations in CRHC, *Slum Clearance* (1934).

360   **Slum Report:** CRHC, *Slum Clearance* (1934), 21-2, 27; **Compulsory purchase:** TNA, HLG/23/5761; **Gwavas estate:** Sagar-Fenton, *Rosebud*, 35, 75.

361   **Navy Inn Court:** TNA, HLG/23/6373; **Lower Green Street:** TNA, HLG/23/14188-90; **Fore Street:** /14191-2; **St Peter's Hill:** TNA, HLG/23/14187 (order no. 2 only); **Vaccination Court:** /14193 and RIC, CLG/2006/22-4.

362   **Public enquiry:** Sagar-Fenton, *Rosebud*, 38-42; **petition:** committee minutes, 4, 8 (Garnier archive).

363   Sagar-Fenton, *Rosebud*, 47-8, 65.

364 **Richards quote:** *Cornishman*, 30 Oct. 1937; **Roberts:** *Swansea Daily News*, 23 Oct. 1937 (Garnier archive).

365 **1938 orders:** TNA, HLG 23/19421-4, 201907; Sagar-Fenton, *Rosebud*, 74, 76; **evictions:** 77-8; **replacement buildings:** 24; **demolitions:** 81; **quote:** EMMPTI (Penwith tape).

366 **Sidney Vivian Hitchens:** TNA, ADM/188/895.

367 **Bombing:** http://www.bbc.co.uk/ww2peopleswar/stories/88/a3339588.shtml (Accessed 7 April 2009); **Penzance Battery:** TNA, WO/192/146; **Rescue Launches:** TNA, AIR 29/447.

368 **Belgian refugees:** *WB*, p.2; W. Stevenson, *Growing Up with Boats* (2001), 141-2; Jenkin, *Newlyn*, 190-7; **evacuees:** A. Calder, *The People's War* (1969), 39-40; R. Clitheroe, *Away from the Bombs* (1990), 10.

369 **Alverton estate:** M. Williams, 'Housing the Cornish in P. Payton ed., *Cornwall Since the War* (1993), 157; **'Pirates':** B.Batten, *Newlyn, Penzance and the 'Pirates'* (1978), 21; HOAWT1, pp.6-8 (Penwith tape); **Memories:** HOAWT1, pp.6-8 (Penwith tape); **Kenstella:** information from M. Perry and Mrs Lockett; **plans:** TNA, HLG 111/1007.

370 **Post-war clearances:** Sagar-Fenton, *Rosebud*, 81; **quote:** Bodleian MS. Top.gen.d.87, 76-7.

371 **Artist model quote:** EMMPT1 (Penwith tape); **policy change:** J. English and P. Norman, *Slums*, 28, 35; **survivals and last clearance:** Sagar-Fenton, *Rosebud*, 81, 87-94.

372 **Canning etc:** *WB*, 28 Sept. 1939; Pawlyn 'Fisheries of the Westcountry', 198; **Pilchard Works:** C. Trewin, *Cornish Fishing and Seafood* (2006), 42-7; **Mackerel fishery:** Pawlyn 'Fisheries of the Westcountry', 200-1.

373 **Trawling:** Pawlyn 'Fisheries of the Westcountry', 198-200; **fleet:** Stevenson, *Growing up with boats*, 90, 98, 121, 127, 143-4; **Trevelyan Richards:** M. Sagar-Fenton, *Penlee – The Loss of a Lifeboat* (1991), 30.

374 **Truman Proclamation:** J.T. Thor, 'The Extension of Iceland's Fishing Limits in 1952 and the British Reaction', in *Scandinavian Journal of History*, 17, 25-43; **Chronology of Cod Wars:** http://news.bbc.co.uk/onthisday/hi/dates/stories/may/20/newsid_250000/2510837.stm (accessed 25/05/09)

375 **Port hierarchy:** D. Whitmarsh, 'Adaption and Change in the Fishing Industry since the 1970s', in *ESF*, 231 (table 24.5);and information from Nick Howell; **Mary Williams Pier:** M. Perry, *Newlyn* (1998), 44; **value:** J.Corin, *Fishermen's Conflict* (1988), 107; **today's catches:** information from Andrew Munson, Newlyn Harbour; **2006:** Report of the Cornwall and Isles of Scilly Economic Forum on Fishing, December 2008.

376 **Penlee crew:** Sagar-Fenton, *Penlee*, 29-30; **Chapel trustees:** CRO, MR/PZ/231, 1.

377 CRO, MR/PZ/231, 166-76; M. Sagar-Fenton, *Serpentine* (2005); other information from M. Perry and J. Barry.

378 **Beaches:** W.J. Bennett, 'A Century of Change on the Coast of Cornwall', *Geography*, 37, 214-224; **Bird hospital:** D. Yglesias, *The Cry of a Bird* (1962), 19, 124, 150-1; **quotes:** M. Perry.

379 **Guide to Penzance:** TNA, ZLIB 19/434.

380 information from M. Perry and Penwith District Council.

381 **Penlee:** Sagar-Fenton, *Penlee*; J. Corin and G. Farr, *Penlee Lifeboat* (1983), 69ff; *Cornishman* 24 Dec. 1981; **Southport disaster:** http://en.wikipedia.org/wiki/Southport-lifeboat-disaster (accessed 30 December 2006).

EPILOGUE Into the 21st Century, pp. 171-172

382 **2001 Census:** Office for National Statistics (accessed 1 June 2009).

383 **Property Prices:** http://property.timesonline.co.uk /tol/life_and_style/property/article4999629.ece (accessed 1 June 2006).

Bibliography

Local History Sources

Among the most up to date guides consulted are:

Arkell, T., Evans, N. and Goose, N., *When Death Do Us Part – Understanding and Interpreting the Probate Records of Early Modern England* (Oxford: Leopard's Head Press, 2000)

Carter, P. and Thompson, K., *Sources for Local Historians* (Chichester: Phillimore, 2005)

Dymond, D. *Researching and Writing History- a guide for local historians (Lancaster: Carnegie and BALH, 2009)*

VCH publications on Cornwall

Haverfield, F., Taylor, M.V., Collingwood, R.G. and Page, W. ed., *Romano-British Remains* II, pt 5 (London: The St. Catherine Press, 1924)

Page, W. ed., *The Victoria County History of the County of Cornwall* I (London: Archibald Constable Company Ltd, 1906)

Page W. ed., *The Domesday Survey*, II pt 8 (London: The St. Catherine Press, 1924)

Page, W. ed., 'Social and Economic History'. 001-0040 (unpublished proof copy, 1908)

Taylor, T. and Page, W. ed., 'The Hundred of Penwith', 110 pp. (unpublished proof copy, 1908)

These can be consulted in the CRO, CSL or RIC.

Archaeology, Crosses, Geology and Landscape

Bristow, C.M., *Cornwall's Geology and Scenery – An introduction* (St Austell, Cornish Hillside Publications, 1996)

Cooke, I. McNeil, *Crosses and Churchway Paths in the Land's End Peninsula West Cornwall, iv, Paul & Sancreed* (Penzance: Men-an-Tol Studio, 2001)

Johnson, N. and Rose, P., *Cornwall's Archaeological Heritage from Prehistory to the Tudors: 8000 BC – AD 1540* (1990)

Kain, R. and Ravenhill, W. ed., *Historical Atlas of South-West England* (Exeter: Univ. Press, 1999)

Langdon, A., *Stone Crosses in West Penwith* (Penryn: OC, 1997)

Selwood, E.B., Durrance, E.M. and Bristow, C.M., *The Geology of Cornwall* (Exeter: Univ. Press, 1998)

Turner, S. ed., *Medieval Devon and Cornwall – Shaping an Ancient Countryside* (Macclesfield: Windgather Press Ltd, 2006)

Cornish Society

There are many books about Cornish society and these include:

Coate, M., *Cornwall in the Great Civil War and Interregnum 1642-1666* (Truro: Bradford Barton rep. 1963 of 1933 edn.)

Lorigan, C., *Delabole – The History of the Slate Quarry and the Making of its Village Community* (Reading: Pengelly Press, 2007)

Orme, N. ed., *Cornish Wills 1342-1540* (Exeter: DCRS, 2007)

Overton, M., Whittle, J., Dean, D. and Hann, A., *Production and Consumption in English Households 1600-1750* (Oxford: Univ. Press, 2004). A comparison of Cornwall and Kent.

Payton, P., *The Making of Modern Cornwall* (Redruth, Dyllansow Truran, 1992)

Payton, P., *Cornwall* (Fowey: Alexander Associates, 1996)

Rowe, J., *Cornwall in the Age of the Industrial Revolution* (St Austell, Cornish Hillside Publications, 1953, 2nd edn. 1993)

Rowse, A. L., *Tudor Cornwall* (Oxford: Univ. Press, 1941)

Stoyle, M., *West Britons – Cornish Identities and the Early Modern British State* (Exeter: Univ. Press, 2002)

Fishing and Trade

For useful articles on this subject see text. Key books include:

Fox, H., *The Evolution of the Fishing Village – Landscape and Society along the South Devon Coast, 1086-1550* (Oxford, Leopard's Head Press, 2001)

Gray, T. ed., *Early Stuart Mariners and Shipping – The Maritime Surveys of Devon and Cornwall 1619-35* (Exeter: DCRS, 1990)

Hutchinson, G., *Medieval Ships and Shipping* (London and Washington, Leicester University Press, 1994, rep. 1997) includes a whole chapter on medieval fishing.

Kowaleski, M. ed., *The Havener's Accounts of the Earldom and Duchy of Cornwall, 1287-1356* (Exeter, DCRS, new ser. 44, 2001)

Razzell, P.E. and Wainwright, R.W. ed., *The Victorian Working Class – Selection from Letters to the* Morning Chronicle (London: Frank Cass, 1973), 16-21. A useful account of Cornish fishing communities in 1849.

Smart, D., *The Cornish Fishing Industry – a brief history* (Penryn, Tor Mark Press, 1992). This small book includes a number of interesting Newlyn photographs including screw pressing of pilchards in 1925.

Starkey, D.J., Reid, C. and Ashcroft, N., *England's Sea Fishing – The Commercial Sea Fisheries of England and Wales since 1300* (London, Chatham Publishing, 2000).

Cornish Language

Ellis, P. Berresford, *The Cornish Language and its Literature* (London and Boston, Routledge & Kegan Paul, 1974)

Murdoch, B., *Cornish Literature* (Bury St Edmunds, D.S. Brewer, 1993)

Padel, O.J., *The Cornish Writings of the Boson Family* (Redruth: ICS, 1975)

Pryce, W., *Archaeologia Cornu-Britannica; or An Essay to Preserve the Ancient Cornish Language …* (Redruth, 1790)

Williams, D.R., *Henry and Katharine Jenner- A Celebration of Cornwall's Culture, Language and Identity* (London: Francis Boutle Publishers, 2004)

Cornish Studies, Old Cornwall and the *Journal of the Royal Institution of Cornwall* also have articles on this subject.

Cornish Names

Gover, J.E.B., 'Place Names of Cornwall' manuscript at RIC (vol. 6 includes Penwith) and Henderson, C., 'The Topography of the Parish of Paul', *RCPS*, n.s. ix (1941), 56-67 are both now superceded by O.J. Padel's Cornish place-names index (a copy is available on microfiche at the ICS). See also:

Padel, O.J., *Cornish Place-Name Elements* (Cambridge: Univ. Press, 1985)

Padel, O.J., *A Popular Dictionary of Cornish Place-names* (Penzance: Alison Hodge, 1988)

Pool, P.A.S., *The Place-Names of West Penwith* (Penzance: OC, 1973, 2nd edn, 1985)

Pool, P.A.S., *The Field-Names of West Penwith* (Penzance: OC, 1990)

Folklore and customs

Courtney, M.A., *Folklore & Legends of Cornwall* (Exeter, Cornwall Books 1989 facsimile of 1890 original)

Hunt, R., *Popular Romances of the West of England* (Edinburgh and London, Chatto & Windus, 1880s 2nd edn.)

Articles in *OC* and elsewhere.

Religion

Orme, N. ed., *Unity and Variety – A History of the Church in Devon and Cornwall* (Exeter: Univ. Press, 1991)

Orme, N., *The Saints of Cornwall* (Oxford: Univ. Press, 2000)

Pearce, J., *The Wesleys in Cornwall: extracts from the journals of John and Charles Wesley and John Nelson* (Truro, D. Bradford Barton, 1964)

Probert, J.C.C., *Primitive Methodism in Cornwall (a history and sociology)* (Redruth, 1960s)

Shaw, T., *A History of Cornish Methodism* (Truro, D. Bradford Barton, 1967)

Population

Population tables, 1801-1901 appear as pages 035-040 of W. Page's unpublished 'Social and Economic History of Cornwall' produced for the VCH in 1908 There are proof copies in a number of libraries. T. Arkell's unpublished tables were also used for Penwith. See also:

Gray, T. ed., *Harvest Failures in Cornwall and Devon – The Book of Orders and Corn Surveys of 1623 and 1630-1* (Plymouth, ICS, 1992)

Thorn C., and F., *Domesday Book: Cornwall* (Chichester: Phillimore, 1979)

Several transcripts of Cornish tax lists were published at Bristol in the 1980s by T.L. Stoate and H.L. Douch, see abbreviations and text.

Artists

Bednar, G., *Every Corner was a Picture – 120 artists of Newlyn and the Newlyn Art Colony 1880-1900* (Mount Hawke: Truran Books, 2nd edn., 2005). A work in progress.

Berriman, H., *Arts and Crafts in Newlyn 1890-1930* (Penzance: Newlyn Orion, 1986)

Berriman, H., *Cryséde – the unique textile designs of Alec Walker* (Truro: RIC, 1993)

Cook, J., Hardie, M. and Payne C., *Singing from the Walls – the Life and Art of Elizabeth Forbes* (Bristol: Sansom & Company, 2000).

Cross, T., *the Shining Sands – Artists in Newlyn and St Ives 1880-1930* (Tiverton: West Country Books, 1994)

Fox., C., *Painting in Newlyn (1900-1930)* (Penzance: Newlyn Orion, 1985). Good potted biographies of second generation.

Fox, C., *Stanhope Forbes and the Newlyn School* (Newton Abbot: David & Charles, 1993)

Fox., C. and Greenacre, F., *Artists of the Newlyn School (1880-1900)* (Penzance: Newlyn Orion, 1979)

Green, I.M., *Artists at Home- Newlyn 1870-1900* (Penzance: privately published, 1995, rep. 2000)

Green, I.M., *Posing the Model* – study of students of the Stanhope Forbes School of Painting 1899-1941 (privately published, 2002). A small sample of those who attended the school, but includes the best known artists.

Hardie, M. ed., *100 Years of Newlyn – Diary of a Gallery* (Penzance: Patten Press, 1995)

James, A., *A Singular Vision: Dod Procter 1890-1972* (Bristol: Redcliffe Press, 2007)

Langley, R. and Knowles, E. ed., *Walter Langley – Pioneer of the Newlyn Art Colony* Bristol: Sansom & Company, 1997)

Lomax, P.A., *The Golden Dream – A Biography of Thomas Cooper Gotch* (Bristol: Sansom & Company, 2004)

Mitford, M.R., *Sketches of English Life and Character* (Edinburgh and London: T.N. Foulis, 1909) includes 16 reproductions from paintings by Stanhope Forbes of Newlyn scenes in the early 1900s.

Newton, L. ed., *Painting at the Edge – British Coastal Art Colonies 1880-1930* (Bristol: Sansom & Company, 2004)

Pryke, R., *Norman Garstin – Irishman & Newlyn Artist* (Reading, Spire Books Ltd, 2005)

Wallace, C., *Under the Open Sky – The Paintings of the Newlyn and Lamorna Artists 1880-1940 in the Public Collections of Cornwall and Plymouth* (Mount Hawke: Truran, 2002)

Slum Clearances

CRHC, *Slum Clearances and Rehousing – The First Report of the Council for the Research on Housing Construction* (London: P.S. King & Sons Ltd, 1934)

English, J., Madigan, R. and Norman P., *Slum Clearance – The Social and*

Administrative Context in England and Wales (London: Croom Helm, 1976)

English, J. and Norman P., *On Hundred Years of Slum Clearance in England and Wales – Policies and Programmes 1868-1970* (Glasgow: Univ. Research paper, 1974)

The Garnier archive consists of scrap books of newspaper cuttings (now in Morab library) and committee minutes compiled by Jill and Geoffrey Garnier and has been preserved by their daughter-in-law Pat Garnier. See also Newlyn section below.

Mousehole

Harvey, P., 'Mousehole alias Porthennys, a Chronicle of a Seafaring Community' (1994) – typescript in Morrab.

Pender, N.M., *Mousehole – History and Recollections* (Penzance: OC, 1970)

Perry, M.E., *Mousehole – A Brief History* (Penzance, 1998)

Sagar-Fenton, M., *Penlee - The Loss of a Lifeboat* (Mount Hawke: Dyllansow Truran, 2000). This is a revised and enlarged edition of a book first published in 1991.

There are in addition a large number of books of Mousehole reminiscences.

Newlyn

Chesher, V. ed., *Newlyn Life 1870-1914 – The Village That Inspired The Artists* (Penzance: PHG, 2003)

Corin, J., *Fishermen's Conflict – The story of a Cornish fishing port* (Newton Abbot: Tops'l Books, 1988)

Jenkin, J.C., *Newlyn – A View from Street-an-Nowan* (privately produced, 2002). Has a useful bibliography. An enlarged edition was produced in 2008.

Perry, M.E., *Newlyn – A Brief History* (Penzance, 1999).

Phillips. K.C. ed., *The Cornish Journal of Charles Lee* (Padstow: Tabb House, 1995).

Russell, S., *Newlyn – Historic characterisation for regeneration report* (Truro: CAU and CCC, 2003)

Sagar-Fenton, M., *The* Rosebud *and the Newlyn Clearances* (Mount Hawke: Truran, 2003)

Stevenson, W. (and Perry, M.E. ed.), *Growing up with Boats* (Penzance, 2001)

There are also several older sources and reminiscences by Ben Batten, who grew up in Newlyn Town, and others. Found too late for inclusion was G. James, *A Holiday and Fishing Village* (London and Harlow: Longmans, 1969). This geography school text book, which features Newlyn, is now an archive item in its own right giving a good impression of the town nearly 40 years ago.

Paul Parish and Penwith

Beaufort-Murray, H. ed., *Penwith at the Time of Charles II* (St Ives: PLHG, 1997)

Chesher, V. and Palmer, J. ed., *Three Hundred Years on Penwith Farms* (Liskeard: PLHG, 1994)

Cullum, D., 'Society and Economy in West Cornwall *c*.1558-1750' (Univ. of Exeter PhD thesis, 1993)

Hosking, J., *People & Places in Paul Parish* (Penzance: 2005)

North, C. and Palmer, J., *The Charter Town of Marazion* (Marazion, Town Trust, 1995)

Palmer. J. ed., *Treasures of the Morrab – a Penzance Library that Has More than Books* (Penzance, PLHG, 2005)

Palmer. J. ed., *In And Around Penzance in Napoleonic Times* (Penzance, PLHG, 2000)

Perry, M. ed., *Looking at Penzance – from the archive of Penzance Old Cornwall Society 1926-2006* (Penzance, OC, 2006)

Pool, P.A.S., *The History of the Town and Borough of Penzance* (Penzance: The Corporation of Penzance, 1974)

Soulsby, I.N., *A History of Sancreed Parish* (Sancreed, 2006)

Trelease, G.M., *The History of the Church in Paul Parish* (Newlyn, 2006)

Index

Picture Credits

The authors and publishers wish to thank the following for permission to reproduce their material. Any infringement of copyright is entirely accidental: every care has been taken to contact or trace all copyright owners. We would be pleased to correct in future editions any errors or omissions brought to our attention. References are to page numbers except where stated.

Vince Bevan, (Private Collection) 84, 155 (Fig. 107)
Birmingham Museums and Art Gallery (W.Langley *Memories*), 115
Bodleian Library, Oxford, 35
British Library, 24, 78
British Museum, 9
Cornish Studies Library, 97 (Fig. 62), 125
Cornwall Historic Environment Service (Steve Hartgroves), 16
Cornwall Record Office, 38, 45 (Fig. B), 73, 128
English Heritage (Peter Williams), 4, 13, 37, 45 (Fig. A), 58, 59, 83, 92, 141, 146, 148, 156, 166, 169 (Fig. 121), (Private Collection) 143, 154, 155 (Fig. 106)
English Heritage (NMR), 121, (NMR - Alfred Newton & Son Collection) 106, 126
Eric Berry, 17, 20, 26 (Figs B and C), 62, 65, 68, 69, 71, 79, 82, 93 (Fig 58), 95, 98, 99, 101, 102, 111, 123, 157,160, 164 (Fig. 115), 165, (Private Collection) 134, (The Gwavas Collection) 138 (Fig. 92), 140, 153 (Fig. 103)
J.M. Dent & Sons Ltd., 109 (Fig. 74)
The Francis Frith Collection www.francisfrith.com, 44
Hatfield House (Lord Salisbury), 6
Charles Hoyland Estate, 161
Images of England (Terry Newman), 162
Adrian Langdon, 29
Andrew Langdon and Ann Preston-Jones, 11
Morrab Library Photographic Archive, 26 (Fig. A), 64, 93 (Fig. 59), 97 (Fig. 63), 117, (Private Collection) 132, 144
The National Archives, 131 (Fig. 86)
The National Library of the Czech Republic, Prague, 34
Penlee House Gallery and Museum, Penzance, 39, 46 (Fig. 26), 52, 53, 57, 60, 67, 81 (Fig. 49), 85, 104, 105, 107, 108, 109 (Fig. 75), 116, 135, 136, 139, 150
Plymouth City Museum and Art Gallery, © Artist's Estate / Bridgeman Art Library, 138 (Fig. 93)
Andrew Taylor, 170
John F. Tonkin & Valentine Tonkin, (photographed by Eric Berry), 114, 131 (Fig. 87)
Royal Institution of Cornwall, 18, 46 (Fig. 27), 49, 50, 56, 80, 81(Fig. 48)
Science and Society Picture Library, 151, 152, 168 (Fig. 119)
St Neot PCC, 30
Steve Tanner, 76
Trinity College Library, Cambridge, 41, 42
University of London, 1, 55, 63, 94, 110 (based on Tony Pawlyn original), 153 (Fig. 104), 164 (Fig. 116), 169 (Fig. 122)
www.lookaroundcornwall.com168 (Fig. 120)
Angela Wigley, www.intocornwall.com3

The following maps were drawn by Cath D'Alton Figs 1, 5, 15, 54, 55, 80,111, Panel 1 (Fig. A), Panel 2 (Fig. A) and Alan Fagan Figs 9, 56, 66, Panel 7 (Fig. A) © University of London